AMERICAN STUDIES
THE BASICS

American Studies: The Basics is an accessible and concise introduction that aims to unpack what American studies does and why it matters.

From *Moby-Dick* to baseball, Hollywood westerns to #BlackLivesMatter, and Disneyland to the U.S. Supreme Court, American studies engages with a myriad of topics in its efforts to understand what the French sociologist Jean Baudrillard called 'social and cultural America'. The book begins by considering how America was studied before American studies' emergence as a recognised discipline in the mid-twentieth century. Successive chapters then explore the rise of American studies, its varied subjects, its distinctive methods of research, its geographical framing and its politics. Throughout the book, explanatory examples are drawn from across American history and culture. Photographs are examined alongside novels, and historical monuments discussed next to films. The text offers an ideal way into an exciting academic subject of continuing growth and relevance.

This book is a must-read for those studying and with an interest in American studies.

Andrew Dix teaches American studies at Loughborough University, UK. His research interests include African American culture, Hollywood stardom and film exhibition.

AMERICAN STUDIES
THE BASICS

Andrew Dix

LONDON AND NEW YORK

First published 2022
by Routledge
2 Park Square, Milton Park, Abingdon, Oxon OX14 4RN

and by Routledge
605 Third Avenue, New York, NY 10158

Routledge is an imprint of the Taylor & Francis Group, an informa business

© 2022 Andrew Dix

The right of Andrew Dix to be identified as author of this work has been asserted by him in accordance with sections 77 and 78 of the Copyright, Designs and Patents Act 1988.

All rights reserved. No part of this book may be reprinted or reproduced or utilised in any form or by any electronic, mechanical, or other means, now known or hereafter invented, including photocopying and recording, or in any information storage or retrieval system, without permission in writing from the publishers.

Trademark notice: Product or corporate names may be trademarks or registered trademarks, and are used only for identification and explanation without intent to infringe.

British Library Cataloguing-in-Publication Data
A catalogue record for this book is available from the British Library

Library of Congress Cataloging-in-Publication Data
Names: Dix, Andrew, 1960– author.
Title: American studies : the basics / Andrew Dix.
Description: First edition. | Abingdon, Oxon ; New York, NY : Routledge, 2022. | Series: The basics | Includes bibliographical references and index.
Identifiers: LCCN 2021019524 (print) | LCCN 2021019525 (ebook)
Subjects: LCSH: United States—Study and teaching—History. | United States—Study and teaching—Historiography. | United States—Civilization.
Classification: LCC E175.8 .D59 2022 (print) | LCC E175.8 (ebook) | DDC 973.07—dc23
LC record available at https://lccn.loc.gov/2021019524
LC ebook record available at https://lccn.loc.gov/2021019525

ISBN: 978-1-138-77503-9 (hbk)
ISBN: 978-1-138-77504-6 (pbk)
ISBN: 978-1-315-72674-8 (ebk)

DOI: 10.4324/9781315726748

Typeset in Bembo
by Apex CoVantage, LLC

For Mandi and Ronan

CONTENTS

List of figures   x
Acknowledgements   xi

Introduction   1

A photograph of Mrs. Watson   1
What is American studies?   7
About this book   10
About the name, briefly   14
Further reading   16

1 **Studying America before American studies**   17

Naming America   17
Dreaming America   20
Towards American studies   30
Summary   35
Further reading   36

2 **The rise of American studies**   38

American studies in 'the American Century'   38
Main Currents in American Thought   41

Three founding narratives 45
The internationalisation of American studies 55
Summary 58
Further reading 59

3 The subjects of American studies — 61

American studies and the humanities (1) 63
The visual in American studies 75
American studies and the humanities (2) 77
American studies and the social sciences 84
America outside American studies 90
Summary 93
Further reading 94

4 Methods and models of American studies — 96

An archive of the Viet Nam War 96
In praise of interdisciplinarity 100
Against interdisciplinarity 103
Totality and fragmentation in American studies 106
Comparative American studies 110
Summary 114
Further reading 115

5 The scales of American studies — 117

Subnational American studies 118
Hemispheric American studies 123
Transpacific American studies 128
Global American studies 131
Summary 135
Further reading 136

6 The politics of American studies — 138

Edna Pontellier's swim 138
American studies and the Cold War 144
Liberating American studies 147

Ecopolitical American studies 151
Coda: resources of hope 155
Summary 157
Further reading 158

Conclusion 159

Glossary 168
Timeline 174
References 183
Index 192

FIGURES

0.1	Gordon Parks, *Ella Watson* (1942)	2
0.2	Grant Wood, *American Gothic* (1930). Art Institute of Chicago	3
1.1	George Alfred Williams, *Pocahontas Saves Captain John Smith*. Illustration in Kate Dickinson Sweetser, *Ten American Girls from History* (New York: Harper, 1917)	26
1.2	U.S. territorial acquisitions 1783–1853, including the Louisiana Purchase of 1803. Map in Edward Channing, *A Short History of the United States for School Use* (New York: Macmillan, 1900)	32
2.1	Margaret Mead *(left)* at the Harvard Student Council's Seminar in American Civilization, Salzburg, 1947 (photographer unknown)	56
3.1	The defaced Albert Pike Memorial, Washington, D.C., 2 July 2020 (photograph: AgnosticPreachersKid)	70
3.2	Edward S. Curtis, *Acoma from the South* (1904)	78
4.1	Vietnam Memorial Wall, Washington, D.C. (photograph: David J. Jackson, 2018)	99
5.1	Solomon D. Butcher, *Miss Mary Longfellow holding down a claim west of Broken Bow, Nebraska* (undated)	122
6.1	Information Centre at Grand Isle East State Park, destroyed by Hurricane Katrina (photograph: Marvin Neuman/FEMA, 2005)	142

ACKNOWLEDGEMENTS

This short book has, for several reasons, been a long time in the making. I should begin by acknowledging the support and understanding shown during this period by members of Routledge's editorial teams on both sides of the Atlantic, including Eve Mayer, Iram Satti and Amy Welmers. Particular gratitude is owed to Siobhán Poole, who invited me to write the book, and to Emily Irvine and Kimberley Smith for their great help during the project's final stages. I only hope that the result is a suitable reward for everyone's patience.

I am grateful for the support of colleagues in the School of Social Sciences and Humanities at Loughborough University who double as both fellow Americanists and close friends: in particular Brian Jarvis, Paul Jenner and Pete Templeton. Near to the book's completion, the opportunity generously offered by Catherine Armstrong to teach with her a module in late nineteenth-century and early twentieth-century American cultural history was invaluable, as were the support and advice of another Loughborough colleague and friend Siân Adiseshiah. I owe a good deal, also, to the anonymous reviewers of the original proposal for their constructive suggestions as to how the volume might be strengthened. Other intellectual debts to the many Americanists whose work has informed and inspired my own over several decades are honoured, I hope, by comments and references in the text that follows.

The friendship and humour of Francis Bowdery, Mandi Connolly, Ronan Connolly, Denise Ollerenshaw, Andy Smith, Gill Smith and Russell Wilson have been vital along the way, especially during that part of the writing done during the global lockdown in the face of COVID-19. Thanks are due also to Ichrak Dik for many engaging conversations about the United States. Finally, this book would not have been written without the companionship, support and encouragement of Karen Kennedy.

INTRODUCTION

A PHOTOGRAPH OF MRS. WATSON

To begin thinking about the theory and practice of American studies, take a look at Figure 0.1 on the following page. The bottom half of this monochrome photograph shows an African American woman, pictured from just below the waist in an interior setting. Her gaze is directed slightly towards the left of the frame, rather than engaging the viewer directly. The broom she holds and the mop propped nearby suggest, along with the plain dress she is wearing, that she is employed as a cleaner. A further supposition might be made that she works in a government building of some kind, since hanging on the wall behind her is the flag of the United States, unfurled downwards rather than extended horizontally.

Other details, too, can be accumulated in an initial inventory of the photograph: the woman's carefully parted hair and round-rimmed glasses, for example, give her an air of sobriety or seriousness rather than frivolity. The image also appears *posed*, evoking a formal portrait rather than a shot which the photographer has grabbed fortuitously from the flow of daily events.

Having described the image with some care, how then to *interpret* it? Our analysis might begin by considering the photograph's title. To complicate matters, however, this picture is variously titled, rather than having a single or definitive label. In some reproductions (including the one used here), it is known simply by the name of its subject: Ella Watson. Elsewhere, as in the Library of Congress archives, it is entitled *Washington, D.C. government charwoman*. As against the humanising reference to Ella Watson, this choice of

Figure 0.1 Gordon Parks, *Ella Watson* (1942).

Source: Wikimedia Commons. Courtesy of the Library of Congress, LC-DIG-fsa-8b14845.

title depersonalises, erasing any trace of the woman's individuality and instead understanding her in terms of the function she performs within the apparatus of American government. More often still, however, the image has circulated under the different title of *American Gothic*. Through this act of naming, the photographer initiates a dialogue with another *American Gothic* in U.S. visual culture: Grant Wood's iconic painting, which was produced in Iowa in 1930, twelve years before the portrait of Ella Watson. As can be seen in Figure 0.2, Wood focuses on a white man and woman of differing ages and indistinct relationship to one another, positioning them in front of a white clapboard house emblematic of small-town America. While the woman, who is younger than her counterpart, looks towards the right of the frame, the man challenges us frontally, brandishing a pitchfork that expresses male agency as efficiently as Watson's broom in the photograph signifies feminised labour.

Almost from the moment of its composition, Wood's version of *American Gothic* has been an object of contention and controversy. Opinion as to what the image means is radically divided.

Figure 0.2 Grant Wood, *American Gothic* (1930). Art Institute of Chicago.

Source: Wikimedia Commons.

For some observers, these plain and upright figures pictured in a plain and upright environment are intended by Wood to pay tribute to 'the denizens of Iowa' and their 'values of sobriety, moral vigilance, patriarchy, and the rest' (Hughes 1997, 442). Other viewers, however, sense an impulse towards *critique* or *satire*, not celebration, with the man's unbending features and the pitchfork's phallic prongs exposing an America given up terrifyingly to judgement, control, even violence.

The 1942 version of *American Gothic*, by the African American photographer and filmmaker Gordon Parks, is similarly plural in its significances and implications. The alternative title of *Washington, D.C. government charwoman*, preferred by the Library of Congress and other institutions, has the effect of situating its African American subject in the administrative centre of the United States: not in a position of great authority or power, admittedly, but nevertheless near to the heart of things. This suggestion of rapport between African Americans and the nation-state is abetted, perhaps, by aspects of the picture's iconography: Mrs. Watson is photographed, after all, in front of the Stars and Stripes. Yet such an optimistic or affirmative reading of the image soon comes under pressure. For, while there is indeed proximity here between the Black woman and the national flag, there is not intimacy: she is physically a little separated from it, and in its scale and positioning it looms over her, rather than offering her any kind of embrace.

The photograph prompts consideration of varying engagements with the U.S. flag in African American culture. For some Black Americans, at least, the flag, along with other icons of U.S. nationalism, has been an object of aspiration rather than something provoking anxiety or fright. An exemplary figure in this tradition is the intellectual and activist Anna Julia Cooper (1858–1964), who attempted in her 1902 speech 'The Ethics of the Negro Question' to convince sceptical whites of African Americans' patriotic fervour and hence their civic entitlement. As Cooper testified:

> With hearty earnestness the million and [a] half colored boys and girls in the public schools [of the] South repeat on June 14 the salute to their country's flag: "I pledge allegiance to my flag and to the country for which it stands".

(1902, 25)

These Black children comprise, in Cooper's words, 'as staunch and loyal a yeomanry as any country can boast' (25). Such a tradition of African American respect for the flag endures to the present day, as can be seen in Barack Obama's recent autobiography, *A Promised Land*. Describing night-time walks that he took early in his presidency among Washington, D.C.'s symbols of U.S. nationalism, Obama recalls seeing 'the regal mass of the White House, its flag aloft on the roof, lit bright' (2020, 5).

Yet while such gestures of Black patriotism should not be disregarded, it is undeniable that often for African Americans the U.S. flag has been bound up instead with terror. Take, for example, the former enslaved person Frederick Douglass's puncturing of nationalist complacency when in 1845, seven years after his escape, he addressed an abolitionist meeting on the subject of 'My Slave Experience in Maryland': 'in this land of liberty, I'm a slave. The twenty-six States that blaze forth on your flag, proclaim a compact to return me to bondage if I run away, and keep me in bondage if I submit' (Douglass 1999, 13). Or consider Spike Lee's 1992 biopic of the radical Black leader Malcolm X. Here the flag is the first image we see, pristine and filling the screen; however, as the opening credits proceed, it is cross-cut with video footage of Los Angeles police officers' vicious and sustained beating of the African American Rodney King in 1991. The promise signified by the flag is immediately annulled by its association in Lee's subversive montage with racist thuggery. Lee jolts us into recalling how the Stars and Stripes has played a key part in rituals of white supremacist violence that extend from lynchings of Black Americans in the late nineteenth and early twentieth centuries to contemporary nationalist rallies. The African American scholar and campaigner Cornel West thus selects only one episode from this history of patriotically infused terror when he describes how a number of Black men who fought for the United States in the First World War were subsequently murdered by racists: 'They put the flag around them to let them know they were not going to be full citizens, even though they had been willing to give their lives for the country' (Muir 2020, n.p.). Here, unlike in the picture of Ella Watson, there *is* enfolding of the African American by the flag, only now as shroud rather than as a source of comfort or warmth.

To further these reflections on the place of African Americans in the United States, we might turn again to the photograph's better-known title. *American Gothic* has ominous resonances, suggesting that its Black subject is not nourished or supported by her nation, but, on the contrary, haunted and menaced. Many other African American artists, working in a variety of media, have also turned to Gothic in order to evoke the Black community's experiences. Numerous literary examples include Toni Morrison's neo-slave narrative *Beloved* (1987) and Richard Wright's anti-lynching poem 'Between the World and Me' (1935), in which the agonised speaker who imagines his own victimisation is reduced to 'dry bones . . . my face a stony skull staring in yellow surprise at the sun' (1935, 19). Films in this vein range from the low-budget shocker *Dr. Black, Mr. Hyde* (1976) to Jordan Peele's more polished *Get Out* (2017), which shows lethal white violence underlying a landscape of stately porticos and manicured lawns. Instances of Gothic can also be found in other domains of African American visual culture besides cinema and photography, including the contemporary artist Kara Walker's striking cut-paper silhouettes of brutalising scenes from slavery. All of this work, including Parks's picture of Ella Watson, fulfils the imperative which Malcolm X set out in his 1964 speech, 'The Ballot or the Bullet': namely, to see America 'through the eyes of the victim' and to speak not of 'any American dream' but 'an American nightmare' (Malcolm X 1989, 42).

Putting the photograph of Mrs. Watson in contact with other examples of the African American Gothic tradition is not the only thing, interpretively, that we can do with it. The image might, for example, be considered alongside other work which Parks did in the course of a long career as a photographer and filmmaker. Though he was always alert to scenes of Black vulnerability or victimisation, he was also interested in contrary evidence of agency and resistance. Thus, in 1963, he photographed Malcolm X himself in commanding pose, arm upraised; while for Hollywood in 1971, he directed *Shaft*, which follows the formulas of the mass-audience private eye thriller, yet, strikingly, has a physically assertive and mentally agile African American protagonist. Or we might acknowledge Ella Watson's *class subordination*, as well as her racial disadvantage, and thus be prompted to enter the photograph into conversation with other images and narratives of exploited labour in the United States. Again, the potential archive is abundant. Examples extend from Herman Melville's harrowing account of exploitation at a

New England paper mill in his short story 'The Paradise of Bachelors and the Tartarus of Maids' (1855), through journalism and photography documenting the horrors of work in urban sweatshops early in the twentieth century, to contemporary representations in a variety of media of the American precariat (a social cluster that, like the ranks of oppressed labour to which Ella Watson belonged during the 1940s, includes many people of colour). In these various ways, Parks's photograph ceases to be an object in isolation and instead is positioned as one link in a longer chain of American representations.

WHAT IS AMERICAN STUDIES?

The discussion that has taken place over the last few pages, beginning with a close study of a single photograph before spooling outwards, is intended as a specimen of work that may be done by practitioners of American studies. Small-scale as it is, the example nevertheless allows us to identify several of this academic subject's key principles and processes. Four of these are briefly considered here, ahead of their lengthier unpacking later in the book.

To start with what seems a declaration of the obvious, American studies finds the bulk of its primary materials in the cultural and social life of the United States. Hence, a photograph of a government charwoman in Washington, D.C. comes within its ambit, while an equivalent picture of a cleaner in Warsaw or in Wuhan does not. Yet, such apparently irreproachable statements need to be qualified. For American studies' interest in the products of U.S. culture and society is geographically expansive or elongated, and thus liable to take practitioners of the subject far beyond the national borders. People may find themselves studying not only territorially restricted phenomena such as surfing subcultures in contemporary California or the poetry of nineteenth-century Nebraska, but globally scattered topics that might range from Japan's importation of baseball from the United States in the 1870s through the proliferation of Wild West clubs in Germany to the repurposing of beats from U.S. hip hop by performers in Nigeria and Senegal. In addition, many professionals in the field have chafed recently against its long-standing confinement to matters relating to the United States and propose instead much more spatially generous understandings of the term 'American'. This is an important topic to which we will return, especially in Chapters 1 and 5. A few preliminary thoughts, however, are offered near the end of this Introduction.

Secondly, American studies is constitutionally uneasy about traditional disciplinary boundaries and often works *across* rather than *within* these. In the example sketched earlier, the starting point was a photograph and the analysis observed the protocols of photography studies by thinking about such things as the image's formality and its framing and iconography. Even as it considered these elements, however, the discussion began to cross over into other disciplines, including *social history* (inquiring what the photograph might tell us about Black experience in the mid-twentieth-century United States) and *cultural studies* (positioning the image alongside other instances of African American expression that span multiple media while sharing core aims of uncovering and contesting unjust power structures). Several larger-scale projects were also outlined, with these potential lines of research encouraging the American studies scholar to traverse the borders between disciplines and to analyse not only photography but cinema, say, or fiction or poetry. This core commitment in the field to *interdisciplinarity* is examined in Chapters 3 and 4.

The case study above allows us, thirdly, to witness the field's keen interest in questions of America's *meaning*. What is suggested or signified about America by the conjunction in Parks's picture of a working-class Black woman and the flag of the United States? Work done within American studies shows us that, far from being fixed, the meaning of America is actually fluid, unstable, and open to ceaseless reinterpretation. This can be seen in miniature by positioning Parks's image, with its ironic or subversive treatment of the U.S. flag, against other well-known photographs in which the flag is offered as a symbol of national unity that dissolves or renders inconsequential racial hierarchies and class divisions. Examples of such patriotic photography include Joe Rosenthal's picture of U.S. Marines raising the Stars and Stripes at Iwo Jima in Japan near the end of World War II, and Thomas E. Franklin's image of firefighters performing the same action amidst the rubble of the World Trade Center in New York City soon after the 9/11 attacks in 2001. Yet, American studies also teaches us that differing assessments as to what America means or signifies are not abstract matters, comprising merely the stuff of disinterested debate in university seminar rooms; rather, these variations in interpretation have powerful consequences for people's lives. The effects of white supremacist visions of the United States, descending from the Declaration of Independence itself in 1776 with its reference to the threat posed by 'merciless Indian Savages' (Beeman 2010, 9), are felt acutely by communities of colour who have endured horrifying disadvantages. To be excluded from the dominant models or blueprints of the United States is also, potentially, to be deprived of adequate life chances – or even of life itself.

Finally, as the last paragraph suggests, American studies is worldly in its outlook, being deeply interested in issues of injustice and inequality in the territory it covers. Not only interested in these, in fact, but profoundly energised by them and seeking to contribute to their redress. This is in the spirit of socially engaged intellectual work as it was set out in a famous remark by Karl Marx. In the eleventh of his 'Theses on Feuerbach', originally drafted in 1845 though not published until 1888, Marx writes that 'The philosophers have only *interpreted* the world in various ways; the point is, to *change* it' (1994, 101, emphases in original). Practitioners of American studies might be wary of comparing their field with the discipline of political philosophy which Marx has in mind, given the latter's immediate and fundamental concern with questions of how society is organised. Nevertheless, in ways that should be neither overstated nor downplayed, American studies participates through its own scholarly activity in campaigns for social justice. While much more will be said about the field's political consciousness in Chapter 6, it might be helpful to illustrate the point here by returning one last time to the photograph of Ella Watson.

Mrs. Watson herself told Parks as he was photographing her that she was only 'muddling through in Washington' rather than 'loving' life in the capital city, and that she was 'bringing up two grandchildren on wages barely enough for one' (Parks 2005, 65). Even without the benefit of biographical knowledge of this sort, however, the American studies scholar is well equipped by training to observe and communicate the picture's ironies – how it alludes to a situation whereby African Americans were ruthlessly exploited for their labour at the same time as being denied full membership of the nation. Yet, the image is not simply a museum artefact that records inequities of the past; it is also a live object which prompts us, as we scan it, to draw comparisons with *ongoing* economic, social and cultural deficits faced by minority communities in the United States. The scholar who discusses this photograph thus has the opportunity to perform not only an archivist's but an *activist's* work. Here it is suggestive to recall briefly the commendation which Parks received from his boss Roy Stryker, of the Farm Security Administration, for the portraits he took of Mrs. Watson (there were others besides *American Gothic*). Parks was showing through this work, Stryker said, how he could use his preferred discipline to 'involve' himself productively 'in people's problems' (Parks 2005, 66). Anyone operating in American studies should, of course, be cautious about claiming similar immediacy and relevance for their chosen activity as scholars. Humility is indispensable here: after all, an unsolicited academic essay about a photograph differs significantly in its potential circulation and impact from the photograph itself. Nevertheless, even when focusing on topics ostensibly rooted in the past, practitioners of American studies may still establish a connection through their work to current 'problems' in the United States. Hence, as I hope to show in this book, much of the field's excitement and purpose.

ABOUT THIS BOOK

American Studies: The Basics comprises six main chapters. The first begins by acknowledging that, compared with philosophy, say, or with medicine or history, American studies is a very young subject, only emerging under this name in the middle third of the twentieth century. Yet, America had, of course, been an object of extensive scholarly inquiry for hundreds of years before this moment of academic formalisation. Knowledge producers extending from natural historians to political philosophers, and from geographers to literary critics, had written about America with agendas as disparate as their specialisms. Chapter 1, then, surveys what we might think of as predisciplinary American studies, taking this phase to stretch roughly from Puritan settlers' arrival in New England early in the seventeenth century to a time early in the twentieth century when scholars situated in numerous traditional disciplines turned increasingly to the United States as an object of research. The chapter will uncover in this pre-institutional stage of American study a number of themes and approaches that later recur in professionalised American studies itself.

Following on from this prehistory, so to speak, the book's remaining chapters are all concerned with aspects of American studies as a codified discipline (or, as we might more aptly call it, an *interdiscipline* or field, since typically it operates across the lines of established subjects). Chapters 2 to 5 explore, in effect, the 'when', 'what', 'how' and 'where' of American studies. Chapter 2 begins by documenting the field's emergence and recognition either side of World War II, aligning this with the increasing potency of the United States in terms of military capability, economic activity and cultural reach. While aiming to avoid a simplistic genealogy that traces the subject's institutional origins to a tiny set of progenitors, thereby overlooking the contributions made by countless other scholars, the chapter nevertheless discusses several figures in American studies' first wave whose work had a galvanising effect. Some of the conceptual frameworks and analytical styles developed by this generation continue to be productive today; others, though, as we will see, are now regarded with suspicion as both methodologically flawed and politically compromised. The chapter also considers how American studies' post-war institutionalisation in the United States coincided with the establishment in numerous international locations of centres and programmes devoted to the subject. Then, as now, American studies was advanced not by U.S. academics alone but by globally dispersed scholars.

Chapter 3, addressing the question of 'what', aims to identify the subject areas that feed into American studies. This task is not so simple, since, historically, the field has been supplied by multiple academic disciplines with widely varying objects and approaches. Something of this disciplinary range can be gauged by listing only a selection of the many cultural and social outputs emanating from or in some way traceable to the United States that have been or still are explored in American studies curricula and research projects. So: novels, poetry, films, TV shows, paintings, photographs, theatrical performances, dialects, geopolitical manoeuvres, military campaigns, political parties, economic structures, industrial innovations, architectural styles, theme parks, prison regimes, educational systems, sports traditions and philosophical ideas. The field is not, however, a perfect democracy in its weighting of constituent disciplines: some academic areas, as we will see, have proved to be more equal than others. For a number of observers, American studies has been skewed in its work by giving too much importance to *literary criticism* at the expense of other subjects (an understandable trajectory, perhaps, given that many of the field's most influential early practitioners found their first academic homes in departments of English). Nevertheless, Chapter 3 begins by considering the key role that literary scholarship, together with other humanities disciplines such as history, philosophy and religious studies, has played in what has been called the 'field-imaginary' of American studies (Pease 1994, 11). To counter the risk of implying that close reading of verbal texts is American studies' only protocol, however, the chapter goes on to consider also two other strands that are crucial to the field. The first of these is work in the humanities directed not towards the verbal, but the *visual* (or the *audio-visual*): for example, the study of painting and cinema. The second is work in the social sciences, principally sociology and anthropology. If the influence which these latter subjects have had on American studies has been intermittent, it has nevertheless been important (and will continue to be so). For the social sciences propose not only new objects of study but also new methodologies, departing from humanities-style textual interpretation in favour of an examination of larger data sets that, it is hoped, can elucidate major structures and processes in the United States.

Chapter 4, on the 'how' of American studies, assesses several of the methods that historically have been dominant in the field. It begins by exploring the key practice of interdisciplinarity. American studies, to be sure, has no monopoly in interdisciplinary work: even the most navel-gazing of academic subjects is liable periodically to advance or reinvigorate itself by broaching topics and approaches that lie outside its traditional boundaries. However, a commitment to the interdisciplinary is rooted more deeply in American studies than in most other fields. It is important, therefore, to assess its contribution to the subject, reckoning mainly with its positive achievements but touching also on its occasional perils. The chapter then moves to consider two other questions of method. Firstly, attempts early in the life of American studies to uncover narratives, symbols and ideas widely shared by people in the United States are juxtaposed with efforts by later practitioners, including in our own moment, to unveil instead difference and dissensus among the nation's multiple communities. Secondly, consideration is given to the notion and the practice of *comparative American studies*. For an enduring strain of U.S. nationalism, the country should be understood as distinctive, even exceptional. However, we will assess the counterforce in American studies that proposes that objects of interest to the field are most illuminated when they are closely compared with materials from other parts of the world.

This reframing of American studies so that it extends its analytical work beyond U.S. borders is examined in detail in Chapter 5, which is devoted to the question of 'where'. The chapter will show that debates about the field's territorial reach have occurred right from its inception. The seemingly uncontentious proposition that the subject should align its borders with the frontiers of the United States itself has rarely held up in the face of the realities of study 'on the ground'. Some researchers in American studies operate in microscopic ways, for example, moving below the level of the nation in order to explore significant cultural and social variations among *regions* of the United States. Many other people, however, work across much larger geographical ranges than that afforded by the nation, insisting that any adequate study of the United States has to burst its territorial boundaries and pursue its many and complex effects across the world. What has been called *the transnational turn* in American studies of the past two or three decades lends itself, though, to granular description. Americanists may, for instance, explore the entanglements of the United States with Central and South America or with nations in and around the Pacific Ocean – or, with greater geographical ambition still, they might model American studies as a field truly *global* or *planetary* in its coverage. Across the chapter, we will assess the strengths of these various attempts to recalibrate the subject's spatial design.

Finally, Chapter 6 assesses shifts in the political positioning of American studies from its beginnings as a formalised subject to the present. The book's earlier chapters consider the ideological implications of individual scholars' work, even of key methods and approaches in the field; this section, however, will give us an opportunity to think more systematically about the political directions taken by American studies in its engagement with the United States. We begin by discussing the part which the subject played during the Cold War, particularly in the 1950s and 1960s. A story often told about American studies in this period describes it as conservative and nationalistic in outlook, supplying intellectual ballast to the U.S. government's attempts to disseminate both at home and abroad an upbeat, affirmative account of the country. Our analysis, however, will suggest that a nuanced assessment of American studies in this era, acknowledging different positions, is more persuasive. Nevertheless, the belief of many scholars and activists by the end of the 1960s that the subject was grounded in a narrow conception of the United States – as white, Anglophone, male and straight – proved powerful and led to lasting changes in both its intellectual design and its political orientation. The chapter will consider how American studies down to our own moment has been reshaped by the activisms of many minority communities and identity groupings in the United States, including feminist, African American, Native American, Latinx, LGBTQ and other social movements. For these struggles, the nation-state is still the principal site of intervention, given their aim of creating a more just and equal United States. The section of the chapter that follows, however, examines an ecologically oriented American studies that tends to work across a variety of scales – from the very local to the planetary. We will ask what the field takes from and what it might contribute to ongoing environmental thought and activism.

Writing just after World War II about the state of U.S. higher education, Robert Spiller situated the emergence of American studies in 'an era of revolution in both ideas and methods'. In the very next paragraph of his article, however, he sounded a note of caution about the prospects for this new academic subject, asking: 'Is it a fad or a lasting reform?' (1949, 166). More than seventy years later, the survival of American studies as a substantial programme of research and teaching suggests that Spiller's question can now be answered with some confidence by choosing the second option. My aim in this book is to unfold the subject's intellectual interest and social purpose which account for its longevity.

ABOUT THE NAME, BRIEFLY

An old joke is told about the name given to the loose assembly of kingdoms and federations which sprawled across Western and Central Europe from 800 AD. The *Holy Roman Empire*, according to humourists, was neither 'Holy' nor 'Roman' nor even, properly speaking, an 'Empire'. As a descriptor, 'American studies' is nothing like as rickety or inadequate. The existence of an extensive network of associations, journals and conferences affiliating themselves explicitly to a programme called 'American studies' suggests that the label remains clear and viable. The commissioning of this book as part of a series on academic disciplines and study objects is itself further evidence of the term's resilience. Nevertheless, as already indicated, many practitioners of the subject have been driven in recent decades to interrogate the name of 'American studies', rather than deploying it instinctively and without self-consciousness. People working in American studies have found themselves pausing in the face of this labelling of what they do – suggesting a terminological difficulty, if not a crisis, that is not encountered by people who identify themselves as working in chemistry, for example, or medicine or geology. American studies scholars feel particular anxiety about incorporating 'American' in the name of the subject, taking this as conceding rather than contesting aggressive claims long made in the United States that the adjective refers exclusively to the nation, instead of applying to the totality of the continent that stretches northwards to Canada and south all the way to Argentina and Chile – and encompassing also the islands of the Caribbean.

Fuller engagement with this issue is deferred until later in the book. In the meantime, though, it is advisable for readers coming across the many references here to 'American studies' to bear in mind that it is contentious as a descriptor, rather than unproblematic. Borrowing a practice from philosophy, the term may lend itself to being put *under erasure*. Philosophers adopt this device with respect to a vexed or unstable part of their conceptual vocabulary when, as Simon Blackburn summarises, 'it is necessary to use it, but it is only doubtfully intelligible' (2016, 160). A word put under erasure is still legible to readers, but its authority or solidity is visibly compromised by striking through it on the page. By analogy, then, this book would be ~~American Studies~~: *The Basics*. While for obvious reasons I have chosen not to follow this method in the text, readers might themselves mentally conjure up the addition of strikethrough whenever they encounter the term 'American studies'. Thinking in this way from the outset is certainly not intended to have a confusing or demoralising effect, giving the impression that scholars are so unsure about their activity that they are unable even to find a name for it. Rather, considering 'American studies' as under erasure both acknowledges the label's continuing usefulness (not least because of its history and its many institutional applications) *and* its openness to debate (evidence in itself of an energetic, inquisitive discipline that is unafraid to ask searching questions, including about something as fundamental as what it calls itself).

FURTHER READING

A very engaging starting point, both playful and sympathetically attuned to the reader new to the field, is Philip J. Deloria and Alexander I. Olson, *American Studies: A User's Guide* (Oakland: University of California Press, 2017). Also recommended as beginnings are the succinct essays in *Keywords for American Cultural Studies*, 2nd ed., ed. Bruce Burgett and Glenn Hendler (New York: New York University Press, 2014). See in addition George Lipsitz's short, attractively upbeat overview of the field in 'What is American Studies?: An ASA White Paper' (2015), available online at www.theasa.net/sites/default/files/What_is_American_Studies.pdf.

Heftier volumes, though still sensitive to the needs of readers finding their way in the subject, include Howard Temperley and Christopher Bigsby (ed.), *A New Introduction to American Studies* (London: Pearson Education, 2006); *American Studies: An Anthology*, ed. Janice A. Radway, Kevin J. Gaines, Barry Shank and Penny Von Eschen (Chichester: Wiley-Blackwell, 2009); John Carlos Rowe (ed.), *A Concise Companion to American Studies* (Chichester: Wiley-Blackwell, 2010), which is not so much concise as pleasingly compendious; and Neil Campbell and Alasdair Kean, *American Cultural Studies: An Introduction to American Culture*, 4th ed. (Abingdon: Routledge, 2016). On American cultural history specifically, see two books of disparate scale: Eric Avila, *American Cultural History: A Very Short Introduction* (Oxford: Oxford University Press, 2018) and Karen Halttunen (ed.), *A Companion to American Cultural History* (Chichester: Wiley-Blackwell, 2014).

STUDYING AMERICA BEFORE AMERICAN STUDIES

As Chapter 2 will show, the history of American studies as a consolidated academic subject is quite short, reaching back only to the middle of the twentieth century. However, a full disciplinary paraphernalia of journals and conferences and degree programmes is not essential for something to register as an object of study, a repository of intellectual energies and imaginative investments. Such was the case with 'America', from the early modern period onwards. While the demarcation of American studies as a field and the codification of its methods still lay sometime in the future, America as a focus of inquiry was excitedly engaged by mapmakers and geographers, naturalists and poets, historians and theologians. In this chapter, I consider a number of these pioneering, pre-disciplinary contributions from the beginning of the sixteenth century to the earlier part of the twentieth century. Scattered and fragmentary though it may have been, and powered by the enthusiasm of lay individuals rather than by the organised activity of an established academic community, this work nevertheless identified topics and themes that would later be of interest to American studies itself. It also, on occasion, presented America in ways that American studies would challenge and try to undo.

NAMING AMERICA

Before America could be studied, it had first to be named. Precisely *which* label, however, to affix to part or all of the continent situated between the Atlantic and Pacific Oceans proved a contentious rather than straightforward matter. Indeed, if a proposal made by Bartolomé de las Casas in his *History of the Indies* (1527–61) had been adopted, *Columba*, and not *America*, would have prevailed. Kanye West would subsequently have rapped on 'Who Will Survive in Columba'; Bret Easton Ellis would have written *Columban Psycho*, and this book would be *Columban Studies: The Basics*.

In other of his voluminous writings, as well as in his frequent practical interventions as a Roman Catholic monk and bishop in Central and South America, de las Casas advanced a forceful critique of the brutalities of European colonialism in which he had once played a part. On this occasion, however, his grievance was smaller, having to do with the decision to call the vast landmass at the western edge of the Atlantic 'America'. This name had been chosen in tribute to Amerigo Vespucci, a Florentine merchant who participated in several voyages to the region at the turn of the sixteenth century. Yet to de las Casas, Vespucci was a fraud and an egotist whose self-serving account of his travels was intended to erase memories of the pioneering exploration undertaken a little earlier by the Genoese sailor, Christopher Columbus. In de las Casas' words, 'the said continent ought to be called Columba', after Columbus, 'and not America after Americo [i.e. Amerigo]' (Vespucci 1894, 76).

Evidently, by the time de las Casas came to write *History of the Indies*, 'America' was fully accredited as a geographical label. Yet, the word had only appeared publicly in 1507, on a map produced near Strasbourg in eastern France by a local scholar and poet Matthias Ringmann and a German cartographer Martin Waldseemüller. Having read with excitement Vespucci's reports of a continent far across the Atlantic that was abundant in flora and fauna, Waldseemüller and Ringmann temporarily set aside their work on an atlas and instead rushed into print a large map of the world that would feature prominently this newly described land. To contemporary eyes, however, the 1507 map looks curiously uneven or unfinished. For, while Europe, Africa and Asia are broadly convincing in outline and scale, North and South America appear as weirdly thinned down. The continent is presented with roughly the latitudinal sprawl we know it to have, extending between the two poles, but with nothing like its actual longitudinal stretch. A gap is also apparent between the northern and southern landmasses, fantasising free passage to ships where in reality Central America intrudes. More interesting to us in the present context, however, is that on this map, for the first time in published work, the word 'America' appears. Not, it is true, where present-day usage might lead us to look for it, printed across the northern geographical territory now occupied by the United States. Rather, the word is inscribed horizontally across the lower part of *South* America, with this off-centre placement, together with a modest font size, masking the fact that Waldseemüller and Ringmann meant it to stand as the name of the whole continent.

The naming of this newly mapped territory as 'America' was unexpected and whimsical. At a time when European cartographers were scrambling to convert reports and measurements brought back from across the Atlantic into comprehensible visual form, many other labels would have been possible. Waldseemüller himself, in fact, came to regret his and Ringmann's choice, as one that gave too much credit to Vespucci: one of his later maps, the *Carta Marina* (1516), is notable not only for its much greater topographical detail but for the absence of the word 'America'. Random or fortuitous as its origin may have been, however, 'America' stuck. In Toby Lester's words, 'It was a poetic choice, one that would echo down throughout the ages' (2009, 5). Here, however, rather than reflecting on the name's poetry, I identify briefly three more of its properties.

First is its *narrowing range of reference across time*. Though the makers of the 1507 map took 'America' to designate the continent at large, rather than simply referring to one of its parts, this expansive spatial implication has not always prevailed. Allusions still to North, Central and South America support the original intentions of Waldseemüller and Ringmann but are complicated by frequent use of 'America' now as merely a synonym for the United States. Chapter 5 of this book will build on the point made in the Introduction that much recent work in American studies has aimed at decoupling 'America' from the United States and at restoring a sense of the name's broad territorial range.

Second is the name's *European origin*. Later parts of the book will document and evaluate the transnational turn that American studies has taken in the last two decades. We will witness increasing recognition of the extent to which the United States is constituted by ongoing interplay with peoples and ideas and cultures originating from beyond the national borders. However, such transnational dynamics have a long history, as can be seen by Europe's naming of 'America' at the dawn of the sixteenth century. In an interesting meditation on this word, Kirsten Silva Gruesz offers the alternative suggestion that it may actually be derived from 'Amerrique', a label applied to part of its territory by an Indigenous community in what is now Nicaragua. The 'radical proposition' here, as Gruesz puts it, is that 'the name "America" comes from within the New World rather than being imposed on it' (2014, 22). Unfortunately, however, this counter-narrative of America's naming has much less traction among scholars than the Eurocentric account which traces the word back to Vespucci.

Thirdly, the name's *imperialism*. To say that the word 'America' is European in origin is also to say that it is informed by imperial ambitions. Just as the map could be filled in with little or no attention paid to Indigenous peoples' own labels, so too the terrain it referenced could be profitably occupied by Europeans with relatively slight resistance, condemning the native inhabitants to fates variously of being exploited, enslaved or exterminated. One of Vespucci's letters, written after his second voyage of 1499–1500, evokes these radical asymmetries of power between native and incomer. He describes how, in return for acquiring more than twenty-five kilograms of pearls from one American community, his expeditionary force offered 'nothing but . . . looking glasses, and beads, and ten bells, and tin foil' (1894, 29). This references an opportunistic and fleeting act of appropriation; soon afterwards, however, systemic European colonisation of America would begin, fulfilling the threat of imperial control carried by the very choice of name for the continent.

DREAMING AMERICA

Given their tightly defined fields and systematic methodologies, and their frequently dry institutional arrangements, we tend not to think of academic disciplines as having dream lives. But if academic American studies has a relatively sober disposition, the same cannot be said of pre-disciplinary accounts of America, produced from the sixteenth century onwards. On the contrary, these are clearly infused with desire and yearning. For multiple constituencies, extending from religious radicals through merchants and entrepreneurs to naturalists, America was not only a location in geography but a dreamscape (Lawrence Buell, the contemporary Americanist, speaks of 'its centuries-old history as a dream space' [2013, 24]). The name itself, in fact, rapidly became a metaphor for a heightened object of aspiration. The *Oxford English Dictionary* defines 'America' in such dreamlike terms as 'A place which one longs to reach; an ultimate or idealized destination or aim; an (esp. newly identified) object of personal ambition or desire'. Immediately beneath this definition, the *OED* gives historical examples of the term used in this desiring way. The first is by the English metaphysical poet John Donne (1572–1631), writing most likely in the mid-1590s in his elegy, 'To his Mistress Going to Bed'. In relation to the woman's progressively naked body, as she is imagined undressing, the poem's male speaker casts himself in terms of a contemporary transatlantic explorer: 'Licence my roving hands, and let them go/Behind, before, above, between, below./O my America, my new found land' (Donne 2008, 13). Two lines later, the speaker discloses still more blatantly the contemporary dreams of imperialistic dominion and material acquisition in America, recasting his lover's body as 'My mine of precious stones, my empery [i.e. empire]' (13).

An argument might be made that Donne is able to think of America as a dreamscape or site of wish fulfilment because he had no personal familiarity with the place itself. His main habitats were the law courts and, later, the churches of Elizabethan and Jacobean London, not territories far across the Atlantic; he could therefore fantasise freely about a realm he would never visit. However, a sense of fantasy, an atmosphere of heightened desire, is apparent also in early writing about America done by people who *did* have intimate knowledge of the terrain. To give some indication of this, I discuss briefly now two very different sets of texts which date from the early seventeenth to the late eighteenth centuries: firstly, writings by Puritans who left England to forge a godly society across the Atlantic; secondly, accounts of this 'New World' aimed more at readers with material enrichment on their minds. The point is not to establish a stark divide, whereby in this chapter are pioneering reflections on America that we understand to be false or fictional because of their patently wish-fulfilling quality, while in later parts of the book is a professionalised American studies committed soberly to rigorous scholarship and to truth-telling. So pure a distinction is untenable: the work that contributes to academic American studies itself emerges from multiple moments and locations, directed by a host of perspectives and agendas, and so cannot claim in any simple sense to be expressing the 'truth' of America. Thus, the aim of the present section is not to expose falsehoods in these early attempts to study America, but rather to identify their orientations and assess their worldly effects.

One last preliminary observation: all of the texts discussed here orbit around territory now comprising part of the United States. As indicated previously, the name of 'America' gradually became more parochial, referring most often not to the continent in its entirety but only to a portion of the northern landmass. When, for example, the Puritan minister and scholar Cotton Mather began his colossal *Magnalia Christi Americana; or, The Ecclesiastical History of New-England* (1702) by declaring, 'I write the Wonders of the Christian Religion, flying from the Depravations of Europe, to the American Strand' (Mather 1855 [1702], 25), his readers would readily have understood that he meant America in this geographically circumscribed sense.

1) PURITAN VISIONS

By the time Mather came to write his book at the start of the eighteenth century, there was a lot of New England history for him to narrate. Since the 1620s, English emigres had settled in the north-eastern quadrant of the present-day United States, concentrating especially in Massachusetts, Connecticut and Rhode Island. They came, at least initially, for mainly religious reasons, seeking a terrain that was more hospitable than their own country to their Calvinist or 'Puritan' version of Protestantism. America, as a potential community of 'saints', was thus often figured in early Puritan representations in *utopian* terms. The most enduring trope in this tradition was probably first put into circulation at sea, rather than on American soil itself. As the flagship *Arbella*, packed with Calvinist emigrants, sailed towards the port of Salem in Massachusetts in 1630, John Winthrop is said to have preached the sermon that would later be called 'A Model of Christian Charity'. Near the end of an address which bracingly reminded his listeners of the many trials they would face in raising their new settlement, Winthrop offered a vision of America as a transfigured and resplendent space: 'we must consider that we shall be as a city upon a hill. The eyes of all people are upon us' (2015 [1630], n.p.).

The notion here of American distinctiveness, even *exceptionalism*, has survived from these precarious beginnings even into contemporary discourse in the United States. Metaphors may vary – President Donald Trump's American 'city', for instance, was not so much visible on a hill as hunkered down behind a militarised wall – but the promise of utopia remains. Yet any utopian vision is inevitably accompanied, as its shadow, by a *dystopian* counter-narrative. This notion is captured in Margaret Atwood's term *Ustopia*, a word that she coined 'by combining utopia and dystopia – the imagined perfect society and its opposite – because . . . each contains a latent version of the other' (Atwood 2011, n.p.). Thus, if America is considered exceptional in its possibilities, it is thereby exceptional too in its potential iniquities and its capacity to disappoint – something acknowledged by Buell when he describes it as 'a dream space, meaning simultaneously also of course a nightmare space' (2013, 24). Such a pessimistic turn is apparent in this early Puritan discourse. The supposedly devout were often portrayed by sermonisers as falling all too easily into ungodliness, thus squandering rather than realising America's unique promise. So, for example, the Massachusetts pastor, poet and astronomer Samuel Danforth assailed his congregation in a sermon entitled 'A Brief Recognition of New-Englands Errand into the Wilderness' (delivered in 1670, published the following year): 'Doth not a careless, remiss, flat, dry, dead, cold frame of spirit, grow in upon us secretly, strongly, prodigiously?' (2006 [1671], 14). Rather than surviving in piety, Danforth's listeners were in danger of perishing in 'the Gulf of Sensuality and Luxury' (17). For Michael Wigglesworth, Danforth's fellow Massachusetts minister, imaginings of an American dystopia were similarly omnipresent. In his poem, 'God's Controversy with New-England' (1662), he detected in the Puritan 'folk' not 'holiness' but 'Carnality'; not 'flaming Love' but 'key-cold Dead-heartedness' (Gunn 1994, 212, 213).

For our purposes here in introducing American studies, several points can be made about this Puritan stencilling of America in alternately utopian and apocalyptic terms. The first is that New England religious discourses of these kinds would later be of great interest to American studies in its first institutionalised phase during the mid-twentieth century. One of the books by Perry Miller, the great U.S. scholar of Puritanism, actually echoes Danforth's sermon in being called *Errand into the Wilderness* (1956) – and Miller's work on this period will be discussed in detail in Chapter 2.

Secondly, the Puritans' oscillation in mood between a euphoric celebration of and crushing disillusionment by the society they fashioned valuably alerts us to one of American studies' key insights (noted briefly in the Introduction): namely, that the meaning of America has never been settled or uncontentious, but on the contrary is always open to struggle and negotiation. Interventions in America's discursive framing or rhetorical construction are ongoing, as can be seen by attending for a moment to Trump's presidential inauguration address, delivered in Washington, D.C., on 20 January 2017. Updating Puritan accounts of a community in crisis, Trump painted a picture of 'American carnage'. The 'forgotten men and women of our country' were portrayed by this 'America First' president as laid low by aggressive economic competition from other countries (The White House 2017, n.p.). In its work, American studies aims to make us conscious to a heightened degree of such attempts to model or imagine the United States, helpfully uncovering their origins in particular sociocultural situations and their underpinning by particular political agendas. And American studies is not simply diagnostic in this way but also constructive or interventionist in its own right. Admittedly with less firepower at its disposal than is available to a U.S. president, it presents its own, competing versions of America (as we will see especially in Chapter 6 of this book).

Thirdly, the example of the Puritans helps us understand that imagining America in one way rather than another is not a neutral or disinterested activity. Rather, each such projection or blueprint has measurable effects, shaping outcomes that are variously regressive or liberating. For their perceived failure to live up to America's godly promise, members of Puritan communities in New England were liable not merely to be on the receiving end of colourful tongue-lashings like those meted out by Danforth and Wigglesworth, but to suffer a host of punishments that extended to banishment and even execution. Likewise, those people recently who did not meet the Trump administration's description of the ideal American were vulnerable to various sanctions and exclusions. Reminding us how visions of America from the Puritans onwards have materially affected people's well-being, even their chances of survival, is among the most important tasks that American studies has fulfilled in its life as an academic enterprise.

2) ECONOMIC PROSPECTUSES

Viewers of Disney's *Pocahontas* (1995) will recall John Smith as the fair-haired, square-jawed love interest of the title character. He can also be seen prone and imperilled in Figure 1.1, in the very different visual style of early twentieth-century book illustration. But if he can be freed from these images, he is a figure of significant interest to us here as an early student of America.

For Smith was not only a swashbuckling man of action who fought his way across the battlefields of Europe and later played a leading role in the first permanent English settlement in North America, established at Jamestown in Virginia in 1607. He was also a prolific writer, recording his findings of the 'New World's' history and topography, and its flora and fauna, in a series of carefully detailed books. *The General History of Virginia, New England, and the Summer Isles*, for example, appeared in 1624, eight years after the short volume I wish to consider for a moment: *A Description of New England*.

Smith's book traces 300 miles of America's Atlantic coastline, from Cape Cod in Massachusetts to Penobscot in present-day Maine. Though it scrupulously lists the many Native American peoples living in this maritime region, its chief concern is with the area's *natural* rather than human variety: plants growing just inland are itemised, trees found along the shore are inventoried, and fish swimming in the coastal waters are also drawn into the volume's descriptive nets. With this compendious massing of facts, the book makes an important contribution to our understanding of America at a point very early in white settlement. Smith's stance with regard to this natural abundance, however, is not primarily that of botanist

Figure 1.1 George Alfred Williams, *Pocahontas Saves Captain John Smith*. Illustration in Kate Dickinson Sweetser, *Ten American Girls from History* (New York: Harper, 1917).

Source: Wikimedia Commons.

or biologist; rather, he writes more in the mode of an estate agent, intent on enthusiastically introducing a new property to prospective incomers. The information he gives in the text thus functions principally as tips for immigrants' survival, even prosperity. Twenty-five sites along this coastline, for instance, are picked out not for their topographical curiosity alone, but because they offer 'excellent good Harbours', with many of them spacious enough to allow 'anchorage for 500 sail of ships' (Smith 2006 [1616], 22). Part of the Massachusetts hinterland that in other circumstances would be of greatest interest to a geologist because of its diversity of minerals is reframed by Smith as especially significant for its potential to sustain and advance settlers' lives, given that it contains 'Free stone for building, Slate for tiling, smooth stone to make Furnaces and Forges for glass or iron, and iron ore sufficient . . . to melt in them' (24). Mullet and sturgeon, described as plentiful in the summer months, are not so much marvelled at as marine wonders as catalogued as available foodstuffs (30), and so on through the book, taking careful stock of copper and salt, mulberries and otters, haddock and turkeys.

Before coming to such mineralogical and botanical and zoological minutiae, readers of Smith's book have to make their way through thickets of prefatory verses and epistles. One of these dedicatory letters, however, helpfully makes clear the kind of text this is. Addressing 'right Worshipful Adventurers for the Country of New England', whom he imagines as gathering expectantly in London, Bristol, Plymouth and other English towns before their voyages to America (7), Smith hopes that in this work, 'I have made known unto you a fit place for plantation' (8). His book is thus a pioneering contribution to an early modern genre we might call *the American economic prospectus*. Such writing is certainly dedicated to the gathering and organising of data: one of Smith's pages even resembles a scientific table, listing the plentiful contents of the New England biosphere under five headings of 'Herbs', 'Woods', 'Birds', 'Fishes' and 'Beasts' that appear in the left-hand margin (40). But what also characterises the genre is its powerful appeal to desire and imagination. The facts which such texts include may be many and dense (in *A Description of New England*, for example, Smith lists fourteen types of trees in one paragraph [40]); yet they are offered as so much raw material for readers' thoughts of self-transformation on settling in the 'New World'. In these prospectuses, the region of America which is described becomes for all its copious material detail a dreamscape, in which those reading are invited to plot their own thrilling progression from cramped circumstances back home in England.

The prospectus genre in which *A Description of New England* is a notable early entry proved popular as a way of engaging America textually in the seventeenth and eighteenth centuries (offering a broadly secular alternative to the theological visions discussed previously). Though Smith's own voyages across the Atlantic were only patchily successful – a final attempt to set sail in 1617 was becalmed and never actually left English waters – he continued nevertheless to traverse America in his writings. His last book, in fact, published shortly before his death, has as its title *Advertisements for the Unexperienced Planters of New England, or Anywhere* (1631).

By way of concluding this section, one later addition to the genre might be briefly considered. 'Information to Those Who Would Remove to America' was written by the scientist, diplomat and political philosopher Benjamin Franklin in 1784, shortly after he had played an important part in the thirteen American colonies' successful struggle for independence from British rule during the Revolutionary War of 1775–83. Several shifts can be detected when Franklin's essay is set against Smith's body of writing for would-be emigrants to America. The first is that Franklin is motivated as much by a desire to keep out undesirables – a sizeable group he calls 'improper Persons' (2015, 260) – as he is by keenness to coax people to America. Secondly, where Smith in *A Description of New England* conjures up for the prospective incomer an exhilarating scene of material abundance – America pictured as a well-stocked kitchen cupboard, garden centre and fishmonger's counter – Franklin is much more sober in tone: he is anxious to quash potential immigrants' fantasies of a paradise 'where the streets are said to be pav'd with half-peck Loaves, the houses til'd with Pancakes, and where the fowls fly about ready roasted, crying, *Come eat me!*' (263, emphasis in original). Thirdly, while Smith's reader learns more about the country's trees and animals than about its human society, Franklin's is informed principally about matters of class, trade and employment. Specifically, Franklin distinguishes an America of rough economic equivalence between citizens – 'a general happy

Mediocrity' (261), in his approving phrase – from a Europe disfigured by gross disparities between the richest and poorest people.

In rerouting the emphasis in writing about America from the biological and horticultural to the socio-economic, Franklin anticipates the later bias of institutionalised American studies itself. As a field, American studies gives relatively little attention to topics such as the zoology or ornithology of the United States: instead, what the French sociologist Jean Baudrillard terms 'social and cultural America' (2010 [1988], 5) is its preoccupation. So, for example, Americanists are happy to study what birds signify culturally in a feature film like *The Giant Claw* (1957), or a novel like Jonathan Franzen's *Freedom* (2010), but they are usually less absorbed by the feathered creatures themselves. Looked at in other ways, however, Franklin's essay is liable to be resisted rather than embraced by practitioners of American studies. To begin with, it resembles the Puritan writings considered earlier in delineating a vision of America that at heart may be as coercive as it is welcoming. For if the nation is, as Franklin conceives, a site of artisanal endeavour, indeed hard labour, then where does this leave Americans who are drawn instead to lives of thought and imagination? Does a place even exist in Franklin's republic for someone like the U.S. poet Walt Whitman, who challenges such a productivist ethos very near the beginning of 'Song of Myself' (first published in 1855), declaring: 'I loafe and invite my soul,/I lean and loafe at my ease . . . observing a spear of summer grass' (1982, 27)?

And what, too, of the nation's racial politics, as this is evoked by Franklin? In analysing Gordon Parks's photograph of Ella Watson in the Introduction, we broached the subject of African Americans' fraught relationship to or precarious situation in the modern United States. Such disparaged status for the nation's Black inhabitants is even more apparent in Franklin's essay – not surprisingly, since it was written some eighty years before slavery was abolished by the Thirteenth Amendment to the U.S. Constitution. Though at one point Franklin quotes approvingly 'the Observation of a Negro' that all animal species on earth except pigs are destined to work (262), his other references to African Americans strip them of their humanity and present them as material assets, not autonomous beings. Thus, immigrants new to the United States should not expect on arrival to be given 'Land, Negroes, Utensils, Stock, or any other kind of Emolument whatsoever' (263). For African Americans, then, to say nothing of Native Americans who by this time had experienced at the hands of the white population almost two centuries of systematic removal amounting to genocide, there was little to celebrate about the newly acquired independence of the United States that is the backdrop to Franklin's article. As it does with Puritan dreams of the 'New World', American studies as a discipline equips us with the tools to assess the costs of such secular models of the United States.

TOWARDS AMERICAN STUDIES

Near the end of the eighteenth century, the United States became a sovereign country comparable to Britain or France or Russia. The nation-state that was imagined in the American Declaration of Independence of July 1776 was brought to actuality by the signing of the Treaty of Paris in September 1783. This acquisition of national status, however, did not mean that all inhabitants of the United States suddenly regarded themselves and their land as objects worthy of the greatest scholarly interest. On the contrary, a time-lag is observable here between political self-realisation on the one hand and intellectual self-confidence on the other. 'For decades into the nineteenth century', Kariann Akemi Yokota writes, 'Americans felt the enduring pull of Europe, which they continued to believe was the center of knowledge production' (2010, 91). In Yokota's helpful term, a 'structure of intellectual inequality' (101) prevailed for some time between Europeans and Americans, with the latter often internalising a sense of the former's pre-eminence in matters of scholarship. This is evident, for example, in the evolution of university curricula in the United States. Though universities had existed on American soil from the first half of the seventeenth century, with Harvard's founding in 1636 followed by the establishment of the College of William and Mary in Virginia in 1693, Yale in Connecticut in 1701 and the University of Pennsylvania in 1740, their programmes of study even after the moment of national independence remained heavily indebted to models of higher education in the 'Old World'. Students in the United States emulated their counterparts at Oxford and Cambridge in pursuing courses in Greek, Latin, logic, rhetoric and theology.

Only quite tardily, as we will see in a moment, were curricula in U.S. universities *nationalised*, opening up possibilities of studying subjects close to home. However, not every American in the eighteenth and nineteenth centuries was intimidated by Europe's long-held intellectual prestige. Away from institutions of higher education, many citizen-scholars actually engaged in study of the United States, helping to validate it as an object for serious inquiry and contributing thereby to the later emergence of American studies itself. I touch briefly here on early developments in three fields: geography, history and literary criticism.

1) GEOGRAPHY

In the decades following independence, geographers of the United States found they had an increasing amount of material to write about. The nation's territorial mass expanded hugely, most of all through the Louisiana Purchase of 1803, whereby, in one of history's greatest bargains, more than two million square kilometres comprising much of the present-day Midwest and the Rocky Mountain states were bought from France (see Figure 1.2).

Two army officers, Meriwether Lewis and William Clark, were tasked by President Thomas Jefferson with surveying this land. The maps and reports they brought back from an arduous three-year expedition greatly extended the remit of American geographical study. However, since geography's embedding in the curricula of U.S. universities was still almost a century away (the first department solely dedicated to the subject, at Berkeley in California, was not established until 1898), its American strand was first apparent in textbooks for schools and introductory volumes aimed at a general readership. A pioneer in this field was the Reverend Jedidiah Morse, who combined long service as a Congregational pastor in Massachusetts with the publication of best-selling geographical studies, including *The American Universal Geography* (1793) and *The American Gazetteer* (1797). Both of these texts appeared first before the Louisiana Purchase but expanded in later editions to take account of the nation's growing landmass. Followers in Morse's footsteps include a number of significant female geographers. Most notable, perhaps, is Emma Hart Willard, mainly remembered now as a dedicated women's rights activist, but important too for her work in geography,

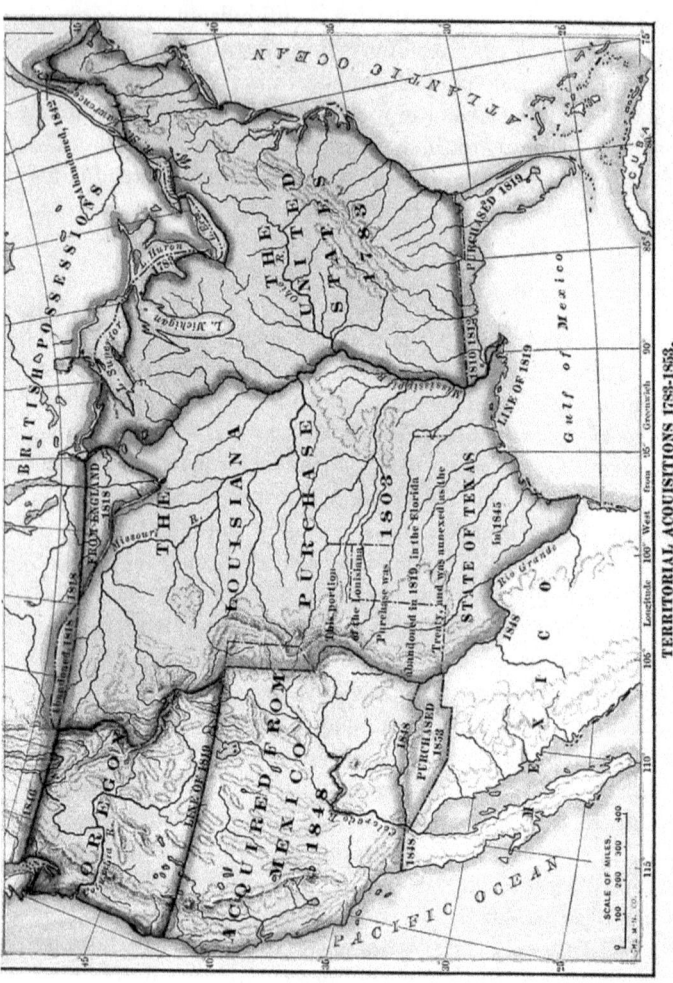

Figure 1.2 U.S. territorial acquisitions 1783–1853, including the Louisiana Purchase of 1803. Map in Edward Channing, *A Short History of the United States for School Use* (New York: Macmillan, 1900).

Source: Wikimedia Commons

including *The Woodbridge and Willard Geographies and Atlases* (co-written with a male scholar and published in 1823).

American studies itself, as a discipline, is highly sensitive to questions of geography. In Chapter 5, for example, we will trace some of the different ways from the mid-twentieth century to the present in which it has demarcated the space it studies. Practitioners in the field are also alert to the political and cultural implications of spatial mapping in the various primary materials with which they engage. The nineteenth-century geographical studies of the United States mentioned earlier are themselves open to such critical review. Lewis and Clark, for example, increased knowledge not only of rivers and mountains in the territory obtained by the Louisiana Purchase but of the biddability of different Native American peoples living there, their degrees of openness to domination by the westward-moving white population. The atlases and gazetteers that followed this pioneering work were similarly not neutral or impartial mappings of American space; rather, they charted the United States according to different political preferences, including southern secessionism as the nation headed towards the outbreak of civil war in 1861.

2) HISTORY

If American studies as a discipline is informed by geography, it has a rich historical consciousness also. Whether scholars in the field are studying novels or photographs, films or poems, they tend to activate in their analysis a highly developed sense of the history of the United States. As with the geography of the United States, however, so with the nation's history: there was a significant delay before it was felt to be a subject fit for systematic study at the university level. The Organization of American Historians was not established until 1907, with its chief scholarly publication, the *Journal of American History*, following seven years later. During the nineteenth century, then, the work of researching and narrating U.S. history was undertaken largely by interested laypersons. Typical here is Benson J. Lossing, the busy author of forty popular books, who in 1854 attempted cannily to reach both educational and general markets when he published *A Pictorial History of the United States: For Schools and Families*. Another bestselling writer was the Honourable Salma Hale, principally a lawyer and politician in New Hampshire, yet with sufficient time on his hands in 1827 to produce a volume with the serpentine title of *History of the United States, from Their First Settlement as Colonies, to the Close of the Great War with Britain in 1815, to Which Are Added Questions for Schools*.

These books aiming at the schoolroom and the fireside tended to tell a particular story about the American past. White possession and domination of the territory were legitimised, indeed celebrated; by contrast, the experiences of numerous, long-established Indigenous peoples were minimised or erased entirely. The study of *Native* American history was decidedly a minority pursuit among whites in the United States during this period, reserved for dissidents such as the Transcendentalist Henry David Thoreau, who reflected on the time prior to white settlement in a series of writings (including the 'Indian Notebooks' which he kept from 1847 until a year before his death in 1862). As the title of Hale's volume indicates, the popular American histories of the first half of the nineteenth century typically had also a nationalistic orientation, choosing as their climaxes one or other triumphant moment in the early life of the independent United States. But as the century wore on, historical narratives, like the atlases of the United States mentioned earlier, came to evoke not a unified nation but one splintering into two bitterly opposed factions.

3) LITERARY STUDIES

Like the study of American history and American geography, the study of American literature struggled in the first decades of U.S. nationhood for recognition, let alone promotion. 'Who reads an American book?' asked the English clergyman and writer Sydney Smith in an article of 1820 that praised the people of the United States as 'brave, industrious, and acute', while nevertheless disparaging their achievements in cultural production, including literature (qtd. in Ricks and Vance 1992, 289). Smith was a professional contrarian, inclined towards witty sallies against everything from gravy to hot weather; thus, his expression of scorn for American literature might seem nothing more than a lone eccentric's audience-grabbing provocation. Such is not the case, however, since across the nineteenth century and even into the twentieth this sentiment was shared by many professional literary critics in the United States itself. When literary study first entered the nation's universities, the literature that counted most was that of *England*. In an article published shortly after World War II but still valuable as a source of information on curriculum development in U.S. higher education, Martin Staples Shockley observes that 'American scholars in American universities teaching American students neglected . . . no other literature like their own' (1946, 24). He also tells the story of 'an elderly English professor [in the U.S.] who, upon learning that a new member of his department had had no training in American literature, remarked approvingly, "A very well-educated man"' (24).

Despite this widespread condescension, however, some significant efforts were still made during the nineteenth century to validate serious engagement with the literature of the United States. As with the study of American geography and history discussed previously, much of this work was undertaken away from academia itself. Major U.S. figures, including Ralph Waldo Emerson, Margaret Fuller and Herman Melville, wrote essays about the lingering influence on American poets and novelists of forms and styles used by their British counterparts. But in some U.S. universities, too, scholars and administrators made space in the syllabus for consideration of U.S. writing. The first course in the subject seems to have been that taught in 1828 at the recently established Amherst College in Massachusetts by the Reverend Nathan Fiske, a polymath initially ordained as a Congregational minister before departing for the academic life. Two decades later, Middlebury College in Vermont 'offered two courses, Critiques on the British and American Classics for third-term juniors and Analysis of American Orators for third-term seniors' (Vanderbilt 1986, 32). Gradually, programmes such as these came to seem not so much quixotic gestures as practical blueprints, anticipating the systematic study which would emerge of the literature of the United States. Suggestive of this growing consolidation of the subject was Pennsylvania State University's appointment of Fred Lewis Pattee in 1895 as the nation's first professor of American literature. Another milestone was the dedication to U.S. writing of four of the eighteen volumes of the prestigious *Cambridge History of English and American Literature*, published between 1907 and 1921.

SUMMARY

This chapter has covered, at a brisk speed, some 300 years of reflection on America prior to the formalisation of American studies itself. 'America' was seen to have shrunk in this period as a geographical descriptor, coming to be applied most often not to the continent at large but to that portion of northern territory now housing the United States. Our analysis began by considering how, before U.S. independence late in the eighteenth century, knowledge of America was produced in a wide range of written forms, including poems, sermons and survival guides for European incomers. The focus then switched to the beginnings, post-independence, of geographical, historical and literary study of America.

Three tendencies were identified in this varied, pre-disciplinary work. First is its *amateurism*, using 'amateur' here not in a pejorative sense, but according to two of the *OED*'s definitions as 'One who loves or is fond of' and 'One who cultivates anything as a pastime, as distinguished from one who prosecutes it professionally'. Even as the U.S. university system expanded in the nineteenth century, knowledge of America was often produced not by specialist scholars but by enthusiasts detouring from their everyday lives as politicians or lawyers or clergymen. Second is the *fluidity* of America's meaning in this body of work, its ongoing openness to contest and renegotiation. Third is the work's political implication, its lack of ideological innocence: each poem or geographical description or history textbook contains within itself, either on the surface or in code, a vision of what America should be.

One final point should be made regarding this inaugural study of America. It was, for the most part, *fragmented*, produced by people in distinct intellectual fields. Historians, geographers, literary critics, art critics, political scientists and others tended to operate within their disciplinary boundaries, rather than imagining and developing crossovers in their work. By contrast, a distinguishing feature of academic American studies from its emergence around the time of World War II is the attempt to resist atomisation, fashioning an interdisciplinary programme from these previously disparate subjects. The beginnings of this project are our topic in Chapter 2.

FURTHER READING

This chapter began by discussing maps, and in print are several expansive, handsomely illustrated books which document cartographers' work on America from early modern mapping to contemporary satellite imaging. Particularly recommended are Derek Hayes, *Historical Atlas of the United States*

(Berkeley: University of California Press, 2007); Tom Howells and Duncan McCorquodale (ed.), *Mapping America: Exploring the Continent* (London: Black Dog, 2010); and Mark C. Carnes and John A. Garraty, with Patrick Williams, *Mapping America's Past: A Historical Atlas* (New York: Henry Holt, 1996). Martin Bruckner's *The Geographic Revolution in Early America: Maps, Literacy, and National Identity* (Chapel Hill: University of North Carolina Press, 2006) is a valuable study of the American geographical imagination into the first decades of the independent United States. Kariann Akemi Yokota's *Unbecoming British: How Revolutionary America Became a Post-Colonial Nation* (New York: Oxford University Press, 2011) has a broader remit, considering in addition to geography the gradual emergence of forms of intellectual history and scientific study focused upon the United States itself.

For a generous sampling of American literary production in the colonial and revolutionary eras, including the texts by Winthrop, Smith and Franklin discussed previously, see the volume edited by Giles Gunn: *Early American Writing* (New York: Penguin, 1994). While this body of writing was initially neglected by scholars, the shortfall has since been made up: illuminating studies include Robert Lawson-Peebles, *American Literature Before 1880* (Abingdon: Routledge, 2014) and Leonard Tennenhouse, *The Importance of Feeling English: American Literature and the British Diaspora, 1750–1850* (Princeton, NJ: Princeton University Press, 2007).

THE RISE OF AMERICAN STUDIES

AMERICAN STUDIES IN 'THE AMERICAN CENTURY'

The previous chapter noted a tendency in the United States during the nineteenth century to continue to cast the nation as subordinate to Europe in terms of complexity and interest. Developing a programme of academic study of traditions and practices in the United States did not seem in these circumstances a matter of urgency. However, as global dynamics shifted in the late nineteenth century and the first half of the twentieth, with the U.S. now an increasingly powerful force, it became more pressing not only for Americans themselves but for others across the world to consider in a systematic way what kind of nation this was. The emergence of American studies as a discipline, then, synchronises with the new muscle and visibility of the United States. This harmonising of national transformation and intellectual shift in the period either side of World War II is explored in this chapter. My starting point is one of the most famous magazine articles in American history.

In February 1941, the U.S. magazine publisher Henry Luce temporarily swapped the executive office for the editorial floor, writing a long piece under the title of 'The American Century'. The outlet he selected for his work was *Life*, one of several titles, including the still-extant trio of *Time*, *Fortune* and *Sports Illustrated*, that he founded in a career that revolutionised journalism in the United States. Writing some ten months before the United States entered World War II in the wake of Japan's bombing of Pearl Harbor in Hawaii, Luce nevertheless begins the article by comparing his nation

DOI: 10.4324/9781315726748-3

unfavourably with Britain that was then under siege by Nazi Germany. Whereas the British in his description are strangely serene, having found a common purpose in fighting for national survival, Americans, by contrast, seem adrift and discontented. As Luce puts it: 'We Americans are unhappy. We are not happy about America. We are not happy about ourselves in relation to America. We are nervous – or gloomy – or apathetic' (1999 [1941], 159). The note of American melancholy here is one we have heard before: recall from Chapter 1 the critiques by Puritan sermonisers of a community that was failing to realise its unique potential. Luce's article remains for much of its length in this mode of national self-flagellation. Although one of the piece's subsections proclaims in shouty upper-case that 'THE 20TH CENTURY IS THE AMERICAN CENTURY' (167), this is offered as a dream or aspiration, rather than as a triumphalist assertion of how things already are.

But while Luce writes in visionary or prophetic style, looking towards a future world order that will be shaped by America, he cannot help but disclose in his article the potency already exhibited by the United States. Early in the text, he acknowledges 'how lucky we are compared to all the rest of the human family – rich in food, rich in clothes, rich in entertainment and amusement, rich in leisure, rich' (160). A glance at statistics collected by Angus Maddison helps us to grasp the astonishing expansion of the U.S. economy that occurred between the middle of the nineteenth century and the middle of the twentieth. In 1870, the gross domestic product (GDP) of the United States was still lower than that of Great Britain, if barely: $98.3 m. to 100.1 m. By 1913, however, the economic activity of the United States was more than twice that of Britain (GDPs of $517.3 m. and 224.6 m., respectively) – while by 1950, as each nation engaged in post-war reconstruction, U.S. GDP was four times higher ($1.4 *billion* as against 347.8 m.) (Maddison 2007, 385). Another of Maddison's tables is helpful, too, permitting us to see that between 1913 and 1950 annual GDP per capita rose in the United States at more than twice the rate in the nations comprising Western Europe (1.61% compared with 0.76%) (383).

Luce is emphatic in his article, however, that it is not material assets alone that define America. Rather than a matter simply of economics, the power that the United States possesses is also cultural and ideological. In this regard, he evokes 'great American ideals' that include 'a love of freedom, a feeling for the equality of opportunity' (170), and argues that these are capable of 'lifting the life of mankind from the level of the beasts to what the Psalmist called a little lower than the angels' (171). The biblically charged language here may remind us of the fact that Luce's parents were Presbyterian missionaries, working in China at the time of his birth. However, a similar transition from economics to culture in thinking about reasons for the potency of the United States can be seen at the start of a text by a mid-century scholar who played a significant part in the development and consolidation of American studies itself.

Perry Miller, who was briefly namechecked in Chapter 1 as a major student of Puritan New England in the seventeenth and eighteenth centuries, recalls a moment of intellectual awakening in the preface to his book, *Errand into the Wilderness* (1956). Miller describes how 'three decades ago', prior to beginning postgraduate research, he found himself 'sitting at Matadi on the banks of the Congo' in West Africa, where he had gone in search of the 'adventure' denied him by having been too young to fight in World War I. The industrial and commercial might of the United States was glaringly apparent to him, given that he was 'supervising, in that barbarous tropic, the unloading of drums of case oil [i.e. kerosene] flowing out of the inexhaustible wilderness of America' (1956, viii). Setting aside on this occasion Miller's first adjective – 'barbarous' might be taken troublingly to be his response to the social world of the Congo, rather than simply to its climate and terrain which would certainly have been challenging for a visitor from Chicago – we might consider instead how the passage goes on. Miller feels compelled to uncover the ultimate source of the American power which he senses at this moment. The sheer commercial reach that has enabled a product extracted from the U.S. interior to reach West Africa might appear answer enough; yet, for Miller, 'the innermost propulsion of the United States' is cultural, rather than economic (viii). The American reserves that matter most for him are of ideas, not oil.

In this fragment of intellectual autobiography, Miller writes that while under the tropical sun he had a vision of what he should do during his forthcoming postgraduate study and subsequent academic career: namely, dedicate himself to exploring 'that interminable field which may be called the meaning of America' (viii). The third section of this chapter will consider Miller's work in more detail, together with that of two other mid-century U.S. academics who framed their projects in comparable terms. These scholars demonstrated great historical and cultural reach, helping not only to establish American studies as an accredited discipline but to make it a scene of intellectual excitement. As well as recognising their achievements, however, we will also discuss the pitfalls of supposing that America has *a* meaning, in the singular, rather than being a site of rival significations that are competing for dominance. In the next section, however, I wish to consider a major scholarly enterprise that was already underway at the time Miller had his epiphany on the banks of the Congo. Though an outlier with respect to American studies' formal establishment, given that it appeared in the late 1920s rather than two or three decades later, Vernon Louis Parrington's three-volume *Main Currents in American Thought* is nevertheless important in the lineage of the discipline. Little read now except by scholars inquiring into U.S. intellectual history during the interwar period, it is recalled here not simply to give it its due as an ancestor, but to assess what might still be learned from it by way of approaching American culture and society.

MAIN CURRENTS IN AMERICAN THOUGHT

Biographies of most literary academics do not set space aside for recording their subjects' sporting achievements. Parrington's story is unusual, however, in that his early career at the University of Oklahoma in the closing years of the nineteenth century saw him combining the teaching of English with success as head coach of the university's American football team. However, we turn to him here not for his tactical innovations on the playing field, but for the intellectual work he did subsequently at the University of Washington in Seattle, resulting in the publication between 1927 and 1930 of the volumes comprising *Main Currents in American Thought*. In its 1,400 pages, the project exemplifies that chronological sweep which would be a feature also of those foundational texts in American studies to be considered in this chapter's next section. Volume 1 covers the colonial era and concludes in the early years of U.S. independence;

Volume 2 ranges from 1800 to 1860. Even the author's premature death did not prevent the third volume, published posthumously in 1930, from being a sturdy one: it was assembled from materials Parrington had already written and substantial research notes he left behind, and takes the narrative of American thought forward to 1920.

It is not difficult, from our current vantage point, to pick holes in Parrington's work. In the first instance, though it is subtitled *An Interpretation of American Literature from the Beginnings to 1920*, it is frequently left unstirred by the literariness itself of the writings it considers. Parrington is open about giving analytical priority to things other than the formal and stylistic features of what he writes about. In the Introduction to the first of his three volumes, he detaches himself from any 'exaggerated regard for aesthetic values' (1930, Vol. 1, vi) – a position he restates in the Foreword to Volume 2: 'With aesthetic judgments I have not been greatly concerned' (Vol. 2, i). Given this frank setting-aside of sensitivity to verbal art itself, he is liable to make decisions as to who and what to include in his history of American writing that strike us now as at best quixotic, at worst indefensible. In the second volume's section on Herman Melville, for example, the novelised travelogue *Typee* (1846) – a book well-attuned to the literary marketplace – gets more attention than the many-stranded and innovatory *Moby-Dick* (1851). More startling still is the treatment of Edgar Allan Poe, a major figure in the development of genres including the Gothic tale, the detective story and science fiction. Poe's work is dispatched by Parrington in a little over two pages, whereas largely forgotten novels by such nineteenth-century southern writers as William Alexander Caruthers, John Pendleton Kennedy and Nathaniel Beverley Tucker are discussed at length. Judgements about literary canons are, of course, provisional and mutable. No one can say for sure that there will never come a day when Caruthers, Kennedy and Tucker return to high critical prestige, relegating Poe to marginal status. At present, however, a shift in critical reputations along these lines is not likely. The result of all this is to suggest that Parrington's literary antennae are underdeveloped or insensitive, reducing the authority of his project more broadly.

Another response to *Main Currents in American Thought*, however, might look more sympathetically on its disengagement from the formal and stylistic properties of the literature it discusses. Parrington is unconcerned by 'aesthetic values' because he wishes to get as quickly as possible to what really interests him in literary texts: that is to say, the ways in which they are caught up in and contribute to a long-running clash of ideologies in America. Rather than comprising a realm set apart from 'our political, economic, and social development' (Vol. 1, iii), American literature is, in Parrington's understanding, fully involved on 'the partisan battle-ground' (Vol. 1, 357). It is to be assessed as a series of interventions in U.S. politics, with variously progressive and reactionary effects.

Several observations can be made about this particular account of literary history. The first is that, unlike some scholars who have tried to find unity or consensus in America, Parrington emphasises the fact of *struggle* between worldviews. The 'currents' of his title are intended to evoke forces of varying mass and strength that cut across each other, rather than flowing harmoniously. A second point is that he does not write in a neutral fashion about the ideological positions of those novelists and poets he studies: on the contrary, he takes up arms himself on this 'partisan battle-ground'. He identifies his political affiliation at the very beginning – 'liberal rather than conservative' (Vol. 1, i) – and this subsequently shapes the narrative of American literature which he tells. Though Parrington often focuses on writers whose work is now found only in the dustiest corners of libraries, the political commitment that runs through his project and is decipherable in each of his critical judgements is still enlivening. Consider, for example, his discussion of Cotton Mather (1663–1728), the New England pastor and author briefly mentioned in Chapter 1. Parrington was hostile to American Puritanism – 'a reactionary theology', he calls it (Vol. 1, iv) – and so it is unsurprising that he identifies Mather as an ideological villain. Even so, there is great rhetorical verve in his critique: 'He was a bourgeois soul who loved respectability and was jealous of his social position; no fraternizing with the poor and outcast for him, no profitless excursions into the realms of Utopian justice' (Vol. 1, 113). Parrington also says memorably of Mather, who was complicit in the trials in Salem, Massachusetts in 1692–3 that resulted in the execution of twenty people on flimsy charges of witchcraft, that 'His speech and writings dripped with devil-talk' (115).

Feted at the time of publication for providing the United States with a substantial intellectual ancestry, *Main Currents in American Thought* fell out of favour after the Second World War. Mid-century practitioners of 'New Criticism', who understood the literary text more as an autonomous object and devoted themselves to carefully elaborating its specificities, were repelled by Parrington's relative lack of concern with verbal art itself. Such scholars, trained in impersonal, neutral methods of study, were also alienated by his openly polemical approach, whereby some writers in the American tradition were celebrated for their politically progressive orientation while others were damned for their regressive ideology. In our own moment, too, particular features of Parrington's project are liable to leave us cold. Despite its colossal scale, the story he tells of literary production in America is oppressively male: Harriet Beecher Stowe, author of the abolitionist novel, *Uncle Tom's Cabin* (1852), is a very rare exception in being granted eight pages of coverage (Vol. 2, 371–378). This history is also, in Parrington's hands, monotonously *white*: for example, no attention is given in the second volume to the genre of African American slave narrative, or in the third to the Black vernacular poetry of Paul Laurence Dunbar. This stencilling of *Main Currents in American Thought* by a patriarchal and white-centred outlook is difficult for contemporary readers to overlook.

Nevertheless, even if the terms of Parrington's radicalism are horribly narrow, his commitment to a progressive manifesto for the United States is one that still animates much work in American studies (as we will see especially in Chapter 6's discussion of the politics of this academic field). There is another link as well that still connects Parrington to twenty-first-century practitioners of American studies. This is his commitment to interdisciplinarity in designing his work. As he tells us in the first paragraph of the first volume, he is conscious of 'the complexity and many-sidedness of the materials, with their ramifications into theology and politics and economics' (i). Literature remains central for Parrington, but literature understood expansively rather than hermetically – less a prison cell for the analyst than a threshold to many other cultural and social domains in the United States.

THREE FOUNDING NARRATIVES

No academic discipline is to be traced to a single starting point. Thus, although a number of writers argue that Parrington's multivolume project should be considered the moment of the formal inauguration of American studies, it is better to imagine a much more complex origin story. Many other accounts of American literature, philosophy, religion, sociology, politics, and so on – including those materials produced from the seventeenth century onwards which were considered in Chapter 1 – are also part of the discipline's elaborate root system. At the same time as not wishing to overpromote *Main Currents in American Thought*, however, it is important to acknowledge that its scale and ambition lent significant support to initiatives to establish an academic field that would be dedicated to studying the United States across its multiple cultural and social dimensions.

Parrington's sudden death in 1929 in the Cotswolds in rural England, where he had gone to find the peace and quiet conducive to sustained work on his third volume, meant that he did not live to see American studies' institutionalisation. Only in the generation that followed his did the study of America begin to accumulate an infrastructure of university faculties and departments, degrees and modules, associations and journals. Harvard was among the pioneers in this regard, establishing in 1937 an interdisciplinary programme in the History of American Civilization. Its first successful PhD student was Henry Nash Smith, who graduated in 1940 after writing a thesis with the title, *American Emotional and Imaginative Attitudes Toward the Great Plains and the Rocky Mountains, 1803–1850*. After the war, Smith reworked his doctoral project into book form as *Virgin Land: The American West as Symbol and Myth* (1950), and this is discussed later, along with two other scholarly texts from mid-century: Perry Miller's *The New England Mind: The Seventeenth Century* (1939) and Leo Marx's *The Machine in the Garden: Technology and the Pastoral Ideal in America* (1964). Referring to Smith, Miller and Marx as authors of 'founding narratives' in American studies is not intended to monumentalise them or to detach them from their peers who, contemporaneously, were also doing important research. Among these other figures are the politically active scholars, connected to social movements as well as to academic locations, who form the dramatis personae of an important book considered in Chapter 6: Michael Denning's *The Cultural Front* (1997). More modestly, the focus here on Miller, Smith and Marx is meant simply to acknowledge their importance in helping to unfold the emergent discipline's intellectual possibilities.

1) *THE NEW ENGLAND MIND: THE SEVENTEENTH CENTURY*

New England Puritanism, which was considered in Chapter 1 for its vision of the godly community, flourished in the seventeenth and eighteenth centuries, though its legacy can still be traced today in the worldview of many Americans. For others now, who are more adrift from its philosophical and moral coordinates, its period of dominance in America is liable to conjure up images of severe dogmatists whose beliefs were as plain and stiff as their dress. A distillation of this popular iconography is offered in 'Mayflower Madman', part of an episode of *The Simpsons* which aired on U.S. TV in April 2006. Here the family finds itself back in 1620, part of the collective of Puritan emigrants sailing from Plymouth in England to Massachusetts on board the *Mayflower*. Early on, we see that Bart's only plaything is a 'toy wood lump' that, unsurprisingly, refuses to bounce: 'What jolly fun', he intones without mirth. The pilgrims' leader then enumerates some of the proscriptions and exclusions which they live by: 'We Puritans have no place for drunkenness or colourful clothes or dreaming or poetry'. Expanding on the last of these banned activities, he declares: 'So if you write a sonnet,/Keep it under your bonnet' – an utterance forcing him promptly to chastise himself for having broken into verse.

Poetry *was* written by American Puritans: simply recall the dystopian example by Michael Wigglesworth cited in Chapter 1. Strikingly, however, it has only a minimal presence in the large-scale account of Puritan culture which Miller attempts in *The New England Mind: The Seventeenth Century*. Miller's reasoning is that, rather than giving licence to unruly or transgressive thoughts as might have been feared by community elders, the poetry that was produced in this context was largely aligned with Puritan orthodoxy. He observes, then, that the primary textual materials in his study are sermons and theological writings, to the relative exclusion of 'other types of expression in New England of the seventeenth century, the histories, diaries, narratives of travel and of special providences, biographies, and above all the poetry' (1939, 359). This self-denying ordinance conflicts with some of the other early ventures in American studies we will come to, in which the archive of useable texts is more varied. For the most part, however, Miller's approach to Puritanism is maximalist, rather than parsimonious. A few years later the English literary scholar E. M. W. Tillyard required barely more than 100 pages to sum up the mental horizons of the late sixteenth century in *The Elizabethan World Picture* (1942). Miller, by contrast, takes over 500 to cover Puritanism's first hundred years in America, unpacking in four lengthy sections the specificities of its religion and learning, cosmology, anthropology, and sociology.

Miller's substantial studies of American Puritanism, in particular *The New England Mind: The Seventeenth Century* and its companion volume, *The New England Mind: From Colony to Province* (1953), have been variously admired and critiqued by later scholars. They remain touchstones for anyone working on this period – even for those who ultimately reject their assumptions and conclusions. For our purposes here, however, a narrower assessment of the seventeenth-century volume is appropriate, setting aside the plausibility or otherwise of the commentary on Puritan thought which Miller offers and thinking instead about the book's broader implications for American studies.

Two points can briefly be made. The first is in response to the reference in Miller's title to the category of 'mind'. Though the book does some work to embed the theology it discusses in the social structures which the Puritans established during their first century in America, its principal interests remain abstract: indeed, Miller is open from the start about his book's framing as 'a chapter in the history of ideas' (1939, vii). This suggestion that scholars should mainly devote themselves to identifying and exploring mental constructions – a viewpoint that, almost two decades later, saw Miller 'compelled to insist that the mind of man is the basic factor in human history' (1956, ix) – is one which we will see was also a guiding principle in other key texts in this first wave of American studies. By contrast, current practitioners of the discipline are drawn not to 'mind' as their chief analytical category, but rather to 'materiality' of various kinds (unequal power dynamics across racial lines, for example, or lived experiences in the face of transphobia). A second observation is that Miller emphasises uniformity and orthodoxy of thinking in seventeenth-century New England. He allots very little of his space to religious dissenters, such as Anne Hutchinson (1591–1643); the word 'Quaker' is missing from his index, even though the Quaker minority suffered persecution at the hands of Puritan authorities. One of Miller's later scholarly defenders argues that 'Far from presenting a static picture of an abstract body of thought, the first volume of *The New England Mind* is dramatic, developmental, and ironic' (Butts 1982, 673). However, Miller rather gives the game away in the book by declaring his intentions to unpack 'a unified body of thought' (1939, vii) and to treat the various texts he discusses as if they were 'the product of a single intelligence' (vii). This hypothesis of cultural consensus is shared by other figures in American studies' early wave. More recent researchers and teachers in the field, though, are frequently concerned to explore Americans' differentiated experiences rather than to follow Miller in looking for 'central tendencies' in the culture (Murphey 2001, 10).

2) *VIRGIN LAND: THE AMERICAN WEST AS SYMBOL AND MYTH*

In a much-discussed essay, 'Can "American Studies" Develop a Method?' (1957), Henry Nash Smith lamented the dominance exerted over mid-century literary scholarship by 'New Criticism'. The New Critics, briefly referenced earlier as resistant to Parrington's attempt to incorporate politics and economics in discussion of American literature, were, in Smith's description, mesmerised by regard for 'the autonomy of the work of art' (1957, 202). For the purposes of analysis, they tended to put the literary text into a sealed-off, hygienically controlled space, rather than considering its embedding in the world. The result was a gain in detailed attention to formal and stylistic particulars, but at the expense of thinking about the text's cultural and ideological dimensions. To underscore his point, Smith considers how to approach the writing of Mark Twain. The critic who comes to *Adventures of Huckleberry Finn* (1884) or *A Connecticut Yankee in King Arthur's Court* (1889) with an eye only for verbal patterns is poorly equipped, since for the novels' effective interpretation knowledge is also required of such phenomena beyond the text as shifts in literary taste in the United States or the class politics of different American dialects.

Virgin Land represents Smith's fullest demonstration of the possibilities of American studies as he outlined them in his subsequent article. Twain himself features only briefly in the book, but many other American writers of multiple generic traditions are considered. There are aspects of Smith's text that remain inspirational for the study of the United States we may wish to undertake now. The first of these is its interdisciplinarity. Smith concludes his 1957 essay by suggesting, in the sexist language naturalised in his period, that American studies is best seen as 'a collaboration among men working from within existing academic disciplines but attempting to widen the boundaries imposed by conventional methods of inquiry' (207). Though the work of a lone scholar, *Virgin Land* itself is such an instance of cross-disciplinary contact. The literary representations of the American West from the late eighteenth century to the late nineteenth that are its principal subject are read by Smith using methods that derive from academic fields extending from history to land economy, and from anthropology to political philosophy.

A second element of the book to applaud is its easy negotiation of the borders between supposedly 'high' and 'low' verbal cultures. While canonical authors such as Whitman and James Fenimore Cooper are discussed, so too are the cheap, throwaway novels that were produced in the period. When Smith acknowledges that the westerns mass-produced from the 1860s by the New York publishing house of Beadle & Adams were 'entirely subliterary' (1970 [1950], 91), this does not mean he is inhibited from analysing them; on the contrary, their repetitive, highly popular plots give him readier access to 'the dream life' of the United States (92).

Thirdly, current readers of *Virgin Land* can still find productive the effort it makes to extend the geographical range of American studies. For Miller, it was axiomatic that 'the meaning of America' he was looking for was to be found on the East Coast. Smith, however, suggests redirecting attention elsewhere in the United States. His choice of region to explore was a bold one. For the condescension that threatened the authors he discusses – 'writers about the West had to struggle against the notion that their characters had no claim upon the attention of sophisticated readers' (1970 [1950],

224) – was something he risked himself in selecting the American West as the object of serious scholarly inquiry.

Yet, if there are still methods and insights to take from *Virgin Land*, there are also elements of the book to question. Firstly, quite briefly, we might point out the narrowness of Smith's archive of primary materials. While he is resourceful and energetic in identifying literary texts for discussion, he is oddly incurious about *visual* representations of the West. Even if it is conceded that the study's cut-off point is just before the flourishing of cinematic westerns, space might still have been made for consideration of how the region's meanings were negotiated in several visual forms, as well as by written texts. Instead, Smith's only concession in this respect is to include as illustrations some of the drawings of iconic western figures such as Buffalo Bill and Calamity Jane that appeared in popular novels. The visual is thereby decorative addition only in *Virgin Land*, rather than substantive material. This contrasts markedly with some later, regionally focused work in American studies: Neil Campbell's book *The Cultures of the American New West* (2000), for example, which considers films, photographs and paintings alongside written fiction and non-fiction.

More troubling, however, in *Virgin Land* are the very terms in which Smith frames the American West. There are traces in his idiom of a long-established discourse that presents the region as empty of prior inhabitants and thus primed for white acquisition: 'the vacant continent beyond the frontier', to quote from early in the text (1970 [1950], 4). Another passage evokes 'the dreary solitudes of the West' (12). But 'dreary' to whom, precisely? The same stretch of the Great Plains or the Rocky Mountains that appeared 'dreary' to the eyes of a white incomer looking for cultivable, lucrative land might well have been charged with profound spiritual significance by one of the many Native American peoples with long traditions of living there. 'Solitudes', too, is problematical phrasing since it reimagines indigenously travelled territory as unsocialised space. In Smith's study, 'Indians' figure often enough as literary *objects*, especially in the popular novels he discusses where they tend to be 'savages' imperilling whites. They are not considered, however, as literary *producers*, with a heritage of representation of this region that often runs counter to the white majority's discourse.

Something very similar might be said about the treatment of women in *Virgin Land*. Like Native Americans, they enter the book largely as characters in the nineteenth-century 'dime novels' it covers, conforming to either of the available types of 'genteel female' (112) or 'softhearted Amazon' (117). No attention is given to women as themselves writers about the West, whether they expressed themselves in accredited forms such as lyric poetry and the novel, or via more fugitive means such as letters or diary entries. As with the racial bias noted earlier, this patriarchal weighting of the material for study is an element of *Virgin Land* that much subsequent critical writing has attempted to undo. In the section of Chapter 5 that discusses American studies' interest in subnational spaces within the United States, as opposed to the nation as a whole, we will consider work done by Annette Kolodny in particular to retrieve female and indeed feminist perspectives on the West that are not captured by Smith.

3) *THE MACHINE IN THE GARDEN: TECHNOLOGY AND THE PASTORAL IDEAL IN AMERICA*

Of the classic texts in American studies' first period that are under review here, *The Machine in the Garden* is perhaps the most ambitious. It has, to begin with, a wider regional focus than both *Virgin Land* and *The New England Mind*, aiming to consider how America more broadly has negotiated the tension between pastoral impulses on the one hand and visions of mechanisation on the other. Secondly, it has a longer chronological reach than either Smith's or Miller's book. Its modern coverage extends to F. Scott Fitzgerald's novel, *The Great Gatsby* (1925). At the other temporal extreme, Marx turns to Ancient Rome to trace pastoral's early development in the poetry of Virgil; he also devotes a whole chapter to *The Tempest* – 'Shakespeare's American Fable', as he calls it (2000 [1964], 34ff.) – which was written in c. 1610–11 and dates therefore from a time before significant English settlement in the 'New World'. Marx's transatlantic manoeuvre here might be reflected on for a moment. For Shakespeare is by no means the only writer from England to figure in *The Machine in the Garden*: later on, there is coverage of the poetry of Alexander Pope, Oliver Goldsmith and James Thomson, together with a discussion of non-fictional prose by Joseph Addison and Thomas Carlyle. Such crisscrossing of the Atlantic is an early indication that research done under the auspices of American studies is not easily or comfortably contained within the national boundaries of the United States; instead, it is often compelled to turn to other parts of the world to consider their fundamental involvement in shaping America. Chapter 5 of this book will consider some of the varying scales and trajectories within the discipline's geographical imagination.

Despite its broader temporal and spatial remit, however, Marx's book can still be aligned with those by Miller and Smith. Parallels with *Virgin Land* in both project and method are especially apparent. Like Smith, Marx is hospitable to a wide range of written materials. Canonised figures in U.S. literature are present, to be sure, and considered in detail: Cooper and Twain, who feature also in *Virgin Land*, but many others including Emerson, Thoreau, Melville, Nathaniel Hawthorne and Henry James. Alongside interpretations of these, however, is analysis of texts that Marx says have 'little or no intrinsic literary value' (2000 [1964], 4). Examples of such disregarded American writing that is recovered by *The Machine in the Garden* extend from government pamphlets on the nation's industrial prospects to James H. Lanman's 1840 report on the 'Railroads of the United States', with its phobic metaphor of trains as 'iron monsters . . . breathing smoke and flame through their blackened lungs' (qtd. 207). In an Afterword written for the book's reissue in 2000, Marx recalled that during his research he collected a great mass of 'technological images' from sources including 'newspapers, magazines, folklore, political debates, and ceremonial oratory' (374). As with Smith, however, his approach towards this written archive remains that of the literary critic rather than social scientist, scanning the texts closely for their significant imagery instead of feeding them into a large-scale quantitative survey. It should also be noted that by 'technological images', Marx means *verbal* rather than visual representations. Like Smith once more, he generally chooses not to expand his repository of primary materials so that it incorporates the many paintings and photographs that have documented the conflict in America between pastoral vision and industrial project. Though he offers some reflections late in the book on Charles Sheeler's painting, *American Landscape* (1930) – a modernist depiction in muted colours of a Detroit car factory, where the title raises expectations of a rural scene – these are brief (355–356) and mainly the prelude to a lengthier discussion of Fitzgerald's description of place in *The Great Gatsby*.

In considering American studies' first phase, when academic work on the culture and society of the United States began to acquire the status of a properly disciplinary activity, I have picked out only three books. Fuller treatment of this moment would involve discussion of many other projects that were enthusiastically received not only for insights into their specific topics but also for delineation of methods that American studies might adopt and directions in which it might travel. Two other books belonging to the period of Miller, Smith and Marx can at least be briefly namechecked here. The first is Alan Trachtenberg's *Brooklyn Bridge: Fact and Symbol* (first edition 1965, second 1979), which, as the subtitle hints, alternates between on the one hand discussion of the bridge's physical construction and on the other analysis of the variable meanings with which it was endowed in artistic productions that include poetry by Hart Crane, photography by Walker Evans and painting by Joseph Stella. Here, admittedly in response to a subject tightly framed rather than the sprawling space which interests Smith in *Virgin Land*, is a pioneering venture in interdisciplinary American studies that navigates between verbal and visual materials. The second influential book in this period to note is R. W. B. Lewis's *The American Adam: Innocence, Tragedy, and Tradition in the Nineteenth Century* (1955). In several respects, this study looks more like conventional literary criticism than a contribution to an innovative academic programme. It is modest in both the historical and the geographical coverage it offers (mainly 'from about 1820 to 1860 . . . New England and the Atlantic seaboard' [1955, 1]); it also restricts its interest to 'articulate thinkers and conscious artists' (1), so that idiosyncrasy here consists in extending the canon to include historians such as Francis Parkman rather than in following Smith's example and enthusiastically analysing popular fiction. Having said all these things, however, Lewis's book belongs with the other texts cited here for a reason I hope the next paragraph will clarify.

Later academic commentators have argued that American studies in this period was dominated by or even reducible to the 'myth and symbol school' (the label deriving from the subtitle of *Virgin Land*). Though this description overstates the extent of professional closeness and intellectual unity within the field – even the few scholars discussed here were institutionally dispersed, with different specialist interests – it is nevertheless helpful in suggesting that there was a paradigm or framework within which much American studies scholarship was done. Especially important in this paradigm was the understanding that researchers in the field would dedicate themselves first to identifying ideas crucial to America – major 'intellectual construction[s]' (Smith 1970 [1950], xi) – and then to pursuing these across stretches of American time and space. Miller's preoccupation with such mental formations is apparent from the title he gives his book, Smith's from the *subtitle*. For his part, Marx declares that the central preoccupation of *The Machine in the Garden* is 'the American view of life' (2000 [1964], 3); he expands by saying that he is concerned with 'the region of culture where literature, ideas, and certain projects of the collective imagination – we may call them "cultural symbols" – meet' (4). It is on this ground that *The American Adam* can also be situated. At the outset, Lewis commits himself to contributing to 'the history of ideas' (1955, 1); specifically, he wishes to follow across his chosen period the heroic American type identified in his book's title: 'an individual emancipated from history, happily bereft of ancestry, untouched and undefiled by the usual inheritances of race and family; an individual standing alone, self-reliant and self-propelling' (5).

The myth and symbol school has an ambiguous place in the story of American studies. Even if some accounts of the togetherness of scholars taken to fall under this heading have been exaggerated, it is undeniable that ideas and approaches were widely shared. As well as enabling American studies to appear orderly and coherent, myth and symbol scholarship also made it seem excitingly ambitious: no field could be described as 'safe' or 'conservative' if it enabled a researcher to move nimbly in the same study from civil engineering to Futurist painting, say, or to follow the trope of the garden in America across 300 years of culture. For all its facilitating of innovative work, however, this earliest phase of American studies also incurred significant political costs as it tended to place straight white male figures at its centre, minimising or even erasing the experiences of other constituencies in the United States. A fuller reckoning with the strengths and weaknesses of the myth and symbol school will be offered in Chapter 4.

THE INTERNATIONALISATION OF AMERICAN STUDIES

American studies is not the first thing that comes to mind when looking at Schloss Leopoldskron, a grand eighteenth-century house near Salzburg in Austria. Dripping with rococo styling, and stuffed with venerable books and paintings, the Schloss is a confident expression of tastes and values of the 'Old World'. Yet it was here, over six weeks in the summer of 1947, that an intellectual event took place which was to play a significant part in the international spread of American studies: namely, the first Harvard Student Council's Seminar in American Civilization. Scholars specialising in different facets of America and based at eight U.S. universities led classes for ninety-two delegates, drawn from seventeen European countries. The participants were mainly university students, but also included teachers, writers, artists and trade union activists. Despite the grandeur of their surroundings, they were offered only modest hospitality, with the prospectus for the seminar cautioning that 'All students should be prepared to sleep in dormitories and to receive a nutritious but plain diet' ('General Session in American Studies' 2020 [1947], n.p.). According to Henry Nash Smith, the scholar of the American West discussed previously, delegates subsisted during these six weeks in 'slightly austere conditions', giving 'a monastic tinge to daily life' (1949, 33).

But if the seminar's bed-and-breakfast facilities were meagre, its intellectual provision was plentiful. The visiting U.S. professors aimed 'to provide instruction in the principal areas of American Studies – history, the social sciences, literature, fine arts' (Smith 1949, 30–31). In accordance with the rationale of the fledgling academic subject, segregation between various strands of inquiry was abolished so as to present those attending with a multidimensional and multi-perspectival understanding of the United States. As Smith reports, delegates crossed adroitly between previously separated disciplines, participating with equal interest in conversations about 'decisions of the supreme court, political parties, labor unions, the American family, American novels and poems' (34).

Why study America, though, at that particular time and place? Sessions on tendencies in U.S. modernist painting or the condition of the U.S. labour movement were not, on the face of it, the most obvious things to offer people who had only recently emerged from a cataclysmic war on their own continent (Schloss Leopoldskron itself, with its bomb-damaged walls and unrepaired windows, was a visible reminder of the conflict). However, the organisers hoped that an event centred upon material far removed from European concerns would help to defuse any residual antagonisms among the participants. Margaret Mead, the distinguished anthropologist who co-chaired the seminar (see Figure 2.1), wrote that the opportunity to reflect upon the United States allowed students 'a certain degree of detachment' from their own politico-cultural circumstances, allowing them to sit 'side by side with men whom two short years ago they might have killed' (1947, 2). From such a perspective, American studies functioned in this first large-scale iteration of the subject on non-U.S. soil as a tool of conflict resolution, even as a form of therapy.

Yet, if there was something altruistic about Harvard's staging of the seminar, it also resulted in a significant payoff for the United States itself. Reading Smith's account, it is possible to see how this event reframed the United States in the participating Europeans' minds, making the nation something which they wished now not simply to study but to *emulate*. Smith describes how delegates from countries

Figure 2.1 Margaret Mead *(left)* at the Harvard Student Council's Seminar in American Civilization, Salzburg, 1947 (photographer unknown).

Source: Wikimedia Commons.

with censorship regimes still in place were startled to encounter 'the relaxed American acceptance of freedom of discussion' (1949, 35). Far from masking any national deficiencies, the visiting academics were happy to initiate a critical conversation about U.S. racial politics or, following a screening of John Ford's film, *The Grapes of Wrath* (1940), about the injustices of Depression-era economics. Mead is careful to detach the event from openly pro-U.S. politicking when she writes that 'To make American civilization a genuine area of communication meant that the Seminar has to be strictly disassociated from any government or propagandist venture' (1947, 4). Nevertheless, it is clear that even without official or state direction of this kind, the seminar at Schloss Leopoldskron positioned the United States as a free and tolerant nation that had the effect of making it an enhanced object of European interest, even desire.

In Mead's account, participants in the seminar left feeling highly energised, but also frustrated by the lack of immediate opportunities for further intellectual engagement; as she reported back to the Harvard Student Council: 'The group was unanimous in feeling that there was a need for a center of American studies in Europe' (1947, 7). Not 'a' centre, indeed, but *multiple* centres of study, dispersed across the continent; in Mead's words, 'many empty castles stand waiting' (8). The kind of baroque splendour exemplified by Schloss Leopoldskron was not generally available, of course, to the other associations for American studies that were established in Europe following this inaugural event. Nevertheless, the high number of these, and their wide geographical spread, testify to the new discipline's significant appeal. There is no need to take a complete inventory of them, but several can be mentioned. The British Association for American Studies (BAAS), for example, was founded in 1955, dedicated, as its website still says today, 'to promote, support and encourage the study of the United States in the Universities, Colleges and Schools of the United Kingdom, and by independent scholars' ('About us' 2018, n.p.). Two years earlier, the German Association for American Studies (DGfA) had been formed, helping to direct the country's intellectual life away from the toxic nationalism of the Nazi era.

Three other points might briefly be made about the post-war internationalisation of American studies. The first is that the proliferation of the discipline was not a narrowly European affair, but global in scope. The Australian and New Zealand American Studies Association, for instance, was founded in 1964; while in Japan, recently defeated in war and still under U.S. military occupation, the America Institute coordinated local study of the United States from 1947. Secondly, despite Mead's warning that agencies of the United States should not leave any impression of propaganda by becoming directly involved in the international development of American studies, some funds were disbursed for this purpose by American governmental, corporate and charitable bodies: in New Delhi in India, for example, 'the Ford Foundation helped establish a Department of American Studies' (Shrivastava 1987, 42). Questions can be asked, therefore, about the relationship between international academic work on the one hand and U.S. sponsorship on the other. Thirdly, the study of America undertaken across the world was not simply a replica of that done in the United States but was often shaped productively by local orientations and agendas. In the Soviet Union, for instance, American studies before the collapse of the Iron Curtain played its small part in the nation's geopolitical struggle with the United States. Note the title of a seminar there that aimed to uncover challenges posed by Soviet-originated ideas to capitalist orthodoxy in America: 'October and the Literature of the USA. The Impact of the Great October Socialist Revolution on American Literature and Journalism' (Antsyferova 2006, n.p.).

Programmes and journals in American studies across the world have frequently not had the resources enjoyed by their equivalents in the parent country. Nevertheless, their multiplicity and longevity tell us that this discipline is and remains a global rather than a proprietorially U.S. enterprise.

SUMMARY

In Chapter 1, we saw that the earliest studies of America tended to be sporadic and improvisatory, lacking the support of a disciplinary infrastructure. This chapter, by contrast, has traced the emergence and codification of the academic field known as 'American studies', beginning in the middle of the twentieth century and synchronising with enhanced interest in the United States itself as the nation ascended to the status of economic, military and cultural superpower. Henry Luce's 1941 article, 'The American Century', was taken as symptomatic of this new sense of the might of the United States. Right from the beginning, however, the scholarly work done under the auspices of American studies has been variable in its politics, sometimes expressing or at least implying a critical view of the nation at odds with the boosterish visions offered by business moguls or presidents. The competing political tendencies of the field will be reviewed in Chapter 6.

This chapter identified Vernon Louis Parrington's three-volume *Main Currents in American Thought*, published in the closing years of the 1920s, as a major precursor of academic American studies. Even if it appeared a little in advance of degree programmes and journals in the subject, it nevertheless anticipated aspects of this field of study, in particular the commitment to interdisciplinarity. Such braiding of different disciplines was also central to the method underpinning important books by Henry Nash Smith, Perry Miller, Leo Marx and others which appeared as American studies established itself after World War II. The label of 'myth and symbol school' was attached to these scholars to reflect their pursuit of ideas they took to be fundamental in America's history. Our evaluation of the legacy of myth and symbol scholarship should be nuanced. Positively, it brought to the new subject a set of intellectual protocols and an energising ambition. Troublingly, however, as indicated earlier and in later discussion in Chapter 4, it also tended to be white, masculinist and heteronormative in its outlook, thereby limiting the scope of American studies and by extension restricting the political possibilities of the United States also.

Finally, the chapter showed that from its earliest moments as an accredited field, American studies has been a collaborative undertaking, pursued worldwide rather than exclusively in the United States. In the wake of the Second World War, the developing subject proved of interest not only to the nation's allies (the United Kingdom) but to its former antagonists (Germany and Japan). This again prompts us to think about what, politically speaking, is at stake when studying the United States.

FURTHER READING

This chapter began by discussing Henry Luce, and Luce's significance as both a commentator on and a contributor to the growing power of the United States is explored by Alan Brinkley in *The Publisher: Henry Luce and His American Century* (New York: Knopf, 2010). Good starting points for readers interested more broadly in the United States' dominance in the twentieth century are two books very different in scale which are also helpful with regard to the earlier period covered in Chapter 1: Paul S. Boyer, *American History: A Very Short Introduction* (New York: Oxford University Press, 2012) and Hugh Brogan, *The Penguin History of the United States of America*, 2nd ed. (London: Penguin, 2001). Helpful specialist studies of 'the American Century' include Jerald Podair and Darren Dochuk (ed.), *The Routledge History of the Twentieth-Century United States* (New York: Routledge, 2018); Thomas C. Reeves, *Twentieth-Century America: A Brief History* (Oxford: Oxford University Press, 2004); and Howard Zinn's chronicle 'from below' in *A People's History of the United States*, 5th ed. (New York: HarperCollins, 2015).

The emergence of American studies in mid-century is well-covered in *Locating American Studies: The Evolution of a Discipline*, ed. Lucy Maddox (Baltimore, MD: Johns Hopkins University Press, 1999). This volume includes not only important texts from the period – Smith's essay on the question of the discipline's 'method' among them – but also reflections by later scholars. For stimulating essays on the internationalisation of this field of study, see *Globalizing American Studies*, ed. Brian T. Edwards and Dilip Parameshwar Gaonkar (Chicago: University of Chicago Press, 2010). Readers can also find valuable materials in the websites of American studies' national or regional associations, including the United States-based American Studies Association, founded in 1951 (www.theasa.net/); the British Association for American Studies (www.baas.ac.uk/); and the European Association for American Studies, established in 1954 (www.eaas.eu/).

THE SUBJECTS OF AMERICAN STUDIES

In the closing paragraph of Jack Kerouac's novel *On the Road* (1957), the narrator Sal Paradise is preoccupied with thoughts of America's magnitude. Living once again in New York City after a series of transcontinental car journeys, he says:

> I sit on the old, broken-down river pier watching the long, long skies over New Jersey and sense all that raw land that rolls in one unbelievable huge bulge over to the West Coast, and all that road going, all the people dreaming in the immensity of it. (2000 [1957], 281)

Sal is hardly alone in having these intimations of American largeness. Many of us are susceptible like him to thinking about the colossal scale of the United States ('one huge unbelievable bulge over to the West Coast') or about the size of its population ('all the people'). Other instances of the hypertrophy of the U.S. come quickly to mind, too: the staggering wealth, say, or the prodigious consumption of natural resources, or the scale of casualties left by white settlement and cultivation of the land. Whether we are speaking of geographical features or economic activities or social phenomena, America is liable to induce thoughts of the inflated or gigantic.

American studies shares in this lavish scale, being ambitious and extensive as an academic programme, rather than compactly designed. This expansive modelling of the discipline is hardly coincidental. For American studies embraces as its object what Sal Paradise calls 'all that raw land' and thereby sets itself the challenge of interpreting a dizzying mass of material that extends, say, from

DOI: 10.4324/9781315726748-4

political traditions of the Iroquois people in the 1770s to Abstract Expressionist painting in the 1950s, or from food cultures in New Orleans to superhero movies in contemporary Hollywood. The task which American studies assumes of analysing the 'general topic of American life' (Smith 1949, 31), including U.S. relations with the rest of the globe, is such that timorousness or modesty in how it presents itself would be inappropriate.

As I hope this book has already established, much of the distinctiveness and the attraction of American studies consists in interdisciplinarity. To describe it as *a* discipline, then, is only partially accurate. Such labelling is efficient enough in capturing a set of institutional arrangements: after all, American studies observes disciplinary norms in having its own professional associations like engineering or geography, and its own university courses like medicine or economics. Nevertheless, the term 'discipline', with its implied singleness, does not get at American studies' characteristic *method*. A sense of new intellectual possibilities was there from the subject's inception during the middle decades of the twentieth century. In Chapter 2, we saw Henry Nash Smith's reference, while reporting on the post-war Salzburg Seminar, to 'the principal areas of American Studies – history, the social sciences, literature, fine arts' (1949, 30–31). What Smith and other pioneers in the field felt to be exciting, however, was not so much the sheer number of interests taken to belong within American studies as the possibility of their combination or interweaving. The commas in Smith's list of subjects are thus to be understood not as barriers, but as bridges, with scholarship in the field transitioning adeptly between history, social sciences, literature and so on.

Given this fundamental commitment in American studies to outwitting the border patrols maintained by distinct subjects, this chapter's intention to consider many of them in sequence might appear misguided. This is a context, after all, in which mixture is everything. As the narrator of Herman Melville's posthumously published novella, *Billy Budd, Sailor* asks: 'Who in the rainbow can draw the line where the violet tint ends and the orange tint begins?' (2016, 300). In this quotation, however, while an impression of blending is paramount, violet and orange can still – just about – be seen separately. Similarly, I would contend that, in discussing American studies, value remains in drawing attention to the individual subjects that have a place in its ensemble. Before it is possible to imagine exhilarating intellectual composites, the specific components that go into making them should be clearly identified.

AMERICAN STUDIES AND THE HUMANITIES (1)

As an academic programme, American studies is usually seen as governed by the humanities or, speaking more loosely, the arts. One simple indicator of this is that university students who choose it as their course graduate with a BA degree, not a BSc. Yet the intellectual work actually done by practitioners of American studies is more varied and complex than can be captured by something administratively clear-cut like a degree certificate. Humanities disciplines are decisive in this field, often dominant; however, they are not monopolistic. Returning one last time to Smith's list of the principal academic strands intertwined to make up this body of study, it can be seen to include not only 'history . . . literature, fine arts', but also 'the social sciences'. Later in the chapter, then, we will consider the role played by social science subjects and methods. We begin, though, with three sections that assess the field's shaping by areas of humanistic study. This survey is substantial, yet, even so, not exhaustive. The first section discusses the contribution made to American studies by several disciplines devoted, broadly speaking, to the examination of *verbal artefacts* (literary studies, history, philosophy, religious studies); the second considers quite broadly the place of the *visual* in American studies; and the third catalogues some of the contributing subject areas that have visual or audio-visual materials as their concern (visual arts, architecture, photography, film, TV, music).

LITERARY STUDIES

By now, readers will have a sense of the many academic subjects involved in the design of American studies. This is not to say, however, that the field is a perfectly level one, with these intellectual strands democratically equivalent in power and prominence; as we noted in the Introduction, some strands have exercised more authority than others. Such is the case with literary studies. Chapter 2 described how scholarship focusing on literary production in America from Puritan settlement onwards played a key role in the twentieth-century theorisation and development of American studies itself. Parrington, Smith, Marx, Trachtenberg and other pioneering figures were literary critics by training, even if their primary interests proved centrifugal and took them into other areas of research (industrial history for Marx, say, or painting and photography for Trachtenberg). This heightened significance of the literary in American studies – perhaps we might even speak of its *privilege* – is still apparent today. A crude way of measuring this would be to glance at the programme drafted for the annual conference of the British Association for American Studies in 2020 (an event that, as it turned out, fell victim to COVID-19). Exact tabulation of subjects covered by the conference panels is tricky since, given the field's interdisciplinary premise, some sessions were due to discuss a formally diverse set of primary materials. Speaking approximately, however, close to two-fifths of the panels – twenty out of fifty-three – had American literature either wholly or substantially as their topic ('BAAS2020' 2020, 1–23). This is, of course, only a single piece of evidence, restricted as to place and time; nevertheless, the importance of the literary to which it testifies is liable to be found also across historically and geographically dispersed sites of American studies.

If American studies is at heart an exploration of the meanings of America, with all of their varied and profound material consequences, then it is unsurprising it should turn so frequently to literature. After all, to differing degrees of explicitness, American literary texts are involved in reflection on what this land signifies. Nevertheless, their promotion from Parrington's moment onwards as objects of serious interest marks quite a shift in critical trends in the United States. As Chapter 1 noted, writings from the 'Old World' rather than from home were often favoured by that Eurocentric culture that persisted in the United States into the first decades of the twentieth century. For a number of nineteenth-century critics, it was problematic even to think in terms of 'American literature', given the significant imprint left on the fiction, poetry and drama produced locally by forms and styles deriving from Europe. Representative of this line of argument was Margaret Fuller, a pioneering feminist as well as writer and critic, who began an article on 'American Literature; Its Position in the Present Time, and Prospects for the Future' (1846) by asserting that:

> Some thinkers may object to this essay, that we are about to write of that which has, as yet, no existence. For it does not follow because many books are written by persons born in America that there exists an American literature. (Fuller 1978, 381)

By the time the first scholars attached to American studies as an academic field began their work in the middle part of the twentieth century, the fundamental questions raised by Fuller and others with regard to the very category of American literature seemed less compelling. There were more urgent things to do with texts that had been produced in the United States than fret about whether they met strict criteria for properly national writing. Parrington, for example, was interested in how they staged a conflict between politically conservative and liberal tendencies; while what mattered to Smith was how they engaged with that western landscape which he judged crucial to the formation of U.S. identity. Nevertheless, there were still occasional traces in this period of a literary nationalism that asserted the importance of identifying and defending a distinctive body of writing done on U.S. soil. One critical study composed along these lines is especially important to mention because of its monumental scale and high analytical quality. This is *American Renaissance: Art and Expression in the Age of Emerson and Whitman* (1941), by Harvard professor F. O. Matthiessen. The book begins in frankly evaluative or canon-building fashion, as Matthiessen speaks of 'our past masterpieces' and observes how many of them were written in 'one extraordinarily concentrated moment of expression' during the middle third of the nineteenth century (1968 [1941], vii). He then reflects on his title's allusion to the fifteenth- and sixteenth-century *European* Renaissance, with its prodigious cultural outpouring. The U.S. literature he is concerned with, Matthiessen says, is 'America's way of producing a renaissance, by coming to its first maturity and affirming its rightful heritage in the whole expanse of art and culture' (vii).

Matthiessen's book contributed to the prestige of American studies as an emerging academic field by virtue of its densely detailed attention to a phase in U.S. culture. It also includes several nods to interdisciplinarity, as in the parallels traced between Walt Whitman's poetry and the realist painting of Thomas Eakins. 'Eakins is most like Whitman', Matthiessen writes, in *The Swimming Hole*, a homoerotically charged picture of 1885. As the passage continues: 'What would have appealed most to Whitman was the free flexible movement within the composition, and the rich physical pleasure in the outdoor scene and the sunlight on the firmly modelled flesh' (610). At the same time as delineating these promising directions for American studies, however, *American Renaissance* also contains a number of dead ends. For example, despite its epic length of nearly seven hundred pages, the account which it offers of American writing is quite constricted. The chronology of significant literary events, included at the end of the book (657–661), begins with the birth of Emerson in 1803 and concludes with Whitman's death in 1891. Matthiessen's period coverage is in effect much more compressed still, with discussion often oriented towards work done in the 1850s. Later scholarship on American writing has sought to reframe the period on which the book focuses, presenting it no longer as a climactic moment but instead as a particular sequence in a much longer literary history that stretches both backwards and forwards.

American literary study during the last half-century is also richer in its demographic coverage. It is not to disparage the great creative achievements of the five writers considered at length in *American Renaissance* to note that they comprise not only an all-male cohort but an *all-white* all-male cohort at that: Emerson, Thoreau, Hawthorne, Melville and Whitman. Emily Dickinson, for example, who rivals Whitman as the major U.S. poet of the second half of the nineteenth century, is referenced only three times in Matthiessen's many pages. No mention at all is made of the African American writer and activist Frederick Douglass, despite the fact that his autobiographical *Narrative of the Life of Frederick Douglass, An American Slave, Written by Himself* (1845) fits both with Matthiessen's chosen period and with his book's theme of American self-invention as Douglass attempts to undo his legal definition as an item of property and claim the same rights to interiority and agency that were asserted by white authors. Such preferences for the white and the male in the choice of examples are also evident in other formative texts in American studies, as we saw in Chapter 2.

It has been imperative, then, for scholars in the field to radically extend the American literary canon so that it incorporates writing by members of other population groups. This began to happen in the 1960s and 1970s in response to second-wave feminism and to campaigns for racial justice that included African American Civil Rights struggle and the American Indian Movement (AIM). Pressure exerted by later social movements forced further canon modifications, as with the inclusion of work by writers of Asian American or Latinx heritages. These last materials have extended the body of American writing not only spatially (making readers aware of many geographies beyond U.S. borders), but *linguistically* also. For a significant development during the past two decades has been the rediscovery by critics of the multilingual nature of American literature, challenging the belief that this is simply an anglophone tradition. As Werner Sollors writes in his introduction to a groundbreaking anthology of U.S.-produced texts in languages other than English that range from Arabic to Welsh:

> Reading, rereading, studying and discussing these works should bring about a much-needed reorientation in historical consciousness and, both in popular debates and in the specialized approaches of many academic fields, a contemporary understanding of the United States as a multilingual country. (2000, 10)

It is clear from Sollors' choice of words that to acknowledge this linguistic diversity is not simply to think differently about American literary history but to reimagine America itself.

Saying that literary scholarship has long had a major impact on American studies goes only so far, of course, since the precise form taken by its input has altered significantly. This is unsurprising: the study of literature has, after all, experienced a series of theoretical and methodological revolutions during American studies' eight or nine decades as a recognised academic programme. One of the most notable shifts, as observed earlier, has been the repopulating of the set of texts felt worthy of study, making it less of a white patriarchal monopoly. However, the very idea of the canon, with its connotations of officially sanctioned reading matter, has itself been questioned within literary studies. From such a perspective, the most pressing task is not to enlarge the canon so that it is demographically more representative, but rather to do away with it altogether and make the tools of literary study available for analysis of writing in general. Early traces of this non-canonical or even anti-canonical method were seen in Chapter 2, with Smith's turn to 'dime novels' in *Virgin Land* and Marx's close reading of U.S. government reports on industry in *The Machine in the Garden*.

For some scholars, however, even this move is insufficiently radical, by virtue of remaining tied to the analysis of purely verbal artefacts; they seek instead 'to challenge the disciplinary identity of literary studies by dissolving the category of "literature" into the more inclusive notion of "culture"' (Moran 2010, 45). Thus, for example, a literary critic investigating representations of Hurricane Katrina that devastated New Orleans and the larger region bordering the Gulf of Mexico in 2005 is not confined simply to canon-extending manoeuvres, whereby non-professional authors' poems and memoirs on the subject are read alongside texts by accredited writers including Dave Eggers and Natasha Trethewey. Instead, following the path which Moran outlines from 'literature' to a more expansive 'culture', the critic could venture beyond an exclusively verbal archive and consider also responses to Katrina in song, painting, photography and film.

HISTORY

Like literary criticism, history has been crucial in the development of American studies. As an already established discipline, it helped in the first instance to endow the newly emerging academic programme with weight and prestige. Historical scholarship has also been important in informing American studies' interventions in topical debates in the United States. For even when historians explore seemingly remote material in the American past – eye-gouging contests in Tennessee in the eighteenth century, for example – there are always connections back to the contemporary. As Gavin Stevens, a character in William Faulkner's novel *Requiem for a Nun*, famously remarks: 'The past is never dead. It's not even past' (2015 [1951], 85). Writing in the American Deep South, a region fashioned by the genocide of Native Americans, slavery and the institutionalised discrimination of the Jim Crow system that succeeded it, Faulkner was highly sensitive to the ongoing effects of history in his own moment. Yet, this quotation is equally resonant today. I want to think for a moment here about some recent events in the United States that show graphically the continuing force of the past and thereby help to underscore why history remains vital as a strand of American studies.

Following the killing of George Floyd, the African American man choked to death by a white police officer in Minneapolis in May 2020, the past emerged as a key site both of protest and backlash. For Black Lives Matter activists and their supporters, it was important of course to attempt to overturn specific policies and practices, beginning with that form of policing replicated across the United States which combines racist impulse with lethal violence. Strikingly, however, protesters also targeted locations of historical commemoration, acknowledging the significant part they have played and continue to perform in the reproduction of a racially unjust society. Statues across the United States of politicians and generals associated with the Confederate, slaveholding side in the American Civil War became especially charged scenes of insurgency. Many examples could be cited. Taking only one instance, however, Figure 3.1 shows the defacing of a classical figure at the base of a statue in Washington, D.C. that honours Albert Pike, who served as a brigadier in the Confederate Army before becoming a leading force in U.S. Freemasonry.

BLM slogans, in a red evoking the blood of slavery's and later racism's victims, have been inscribed on the lower part of the statue. The word 'RACIST', capitalised and in the same red, has been added as a subversive caption beneath Pike's name on the plinth. The figure of Pike himself is missing from its former position of eminence on top of the statue: in an act of symbolic counter-violence, protesters pulled it down and partially burned it before it was removed by local authorities.

In actions of this kind, BLM activists attempt to delegitimise that white supremacist story of the American past to which the statues give marble or brass form. By doing so, they aim to enhance the possibility of a transformed American present. Conservative opponents understand this, recognising the threat to their current powers

Figure 3.1 The defaced Albert Pike Memorial, Washington, D.C., 2 July 2020 (photograph: AgnosticPreachersKid).

Source: Wikimedia Commons.

and privileges in the event of anti-racists' counter-history of America gaining mass support. Thus, President Trump tweeted furiously about damage to statues and even issued an Executive Order stating that 'the violent extremists'' choice of targets is 'indicative of a desire to indiscriminately destroy anything that honors our past and to erase from the public mind any suggestion that our past may be worth honoring, cherishing, remembering, or understanding' (The White House 2020, n.p.). Other conservatives resorted to direct action of their own. In July 2020, in Rochester, New York, a statue of Frederick Douglass was ripped from its pedestal. The figure was found damaged in a gully nearby, recapitulating the historically abusive treatment of the Black body in America.

American history's importance is such that, as these recent events show, it has ceased to be the preserve of a specialist academic caste. Ordinary U.S. citizens, too, often present themselves as unofficial historians, telling stories about the past of America that both derive from and reinforce their radically different political outlooks in the present. By way of concluding this section, however, I want to return to *professional* historians' accounts of the United States – especially those that contribute to the larger programme of American studies – and make two points.

The first is that here, too, as with the laypersons' narratives, we should expect to find ideological dispute, rather than consensus. If there are less obvious signs in historical scholarship now than in the previous historiography of a white supremacist mentality, or a triumphalist outlook on the United States, that is not to say that all work on the American past is progressive in its intent and effect. Secondly, the part played by history in university courses in American studies is also varied. At times the subject appears to observe its traditional disciplinary boundaries, rather than infusing a broader, multidimensional programme of study of America. Undergraduates in American studies at Yale University, for example, can select from modular options that include 'American Indian History', 'Antebellum America' and – focusing on the early decades of the independent United States – 'Age of Hamilton and Jefferson' ('Undergraduate Courses' 2020, n.p.). Elsewhere, however, including in other parts of Yale's course design, history is less a subject sufficient to itself than part of the functioning of American studies in its totality. Practitioners in the field engage in historical scholarship not only when researching the Civil War or the Wall Street Crash of 1929, say, but when they turn to the chronology of U.S. feminism while reading Henry James's novel *The Bostonians* (1886) or when they mobilise the story of Italian immigration to the United States in the course of considering Francis Ford Coppola's *Godfather* film trilogy (1972–90). Instances such as these prompt us to think of history as not only a distinctive strand of American studies, with its subject-specific topics and methods, but as the atmosphere breathed by everyone in the field, whatever their own specialisms.

PHILOSOPHY AND RELIGIOUS STUDIES

In Chapter 2's review of several foundational texts in American studies produced during the middle of the twentieth century, we observed that one of several things they have in common is that they frequently present themselves as contributions to intellectual history. Here, an extended version of a passage already quoted from R. W. B. Lewis's *The American Adam* (1955) can fairly stand as a description of what especially preoccupies these pioneering scholars. Strikingly, Lewis begins his book with a set of exclusions or negations, listing those subjects in which he will *not* be interested: so, no 'anthropology and sociology', no 'folklore and legend', no 'economic geography and political history' (1). He thus clears the terrain for what he *does* want to write about: 'the history of ideas and especially . . . the representative imagery and anecdote that crystallized whole clusters of ideas' (1). Lewis's contemporaries, as we saw, were often similarly austere, bracketing off various social and cultural materials in order to focus on the genealogy of ideas in America.

This tendency in the field's earliest work had a significant effect on the subsequent development of American studies as an academic programme. Many institutions gave space or even, in some cases, pride of place to modules in the history of 'American thought'. As with efforts already discussed to theorise a distinctive American literature, purged of European and other alien influences, so attempts have sometimes been made to identify a tradition of philosophy that by virtue of its key themes or its preferred styles is describable as 'American'. John Kaag, in a book that winningly weaves together conceptual exposition and autobiographical reminiscence, contributes to this nationalistic project. One idea in particular, he suggests, has proved so durable in America that it connects figures as disparate as a white Congregationalist theologian of the antebellum period and an African American intellectual and activist of our own moment: 'American philosophy – from Jonathan Edwards in the eighteenth century through to Cornel West in this one – is about the possibilities of birth and renewal' (2016, 67).

Nevertheless, as an area of study, intellectual history has undergone significant shifts in recent decades. Two of these modifications that have consequences for American studies might be mentioned. To begin with, a patriotic or possessive attitude towards specific ideas has proved hard to sustain in an era increasingly sensitive to the impact of long-running exchanges across national borders, including transfers of intellectual material; ideas may be inflected by local conditions, but cannot easily be confined to them. Taking only one example relevant to us, Emerson, the U.S. Transcendentalist of the nineteenth century, did not conjure his romantic philosophy simply out of the Massachusetts countryside in which he walked, but through intensive reflection on and response to imported traditions of thought ranging from Plato in Ancient Greece to Hindu scripture. Rather than thinking about American philosophy as wholly original and distinctive, as a self-sufficient body of work, it is more compelling to situate it in ongoing interactions with philosophies from beyond the U.S. frontier.

Secondly, philosophers may be increasingly attracted to 'true interdisciplinary co-operation . . . philosophy joining forces with other disciplines' (Hansson 2008, 480). While obvious possibilities here include exchanges with medical practitioners and biologists over questions of human fertility, or with economists concerning definitions of value and need, more relevant to us in the field of American studies is that philosophy specialists might turn to history and politics so as to embed the concepts they are concerned with in richly material circumstances. Returning to Emerson and the other Transcendentalists for a moment, it is not a vulgar or reductive move to interpret their ideas of the visionary and resplendent self as a defence against gathering forces of standardisation and conformity in the rapidly industrialising and urbanising mid-nineteenth-century United States. Likewise, African American thinking from Douglass to Cornel West is most productively understood not as contributions to some disembodied conceptual realm, but rather as a set of urgent attempts to theorise the oppression and plot the liberation of Black citizens. This emphasis on particular sociocultural conditions as the ground for intellectual production suggests a different way of understanding the history of American thought from that sketched earlier by Lewis, who tends to disembed ideas from their worldly situations so as to inspect them abstractly.

A brief word should be said finally about the coverage of religion in American studies. Positioning religious studies alongside philosophy in this section is intended to reflect the extent to which, in America, philosophical and theological traditions have long been intertwined, even synonymous. Much of America's mental energy has historically been devoted to devising, codifying and elaborating religious systems of various kinds. So, for example, the 'New England mind' of the seventeenth and eighteenth centuries, which in Chapter 2 we saw Perry Miller discussing, was preponderantly a *religious* mind, one shaped by or even reducible to the system of Puritan belief (suggestively, Miller refers at one point to 'a philosophy of Puritanism' [1939, 90]). Many later instances of American thought, including nineteenth-century Transcendentalism, bear the traces of this Puritan or more broadly Christian tradition, while nevertheless attempting to break from it in heretical directions. Even such a militantly secular movement as communist struggle in the United States during the Depression of the 1930s borrowed from religious precedent. As evidence, consider John Steinbeck's socially engaged novels, *In Dubious Battle* (1936) and *The Grapes of Wrath* (1939), which feature characters who align themselves with the cause of the labour unions yet continue to utilise a Christian language of sacrifice and martyrdom.

Whether the topic for discussion is seventeenth-century Quakerism in Pennsylvania or nineteenth-century Mormonism in Utah or twenty-first-century Catholicism in New Mexico, the interdisciplinarity of American studies prompts us to think historically and culturally about all spiritualities. Faith communities, after all, are not disembodied in encounters with their god but rather situated in specific social conjunctures. Any temptation to offer a doctrinaire assessment of religion in the United States, viewing it monolithically as either reactionary or progressive in its political effect, should be resisted. For if certain religious traditions in America have indeed contributed to the reproduction of an unjust society, as when Southern Christian pastors legitimised the institution of slavery from the pulpit or when contemporary evangelical ministers give a blessing to homophobia, there are also contrary examples of faith groups on the side of liberation. Applying more broadly some words used by Eddie S. Glaude Jr. to describe Black spiritual traditions, in particular, we might say that religious observance in America has shown itself to have at least the potential to function as 'a *practice of freedom*' (2014, 11, emphasis in original) and to provide 'a powerful site for creative imaginings' of a transformed social order (118).

THE VISUAL IN AMERICAN STUDIES

By comparison with the intensively discussed verbal archives of literature, history and philosophy, visual materials have been patchily addressed in American studies. As we saw in Chapter 2, this tendency towards certain kinds of subject matter at the expense of others was apparent in the mid-twentieth century in some of the work most important to the field's consolidation. To recall briefly: Smith in *Virgin Land* restricts graphic and pictorial representations of the American West to a supporting role only (and ignores cinematic westerns entirely); while Marx, in *The Machine in the Garden*, construes 'the pastoral imagination' in America almost entirely in verbal terms, causing him to pass over such important visual manifestations of American pastoral in the nineteenth century as Thomas Cole's paintings of the Hudson River Valley and Albert Bierstadt's of the Rocky Mountains. Only in Trachtenberg's study of Brooklyn Bridge in New York City, which discusses art by Joseph Stella and photography by Walker Evans alongside poetry, did we encounter a different orientation, seeking to counter the visual's relegation or even outright erasure in the face of the verbal.

In thinking about the history of American studies, it is important not to regard such iconophobia as a short-lived pathology that marked only the discipline's first phase. On the contrary, its traces can be identified in later generations of work in this field, down to our own. Despite American studies' declared openness from the beginning to the analysis of primary materials extending far beyond the traditional literary corpus, there was still a significant time lag before the appearance of prolific work on such visual artefacts as films and TV shows. One piece of evidence of the stubborn hold exercised by verbal subject matter is the startling fact unearthed by Jonathan Auerbach that 'the American Studies Association journal, *American Quarterly*, published only one article on film between 1953 and 1973 out of more than four hundred articles published during this twenty-year span' (2006, 31). Auerbach goes on to acknowledge some subsequent correction of this visual deficit, writing that 'By the late 1970s and early 1980s film had finally shown up on the American studies radar' (31). Looked at carefully, however, his phrasing evokes a relatively modest change in the discipline, rather than its wholesale recalibration.

Anyone who is still tempted to regard the dominance of the verbal in American studies as having ended some decades ago should reckon with the evidence of current books, articles and conferences. If we reopen for a moment the draft programme of the 2020 conference of the British Association for American Studies that was discussed earlier in this chapter, observing the same caveat that this offers only partial testimony of the state of the field now, we see a marked disposition still towards literature, history and politics. Panels organised around film and TV are sparse. Sessions and papers on other visual media are scarcer still – though with exciting exceptions, such as a panel on race, class and landscape in American women's photography and a contribution on the Armory Show of 1913 which introduced audiences in New York City and the wider United States to avant-garde European art ('BAAS2020' 2020, 5–6, 7). To point all this out is certainly not to allege outmodedness or aberration in the British event's approach to American studies. Instead, it is to suggest that the field's initial preference for verbal materials continues to have some gravitational pull over the study choices made by contemporary scholars.

This downplaying in American studies of analysis of exclusively or significantly visual forms of expression is especially surprising where scholarship focuses on the recent and contemporary United States. It was, after all, more than thirty years ago now that W. J. T. Mitchell, the U.S. scholar of both art and literature, observed a major shift from the verbal to the visual in our lifeworlds. Such transformation heightens the responsibility on us to *see* in order to make sense of experience:

> Everything – nature, politics, sex, other people – comes to us now as an image... the very view from one's window, much less the scenes played out in everyday life and in the various media of representation, seem to require constant interpretive vigilance. (Mitchell 1986, 30)

This reorientation towards the image is of course experienced unevenly by people across the globe. More than most societies, however, the United States is in a state of image saturation, asking us as practitioners of American studies to be highly sensitive to the visual and its meanings.

AMERICAN STUDIES AND THE HUMANITIES (2)

STUDIES OF VISUAL ARTS, ARCHITECTURE AND PHOTOGRAPHY

Visually oriented American studies should, of course, be wide in its coverage of primary materials, rather than restricting itself to modern and contemporary forms such as TV, film and video. It might begin by considering *visual arts*, taking this term to apply usefully to artistic work of a very broad range. Thus, potential objects for discussion will vary markedly in their moment of origin (from the early practice of Indigenous peoples in America to contemporary production); their medium (from oil painting or watercolour, say, to ceramics); and their mode of spectator address and engagement (from an Album Quilt woven in a Baltimore household in the 1840s to a conceptual piece exhibited now in a niche Los Angeles gallery). If visual arts have been more lightly discussed than film in American studies over the last few decades, within this category itself there are further inequalities in coverage. More books and articles have appeared on canonical work such as post-war Abstract Expressionist painting or Andy Warhol's Pop Art of the 1960s, say, than on vernacular artistic traditions like the scrimshaw carvings done by New England sailors on the teeth and bones of whales.

Close connections exist between the visual arts and *architecture*, which also falls within the scope of American studies. This particular link is made by Robert Hughes in his monumental history of art in America, as when one of the first works he chooses to analyse is not a painting or drawing, but a cluster of stone and adobe buildings raised 'in utter defiance of environmental reality': the twelfth-century pueblo constructed by the Acoma community of Native Americans in present-day New Mexico (1997, 8). Figure 3.2 shows a photograph of the pueblo taken in 1904 by Edward Curtis, a significant figure to whom we will return shortly. The point to make at the moment is that, as with visual arts, coverage of American

Figure 3.2 Edward S. Curtis, *Acoma from the South* (1904).

Source: Wikimedia Commons.

architecture should be chronologically expansive, extending from these earliest surviving structures on the continent to the contemporary built environment of shopping malls, theme parks and gated communities.

Where American studies turns to architectural criticism to inform its work, it finds an already interdisciplinary and outward-looking subject. For while there may still be some people who construe the history of architecture narrowly as a sequence of building styles, detached from worldly contexts, this is an outmoded, minority position. Most architecture critics insist that to consider a particular construction, whether this is an antebellum plantation mansion in the American South or a twenty-first-century airport, is inevitably to reckon also with social and cultural questions: power, class, environment, the body, and so on. A relevant example of politically oriented work of this kind is offered by the Italian critic Manfredo Tafuri, discussing the active interest taken in U.S. building design by Thomas Jefferson, who served as President from 1801 to 1809.

Tafuri writes of the 'extreme lucidity' with which Jefferson 'recognized the institutional and pedagogical value of architecture' (1976, 25). The buildings in which he had a hand, including the White House in Washington, D.C., were thus not mute additions to the landscape, but rather manifestos in stone for his 'agrarian and anti-urban' vision of America (26).

Surprisingly, perhaps, in view of how a discussion of architecture opens on to topics of urgent worldly concern, comparatively few analyses of buildings themselves and other parts of the built environment are undertaken from inside American studies. There are interesting exceptions, of course, where 'hard' architectural criticism of this sort *does* occur. For example, Yale's undergraduate programme in American studies, mentioned earlier in this chapter, includes 'Material Cultures and the Built Environment' as one of its six 'Areas of Concentration', giving students an opportunity to explore 'the formation of the American landscape from the natural to the man-made, including the development of American architecture' ('Areas of Concentration' 2020, n.p.). More often, however, American studies' engagement with architecture occurs at second remove, so to speak, assessing its textualisation or pictorialisation in various expressive forms. So, while practitioners of American studies may not actually get their shoes dirty by going on a field trip to the Empire State Building, for instance, they might nevertheless consider how the building has been mediated by literary fiction or cinema – or by *photography* (another of the visual forms for inclusion in the repertoire of American studies). Examples here would include the many pictures that Lewis Hine took of the Empire State Building's construction at the beginning of the 1930s. This work might to considered to mimic the real estate project itself in contributing to a triumphalist U.S. narrative of modernisation. However, it also lends itself to alternative readings that take the side of labour, not capital. Significantly, perhaps, one of Hine's photographs is titled *Girders and Workers* (c. 1930), reinforcing that ominous sense of property's dominance which is suggested visually by the human figures' slightness against a grid of metal.

The tradition of photography in the United States has often interested American studies. Both within the work of individual photographers, and in the juxtaposition of different photographers' portfolios, critics have found competing responses to the question of what is meant or signified by America. Again, there is an extensive chronological range here. At one end of the spectrum, scholars have discussed the enormous archive of pictures of Native American communities which Edward Curtis took in the late nineteenth and early twentieth centuries as part of his broader ethnographic project to document ways of life under threat in a modernising and standardising United States. An example of his work, looking from a distance at the Acoma Pueblo was included earlier as Figure 3.2. If Curtis's photographs risk inadvertently abetting the racist case that 'the Indian' is fixated on tradition and thereby doomed to obsolescence, they should not be reduced to this meaning, for in combination with the audio recordings that he made they also disclose the humanity of their frequently disparaged subjects. Nearer to our own moment, photography assessed by American studies scholars includes post-war work that challenges an enduring sense of the American West as an empty and sublime space. For instance, Neil Campbell, the British Americanist mentioned in Chapter 2, turns to photographs of this region by Robert Frank, Michael Ormerod and others that fasten on details of urbanisation, commodification, migration and ecological depletion. Their work thus offers 'more complex, multiple, and dialogical renditions of place' than the monumentalised West of earlier imagery (Campbell 2008, 186).

STUDIES OF FILM, TV AND MUSIC

Representations of the West figure prominently also in American studies' engagement with *film*. Although the output of westerns has declined markedly since 1970 or so, with only spasmodic if interesting recurrences, the genre's earlier popularity and its foregrounding of questions of U.S. identity have long made it of obvious interest to Americanists. Not that cinematic westerns, or indeed films of any category, cropped up much in the first, mid-century phase of American studies. On the face of it, it is puzzling that this new academic programme was slow to make much of what had already become America's paramount expressive form; after all, as Auerbach reminds us: 'American studies in its earliest stages of institutionalization sought to distinguish itself from traditional fields such as literary studies and history by claiming an interdisciplinary ground of investigation, including the myths and symbols of mass culture' (2006, 31). Reasons for this initial neglect of film might be suggested, however. To begin with, as we have already seen, the professional formation of many of American studies' earliest practitioners was in precisely those 'traditional fields such as literary studies and history', inducing perhaps some reluctance to venture into cinema despite a theoretical commitment to diverse primary materials. A less personalised reason may have been a lingering suspicion that, by comparison with literature, film was a debased art form. Among the most forceful exponents of this case in mid-century were the exiled German Marxists Theodor Adorno and Max Horkheimer, who aligned films with radio broadcasts, magazines and other popular media products, characterising them as aesthetically formulaic ('the mechanically differentiated products are ultimately all the same') and politically regressive in serving only the interests of capitalism ('nothing but business') (2002 [1947], 97, 95).

Lively critiques of film of this sort did not, in the end, prevent the medium's thorough absorption into the field of American studies. As Auerbach observes, scholarly work on cinema proliferated in the late 1970s and early 1980s. Since then, it has become a staple, if still not quite rivalling in abundance studies of literature and history. The work done on film under this remit has been expansive in both textual choice and methodological framing. In the first regard, anxiety about the artistic quality of particular films, or even whole genres, has generally proved no obstacle to their potential analysis in American studies. So, Rob Zombie's visceral horror movie *House of 1000 Corpses* (2003), with its exploitation scenes of torture and vivisection, offers as much grist to American studies' mill as a reflective piece of independent cinema by Paul Thomas Anderson or Jim Jarmusch. Perhaps *even more* grist, in fact, given the engagement of Zombie's film with the white rural dispossessed in America (a choice of subject that opens it up potentially to quirky interdisciplinary study alongside, say, traditions of country music or sport). Secondly, if American film studies has learned not to worry about the canon but to embrace discussion of U.S. titles of any type, it has been similarly eclectic and mobile in its methodologies. Campbell's 2013 book *Post-Westerns*, for instance, draws on cultural geography, environmental studies and poststructuralist philosophy in exploring a set of films from the 1950s to the early twenty-first century that utilise the tropes of the classic Hollywood western, while also revisiting and revitalising them so as to reflect such changes in the region as increased ethnic diversity and modified gender codes. It might also be noted in passing that many of Campbell's conceptual influences are French in origin (in particular, Gilles Deleuze and Jacques Derrida), indicating a broader willingness in American studies to treat 'foreign' ideas as invigorating arrivals rather than unwanted intruders.

Historically, research into film has taken its key tools from disciplines in the humanities, notably literary studies and art criticism. The practice of *interpretation* has thus been central, involving us in unveiling the significance of a camera angle or instance of voiceover in Martin Scorsese's *The Wolf of Wall Street* (2013), say, just as we might unpack a metaphor in Mark Twain's *Adventures of Huckleberry Finn* (1884). This form of film *reading* remains paramount and, as demonstrated by Campbell's book on post-westerns, is also open to renewal by fresh conceptual inputs. In the last two decades, however, this approach has been joined by other research programmes that aim to go beyond 'the film text' and to explore instead such topics as the diversified structure of Hollywood conglomerates or the experiences of audiences in venues of film consumption that might range from racially segregated cinemas in the U.S. South to the drive-in. Work of these kinds shows a diversifying set of influences on film studies, with the imprint particularly of economic history and ethnography.

While such a mixing of approaches is relatively new in film studies, it was actually foundational in another branch of visual inquiry that belongs in the field of American studies: namely, *television studies*. In outlining the trajectory of TV scholarship, Jonathan Gray and Amanda Lotz point out that 'the distinctions' right from the start between 'social sciences and humanities approaches have taken different forms and led scholars to identify their work in different ways' (2019, 26). For every person in television studies caught up in interpreting characters and images in David Lynch's and Mark Frost's mesmerising neo-noir series *Twin Peaks* (1990–1, 2017), for example, there has been someone else doing sociologically based work on the part played by TV more broadly in the structuring of the American family or the formation of the American teenager. Qualitative and quantitative types of research thus cohabit in ways that are sometimes prickly, but often mutually enriching. Interestingly, Gray and Lotz refer also to 'the US-centrism' of television studies as an academic subject (2019, 26). This is yet to be fully reflected in the broader field of American studies itself, where scholarship on TV is to date much less prolific than that on film (let alone literature). The situation may change in the future, perhaps, not least given the novelistic scale and density of multiple U.S. drama series that extend from *The Sopranos* (1999–2007), *The Wire* (2002–8) and *Breaking Bad* (2008–13) to *Orange Is the New Black* (2013–19) and *Succession* (2018–). It is a moot question, though, whether 'television studies' is now the best term for academic work on shows such as these, since they are often consumed on devices other than traditional TV sets and in binges unimaginable to a previous generation's schedulers.

Finally, in this section, a corrective comment with regard to some things previously said can help to bring us to another humanities discipline that feeds into American studies. I have considered film and TV here under the heading of visual culture. However, this is only partly accurate as a categorisation and risks contributing to long-standing ocularcentrism in the study of these media. For film and television are *audio*-visual in composition, requiring from us sensitive listening, as well as vigilant spectatorship: indeed, the French critic Michel Chion proposes that we ditch any suggestion of visual monopoly and speak instead of an 'audio-spectator' who is involved in 'audio-viewing' (1994, xxv). One of the things we should listen to here is a film's or TV show's musical soundtrack – and this offers us the chance to note that *musicology*, too, has a place in American studies. Again, this is a part of the field that is relatively underdeveloped. Far more studies exist of *Benjamin* Franklin than of *Aretha* Franklin, the great soul singer; monographs on Ernest Hemingway take up much more shelf space than books about Slipknot. It is true there are signs of growth in certain areas of American musical study, not least in nuanced scholarly work on both the texts and the contexts of gangsta rap. While this is greatly to be welcomed, it is important that research into U.S. music conducted from within American studies be expansive in its coverage of both forms and histories, venturing beyond Tupac and Dr. Dre to consider, say, the minimalist compositions of Steve Reich and Philip Glass or vernacular traditions such as bluegrass and Appalachian folk. Like the study of architecture, considered earlier in this section, any exploration of American music should be eclectic and multidimensional, taking the analyst beyond musical particulars to consider also questions of identity and ideology.

AMERICAN STUDIES AND THE SOCIAL SCIENCES

So far in this chapter, we have considered the varying contributions which have been made to American studies by disciplines belonging to the humanities. The most obvious yield has been in fine-grained analyses of American texts, taking 'text' here in a very broad sense as referring not only to literary materials but also to songs, films, photographs, paintings, even buildings. Through this close reading, the humanities disciplines have helped to advance American studies' core project of identifying and evaluating attempts that have been made to endow America with meaning. For some scholars, however, the field's dominance by humanities subjects is problematical, carrying the risks of restricting the methods used to textual analysis and of giving privilege in thinking about meaning-production in America to elite individuals rather than to social aggregations (thus, more research has been done in American studies on Bob Dylan's songwriting than on, say, the cultural life of the sizeable German American community in Pennsylvania). A key intervention along these lines was made by Gene Wise in an essay of 1979, which alludes to 'the long-lamented gap between humanistic and social scientific approaches to culture' (296, n. 4). His proposal for change in the field was not for humanities' rule simply to be supplanted by a reign of the social sciences; rather: 'A healthy future for American studies lies not in the domination of one or another approach, but in an open dialogue, indeed an open tension, between them' (332, n. 79). Each can repair a deficit in the other, in Wise's estimation, with the social sciences' preference for large data sets offsetting a tendency in the humanities to prioritise discussion of relatively small-scale samples of American high culture, and the humanities' mission to engage with texts in their individual complexity countering 'the decided over-emphasis on quantification in the social sciences' (334).

As early as 1951, the U.S. anthropologist Margaret Mead, mentioned in Chapter 2 in connection with her involvement in the inaugural Salzburg Seminar, had sketched an example of this kind of collaboration between disciplines that are often remote from or even hostile to each other. The project she imagined was 'a study of American civilization of a given region between 1900–1914' (Mead 1951, 13). To undertake this research, she envisaged a group containing not only Americans and Europeans, and locals to the region and incomers, but also 'American anthropologists and American historians' (13). Two points might be made in response to this imaginary project. The first is that Mead presumes that the desired interdisciplinarity of American studies will be achieved at the level of *programme design* (with inputs gathered from specialists representing a range of subjects, such as anthropology and history), rather than by *individual scholarship* (it is not necessary for anthropologists to become expert historians also, or vice versa). Many subsequent practitioners in American studies *have*, of course, been interested in crossing intellectual borders in their own work; however, reflecting what is feasible for individuals in a time of multiple fields that all have their own formidable complexities, these turns to other subject areas have often resembled rapid and localised raids. A second point, however, as suggested by the appearance of Wise's essay almost thirty years after Mead was writing, is that her vision of collaboration between social sciences and humanities proved more utopian fancy than actualised initiative. Yet, opportunities still exist for such a rapprochement. In the rest of this section, then, we consider some of the social sciences that have much to contribute alongside the humanities in American studies.

ANTHROPOLOGY AND SOCIOLOGY

It is appropriate to begin by considering Mead's own specialism of *anthropology*. In the popular imagination, anthropologists tend to be seen as scholars immersed in the study of the organisation of premodern societies. While this picture is outdated – the anthropologist is as likely to be working on the ritual behaviour of contemporary baseball fans as on ancient kinship patterns – it still usefully identifies one anthropological strand that might figure much more strongly in American studies than has historically been the case. The pre-modern life of North America's own Indigenous communities, after all, lends itself to the anthropologist's expertise as regards relationship systems, ceremonial practices, material cultures and linguistic traditions. Such scholarship has the salutary effect of greatly extending the temporal range of American studies. There is a foreshadowing of the exhilarating opening-up to earlier times that the anthropological imagination can bring during a moment in Henry David Thoreau's *Walden*. Thoreau, the nineteenth-century Transcendentalist cited in Chapter 1 for his interest in Indigenous cultures in America, describes a revelation he has while cultivating his small patch of ground in Massachusetts: 'in the course of the summer it appeared by the arrow-heads which I turned up in hoeing, that an extinct nation had anciently dwelt here and planted corn and beans ere white men came to clear the land' (1997 [1854], 141). All of a sudden, following the discovery of this artefact, America is drastically reimagined as both less new and less white.

Scholars contributing to American studies from anthropological perspectives also, of course, work on more modern topics. An example of the kind of research that can be done is given by the career of the mid-twentieth-century U.S. anthropologist Hortense Powdermaker. Though her intellectual formation was quite conventional – doctoral study took her to traditional communities in the Pacific – she subsequently brought anthropological questions and methods to bear on facets of the contemporary United States. In 1939, she published *After Freedom: A Cultural Study of the Deep South*, unpacking small-town social dynamics in Indianola, Mississippi. Subsequently, in *Hollywood, the Dream Factory*, she explored how 'the social system underlying the production of the movies influences them' (1950, 9). While producers, directors, screenwriters and actors obviously differ in preoccupation from the 'headhunters in New Guinea' she had previously studied (10), they nevertheless oddly resemble them in comprising a structured, rule-bound community. To these mid-century ventures in anthropological American studies can be added later work taking the anthropologist into Mormon communities in the United States, or L.A. gangs, or – as with Karen Ho's *Liquidated: An Ethnography of Wall Street* (2009) – New York City's financial community. In each of these cases, as with Powdermaker's earlier projects, anthropology brings to American studies not only an expanded subject range but as a diversified methodology. Anthropological methods of fieldwork and participant observation, applied classically to traditional societies, are mobilised in these modern settings. Ho, for example, writes of her immersion in Manhattan's corporate centre, where a combination of networking and 'chance encounters' enables her to 'assemble a diverse financial crowd at multiple levels of the Wall Street hierarchy' (21). Whereas the literary critic or historian remains at an experiential distance from their object of study, the anthropologist, as in Ho's project among the bond traders, is likely to achieve empathy and even intimacy with those they discuss.

There are obvious risks as well as undoubted gains in anthropological research methods such as these. For one thing, this degree of immersion in the field under consideration may threaten the critical distance often regarded as fundamental to scholarship (in Ho's case, she has to resist internalising the profiteering logic of the bond dealers she interacts with). Secondly, an anthropologist's description of a given social world may be overly parochial, inhibiting awareness of external forces operating upon it. It is because of its constitutive interest in precisely those broad structuring processes that *sociology* has a valuable role to play in American studies. This is not to say that sociologists never adopt the methods of anthropology, such as participant observation. In *Body & Soul*, for instance, the U.S.-based French sociologist Loïc Wacquant faces not only physical pain but also identity transformation when he spends three years training as a boxer in an African American neighbourhood of Chicago: 'Is that really me, decked out in this black leather belt girdling my hips halfway up my belly, with my spindly legs sticking out below in purple sweatpants?' (2004, 73). Wacquant's book, however, is multiple in its genres, combining anthropological fleshing-out of his boxing club's rules and rituals with sociological investigation of the racial and class dynamics in the United States more broadly that shape this specific environment. Elsewhere, sociologists may forego such immersive fieldwork in order to engage more directly with large-scale forces of social structuration in the United States that range from gender formations to education systems or from religious traditions to penal codes. Sociologists thus serve to counter a tendency in some other parts of American studies to analyse the small scale or the fragmentary, rather than engaging with bigger processes and relations.

One other thing about Wacquant's *Body & Soul* is worthy of comment. While it can be described in general terms as an example of sociological research, it is, more specifically, a contribution to the *sociology of sport*. This is a well-established line of social inquiry that, to date, has had only a modest impact on American studies itself. Such a deficit in coverage is surprising when we consider sport's historic importance in U.S. cultural life, the extent to which it has long participated in negotiations of race and ethnicity, gender and sexuality, modernity and tradition, nation and world. This cultural function is only expanding in contemporary conditions, rather than diminishing. It is to be hoped, then, that a recent article on the National Football League by Kellen Hoxworth, published in American studies' premier journal in the United States, signifies not a lone scholar's eccentric choice of field but rather the opening up of territory for mass research. Hoxworth explores how the protest of 'taking the knee' before matches, led by the San Francisco 49ers' quarterback Colin Kaepernick and other African American players, inscribes resistance to 'the NFL's commoditization of the "spectacle of the black body"': 'Collectively, these professional football players made spectacles of their black bodies outside the frames of athletic performance and statistical production, laying claim to their political rights rather than their economic value' (Hoxworth 2020, 171). Viewed in this light, U.S. sport becomes something other than touchdowns and baskets, home runs and putts: it becomes *politics* through and through.

POLITICAL SCIENCE AND LEGAL STUDIES

A sociological perspective, whether applied to American football or to Jehovah's Witnesses, is inevitably also a form of political inquiry. Political investment is apparent, too, right across the portfolio of subjects contributing to American studies covered earlier in this chapter. Literary critics, for example, are doing politics when they examine the portrayal of Native Americans in James Fenimore Cooper's novel, *The Last of the Mohicans* (1826); so are film scholars when they discuss Scarlett Johansson's body image and costuming choices as Black Widow in a series of Marvel movies. But if the political is sometimes liable to enter deviously or in disguise into these subject areas, it is central and overt in another field for which American studies makes space: that is to say, *political science*. Traditionally, in American studies university courses, political science had a patrician character, concerning itself with such topics as the separation of powers between executive, legislature and judiciary under the U.S. Constitution, or the history of the Democratic and Republican parties. More recently, however, political science as a strand of American studies has taken on a radical inflection, given over not so much to analysing traditional forms of power in the United States as to exploring challenges and alternatives to these. To give a flavour of this reorientation, it is worth returning to Yale University's summary of its undergraduate American studies programme, cited previously in this chapter. The 'Politics and American Communities' strand, according to the course description, 'investigates the emergence of social groups and their political struggles at the local and national levels emphasizing the themes of power, inequality, and social justice' ('Areas of Concentration' 2020, n.p.). Elsewhere, too, in political science contributions to American studies, energetic activisms rather than static institutions are favoured for discussion. Movements such as Occupy Wall Street and the Indigenous Environmental Network come to the fore, then, rather than the U.S. Senate.

In considering topics such as civil disobedience, political scientists engage with issues of *the law*. So do sociologists in much of their work, for example when they are exploring the question of environmental determinants of crime. To conclude this section, I want briefly to discuss the place that law, as an academic discipline, has in American studies. Some hesitation is appropriate before situating legal studies among the social sciences, since a number of legal scholars insist that what they do belongs on the contrary to the humanities. This is, in some ways, a persuasive case: after all, they resemble their counterparts in literary criticism in often being engaged in close textual interpretation, while they also overlap with historians when researching, say, shifting theories of common law from the Ancient Greeks to the present. Nevertheless, we place legal studies tentatively in the social sciences here on the grounds that its links with questions central to sociology and political science are more compelling still.

As with political science, it is possible to detect a shift in recent decades in the nature of law's contribution to American studies. During American studies' early period, there was a tendency towards respectful explication of high-level legal institutions and practices, as in the discussion of the powers available to state legislatures or of the varying approaches to interpreting the Constitution taken by successive generations of justices sitting on the U.S. Supreme Court. Contemporary American legal studies, however, animated by a host of political activisms, is notable both for a wider selection of topics and for a less deferential tone. Scholars may, for instance, interrogate the racial bias of sentencing policy in the United States, or explore the abusive gender politics underlying Brett Kavanaugh's appointment by President Trump to the Supreme Court in 2018, even in the face of allegations of sexual assault by Christine Blasey Ford and two other women. Reflecting on this last episode, Michael Salter writes of 'a spectacular deployment of institutional power to suppress good faith allegations of sexual violence' (2019, 135). For Salter and many others, American legal studies now has radical possibilities, being able to contribute in however modest a way to the contesting of established power structures in the United States.

AMERICA OUTSIDE AMERICAN STUDIES

This chapter has attempted to give a sense of the many disciplines drawn into the academic ensemble we call American studies. Aiming to keep to a manageable length, it could not plausibly aim at completeness. One significant omission, however, important to mention if only in passing, is *theatre studies*. While specialists in U.S. literature have sometimes adjusted their focus from fiction or poetry so as to consider plays as disparate as those of Eugene O'Neill and Lynn Nottage, or Tennessee Williams and August Wilson, American studies has also been enriched by the work of drama scholars who are drawn less to the tradition of textual interpretation than to engagement with the specificities of theatrical performance itself. Yet, even without considering research areas such as this, the chapter has already shown American studies as expansive enough to accommodate objects of study that range from sermonising in seventeenth-century New England to tattooing in twenty-first-century Manhattan, and from sentimental American novels of the 1850s to paranoid sci-fi films made in Hollywood a hundred years later. The suppleness and the absorptive power of American studies are indeed such that, rather than saying what the field covers, it seems easier to indicate what it *does not*. Here I touch briefly on two subjects that tend to be excluded, while also noting ways in which they too prove relevant to or recoverable by American studies.

The first of these is *physical geography*. In Chapter 1 I described how, prior to American studies' inauguration as an academic programme, geography featured prominently in scholarly work on the United States. Wishing to celebrate the newly independent nation, nineteenth-century U.S. geographers were drawn to consider its richly variegated physical features extending from the desert spaces of the Southwest through the vast drainage system of the Mississippi and Missouri rivers to the pastoral landscape of New England. In the subsequent phase of American studies itself, however, physical geography in its purest form has often gone missing. Yet, rather than being abandoned entirely, it is liable to be incorporated in the field whenever it bonds with other disciplines that *do* figure in American studies. This process can be observed in an essay by Peter Coates on 'The human and natural environment' that is positioned as the first chapter in a major introduction to American studies. It appears initially that Coates is setting to one side the very stuff of culture on which American studies fastens, as he describes the United States as 'a physical and biological place' that comprises 'trees . . . rocks, soil and water and creatures great and small' (2006, 7). Almost at once, however, this scene of non-human nature is reimagined by Coates as the site also of complex human activity and interaction. Sensitivity to the environment is shown to enhance exploration of social and cultural topics that are fixtures in American studies: 'colonisation; material abundance; the perils of prosperity; notions of property; the tension between individual rights and social responsibilities', and so on (Coates 2006, 7–8).

Much more will be said about an environmentally oriented American studies in Chapter 6. For the moment, we note simply that since American studies is to a significant extent a form of *cultural studies*, it is unsurprising that ways have been found to draw into its orbit the physical geography of the United States. After all, even something as apparently straightforward as a walk in the woods is an experience highly mediated by culture at the same time as it is an immersion in the non-human environment. The point can be underscored by a more extended example.

The Grand Canyon, carved out in northern Arizona by the erosive activity of the Colorado River over millions of years, exhilarates as much by its cultural ramifications as by its natural splendours. There are some dimensions or elements of the Canyon, admittedly, that are unlikely to engage American studies scholars. Practitioners in the field may not feel compelled to take a position on whether the raising of the Colorado Plateau that has been fundamental to the Canyon's distinctive formation is caused either by 'shallow-angle subduction or [by] continued uplift through isostacy' ('Geology' 2018, n.p.). Lack of subject expertise, of course, goes a good way towards explaining this intellectual reticence; more determining still, however, is a sense that such geological processes occurring across deep time are alien to American studies' interests in the social and the cultural. But once such materials are set aside, very little else relating to the Canyon proves unusable by or of no consequence for American studies. For example, scholars may choose to explore forms of human dwelling in the Canyon, from the extended experiences of ancient Pueblo communities to the fleeting stays of backpackers now at Phantom Ranch on the Canyon's floor. Or research activity might be directed instead towards the vast archive of visual representations of the Canyon, beginning with paintings by Thomas Moran and photographs by Timothy O'Sullivan that emerged simultaneously in the 1870s. Or, rather than considering the responses of individual artists, researchers may investigate a larger clash of cultural forces, which has seen believers in the Canyon as a rarefied 'supreme spectacle' pitted against promoters of 'the populist Canyon' for whom it is a site for mass consumption (Pyne 1999, 136). As with America's other natural phenomena, few aspects of the Grand Canyon are *only* physical, without simultaneously being historical and cultural.

The second of the two disciplines highlighted here as not having featured centrally in American studies since its inception is *economics*. Where American studies departments or faculties still exist, they are unlikely to house a specialist economist. Where the field takes other institutional forms, such as conferences, we should similarly not expect to find economics foregrounded in the same way as literature or history. No journal in American studies is going to publish an article entitled 'Endogenous Monitoring in a Partnership Game' (as the *American Economic Review* did in its issue of March 2020), even if the focus of the piece is on economic activity in the United States. The issue, as above with the geology of the Grand Canyon, is partly one of subject complexity: economists speak a forbidding technical language, often steeped in mathematics, that is liable to leave non-specialists tongue-tied. Again, however, there is also the sense of distance between this specialism and the social and cultural substance to which American studies is devoted. Nevertheless, like physical geography, economics can still be drawn into American studies where potential connections exist with academic subjects that are well-represented in the latter. For instance, historians investigating the consequences of the U.S. Depression of the 1930s have, at least to an extent, to familiarise themselves with economics; likewise, analysts of films and novels responding to the financial crisis of 2008. On these occasions, practitioners of American studies set aside economics' more abstract and theoretical registers, and instead look tactically for what can be taken from the discipline into their own materially grounded research.

SUMMARY

This chapter began by noting that, as befits the largeness of America, American studies itself is a large subject. Rather than focusing on a modest number of themes or topics, it ambitiously undertakes to examine the totality of U.S. cultural and social life. Often, in the genealogy of American studies, subjects in the humanities that are dedicated to interpreting verbal materials have been dominant: literary studies and history, above all, but also philosophy and religious studies. Humanities disciplines oriented towards visual and audiovisual contents have historically been underrepresented. However, the analysis of visual arts, architecture, photography, film, TV and music have become better entrenched in American studies, and are likely to become more important still. We saw, too, that the humanities have not been unrivalled in this field of study, since decisive contributions have also been made by the social sciences, including anthropology, sociology, political science and legal studies. These particular disciplines have been especially valuable in American studies in directing research towards larger patterns and tendencies in U.S. life, offering a wide-angle rather than the highly magnified readings of text or image that characterise the humanities. Finally, the chapter acknowledged that, despite American studies' expansiveness, several subjects have tended to be excluded. Yet, the case of physical geography shows us that this situation changes as soon as cultural or social implications become apparent. To give a last example, practitioners of American studies might not be engaged at first by the V-shaped sandstone formation in New Mexico known as the White Place; however, once it enters into artistic representation, as in Georgia O'Keeffe's 1943 painting *The White Place in Sun*, their interest is stimulated.

Two final points should be made about the academic subjects covered in this chapter. The first, anticipating a key concern of Chapter 4, is that American studies frequently aims to draw these subjects into interdisciplinary combinations, rather than leaving them separated from one another. The second, which was indicated in the brief discussion of fields such as history and legal studies, is that none of the contributory disciplines is neutral in its intent, aiming disinterestedly at richer descriptions of America. Rather, these analyses of diverse aspects of U.S. life are all charged with ideological implications, whether radical or conservative. This is a topic we will return to in Chapter 6, devoted to the politics of American studies.

FURTHER READING

Readers wishing to explore in detail the various subject areas of American studies considered in this chapter can choose from many resources. In literary studies, Richard Gray's *A History of American Literature*, 2nd ed. (Chichester: Wiley-Blackwell, 2011) is recommended for its scope and lucidity; while *A New Literary History of America* (Cambridge, MA: Belknap Press of Harvard University Press, 2009), ed. Greil Marcus and Werner Sollors, is suggested enthusiastically for the interdisciplinary quirkiness with which it discusses not only novels and poems but objects such as the telephone and the Winchester rifle. For studies of American history, see Eric Foner's *The Story of American Freedom* (New York: Norton, 1999), together with the books by Boyer, Brogan and Zinn listed in Chapter 2's 'Further reading'. John Kaag's *American Philosophy: A Love Story* (New York: Farrar, Straus and Giroux, 2016), mentioned in this chapter, offers a distinctive, personable introduction to its field. On religion, the essays collected in *One Nation Under God?: Religion and American Culture*, ed. Marjorie Garber and Rebecca L. Walkowitz (New York: Routledge, 1999), are engagingly diverse in their coverage of faith traditions.

Good starting points for reading in American visual culture include: for the visual arts, Robert Hughes's sumptuously illustrated *American Visions: The Epic History of Art in America* (London: Harvill Press, 1997); for architecture,

American Architectural History: A Contemporary Reader, ed. Keith L. Eggener (New York: Routledge, 2004); for photography, Mick Gidley, *Photography and the USA* (London: Reaktion Books, 2011); for film, Robert P. Kolker, *The Cultures of American Film* (New York: Oxford University Press, 2015); for TV, Jason Mittell, *Television and American Culture* (New York: Oxford University Press, 2010).

On music, Richard Crawford's *America's Musical Life: A History* (New York: Norton, 2001) is now in need of a postscript, but is highly recommended for its scope and clarity. *African American Music: An Introduction*, 2nd ed., ed. Mellonee V. Burnim and Portia K. Maultsby (New York: Routledge, 2015), is a wonderfully rich collection of essays.

Anthropological approaches to the United States can be assessed by sampling two studies published more than half a century apart: Margaret Mead's *And Keep Your Powder Dry: An Anthropologist Looks at America* (New York: Berghahn Books, 2000 [1965]) and William H. Westermeyer's *Back to America: Identity, Political Culture, and the Tea Party Movement* (Lincoln: University of Nebraska Press, 2019). Important contributions to sociological study of America, focusing on issues of class, race and gender, include Mary Romero, *Maid in the U.S.A.*, rev. ed. (New York: Routledge, 2002) and Earl Wysong, Robert Perrucci and David Wright, *The New Class Society: Goodbye American Dream?*, 4th ed. (Lanham, MD: Rowman & Littlefield, 2014). In the field of political science, a valuable introduction is Stephen Brooks, Douglas L. Koopman and J. Matthew Wilson, *Understanding American Politics*, 2nd ed. (Toronto: University of Toronto Press, 2013); likewise, in legal studies, Lawrence M. Friedman, *A History of American Law*, 4th ed. (New York: Oxford University Press, 2019).

METHODS AND MODELS OF AMERICAN STUDIES

The focus of Chapter 3 was on the 'what' of American studies, identifying multiple academic subjects that have contributed to the field and assessing their prominence or marginality to date. In this chapter, we turn more to the 'how' of American studies, outlining and evaluating some of its key operating procedures. The discussion begins with the topic of *interdisciplinarity* that has already been raised briefly in this book: that is to say, the attempt to weave together many academic disciplines, each of which has its own objects and protocols of study. Interdisciplinarity has been part of American studies' conceptualisation of itself from the beginning: it is important, therefore, to consider the effects of this crossing between disciplines. The chapter then goes on to assess the rival claims of quite different approaches to the United States that have emerged from this multistranded research activity: firstly, attempts to understand the United States in terms of totality or unity, as against work that emphasises its fragmentation and division; secondly, efforts to theorise the U.S. as distinct unto itself as opposed to scholarship which approaches the nation comparatively.

AN ARCHIVE OF THE VIET NAM WAR

Before assessing the key role that interdisciplinarity has played in American studies, a specific example may help in grounding this abstract term. Imagine a literature specialist who takes on the task of evaluating U.S. responses to the Viet Nam War (or 'the American War' as, understandably, people in Viet Nam call this conflict of the 1960s and early 1970s which caused the

DOI: 10.4324/9781315726748-5

deaths of several million local combatants and civilians, together with over 58,000 U.S. military personnel). Given this scholar's area of expertise, a likely first move would be to visit a set of well-known novels and short stories, written at varying degrees of remove from the events described and spanning a range of styles from attritional realism to self-conscious experimentation that aims to problematise the very enterprise of putting a war into words. These include former soldier Tim O'Brien's *Going After Cacciato* (1978) and *The Things They Carried* (1990); Denis Johnson's *Tree of Smoke* (2007); and Norman Mailer's *Why Are We in Vietnam?* (1967), a novel set during a hunting trip in Alaska that does not mention the war until its last page yet is connected to it thematically by its interrogation of U.S. hypermasculinity and violence.

Looking to go beyond this well-established corpus of texts, however, the literary scholar we are imagining might take their research in several directions. One option would be to incorporate novels such as Bobbie Ann Mason's *In Country* (1985) that move Viet Nam War fiction away from the combat zone itself, positing the home front as a terrain of equivalent social, cultural and emotional importance. Or the researcher could turn to popular fiction, rather than to accredited literary art (both *Going After Cacciato* and *Tree of Smoke* won the prestigious National Book Award for Fiction): the numerous candidates here include Joe Weber's combat yarns, *Rules of Engagement* (1991) and *Targets of Opportunity* (1993). Another possibility would be to consider reportage, in addition to novels, as with Michael Herr's *Dispatches* (1977), a book that presents itself as journalism while nevertheless drawing on fiction's repertoire in its play with voice, perspective and dialogue. Despite considerable variety in the written materials they would have assembled by this point, the researcher might still be sensitive to the danger of prioritising certain perspectives on the conflict to the exclusion of others. Hence, they could also seek out texts deriving from elsewhere in the United States than the white caucus, such as writings by California-based but Viet Nam-born Viet Thanh Nguyen that include both a pair of interconnected novels (*The Sympathizer* [2015] and *The Committed* [2021]) and a critical study (*Nothing Ever Dies: Vietnam and the Memory of War* [2016]).

Already there is the substance here of a major research project, since the quite familiar archive with which this imagined scholar began has expanded significantly and in several directions. The work is still at this stage confined to the single discipline of literary studies, albeit understanding 'the literary' now as sufficiently elastic to include genre fiction and journalistic writing as well as canonised novels and short stories. Operating inside this disciplinary boundary has generated rich scholarship, for example Philip Beidler's *American Literature and the Experience of Vietnam* (2008). Nevertheless, it is possible to think that, in a quiet moment, our literary critic would also be given to reflect on the limitations of their project. However expansively the category of Viet Nam War literature is drawn, and however densely it is populated, these writings remain a relatively small part of the totality of U.S. responses to the conflict. In such circumstances, there may be an incentive to venture beyond disciplinary specialisation, with the protocols of literary study experienced now not only as guidelines that enable coherent, meaningful work but also perhaps as rigid and exclusionary mechanisms. If only tentatively and temporarily, then, the literary critic might enter into fields such as film studies or music studies or even – daringly going outside the humanities – political science or anthropology. Or, mindful of the limits of individual capability, they could instead establish links with other scholars who, between them, command this range of subject expertise. In these new conditions, the critic's original, tightly composed reading list becomes much more sprawling and eclectic – taking on the appearance, perhaps, of a *project archive*, to borrow the attractive metaphor which Philip Deloria and Alexander Olson use to evoke the creative, idiosyncratic quality of American studies research (2017, 166–168).

Possible inclusions in this expanded Viet Nam War archive, now multimedia in its content, can be briefly identified. It is likely, to begin with, that space will be made for films, with examples ranging in genre from combat adventures to ethnographic documentary, and in politics from the crass jingoism of *The Green Berets* (1968; dir. John Wayne and Ray Kellogg) to the cool unpicking of U.S. military machismo in *Full Metal Jacket* (1987; dir. Stanley Kubrick). Also important to analyse are TV responses (for instance, Ken Burns's and Lynn Novick's *The Vietnam War*, a ten-part documentary series shown in 2017, which interweaves archival footage with newly filmed interviews), theatre events (like Megan Terry's politically incendiary rock musical *Viet Rock*, staged as the war escalated in 1966) and works of visual art (of dizzying formal variety, including abstract compositions and performance pieces as well as agitprop photomontages). The primary material for analysis should also extend to the architecture of public commemoration, such as the Vietnam Memorial Wall in Washington, D.C., dedicated in 1982 (see Figure 4.1).

Even such a radically enlarged archive, however, still comprises a series of *individual* responses to the Viet Nam War. There is occasion here, then, for moderating the power of humanities disciplines and for drawing also upon the methods of the social sciences which, as we saw in Chapter 3, have historically contributed to American studies. From anthropology, say, might come minutely detailed

Figure 4.1 Vietnam Memorial Wall, Washington, D.C. (photograph: David J. Jackson, 2018).

Source: Wikimedia Commons.

studies of what the war means for various collectives. This research could include field work at sites of memory and mourning, so that consideration of the Memorial Wall encompasses not only the aesthetics and thematics of architect Maya Lin's design but also the manifold ways in which the structure is 'overwritten' by veterans' families and friends who leave flowers, flags, toys, poems and many other personalised objects. Or political science might supply accounts of different anti-war movements in the United States. And so on, in an ever-widening spiral (with the proviso, of course, that under real-world constraints not all of this research could be done, let alone synthesised). It is not the case, though, that this expanded archive entails the loss of the literary criticism with which the project began. Rather than disregarded, the literary critic's activity is instead *decentred*, no longer seen as dominant in the work but understood, more modestly, as donating one approach to a cluster of analytical methods that enables a fuller evaluation of American responses to the Viet Nam War.

IN PRAISE OF INTERDISCIPLINARITY

In the last few pages, we have sketched a possible research project with regard to the United States that ultimately refuses to privilege any single academic subject and aims instead at a pooling of disciplinary expertise. Such multistranded endeavour has, historically, characterised American studies, as compared with many other fields that more zealously defend their boundaries. This foundational commitment to interdisciplinarity can be glimpsed by attending for a few moments to a primer on American studies written in 1948 by one of its pioneers: Tremaine McDowell, professor of English at the University of Minnesota. In the section of his book devoted to subject provision in U.S. universities, McDowell finds wide variations in how institutions deliver the programme to which they give such varying names as 'American Studies', 'American Civilization' and 'American Culture'. As he puts it: 'No two of the American curriculums which have been established from the University of Maine to the University of California are alike' (1948, 35). This is, for McDowell, not a weakness but a virtue, since a uniform, centralised curriculum would threaten the freedom and creativity that he and other trailblazers valued in American studies. Nevertheless, if he uncovers variations at the syllabus level, he sees constancy in the interdisciplinary method. Barnard College in New York City, for instance, gives students taking its course on 'The Arts in American Civilization' an opportunity to engage with cultural fields as diverse as 'architecture, painting, literature, and music, cartoon strips, and the motion picture' (53). Often, however, the American studies programmes described by McDowell are more expansive still, bridging the gap between humanities and social sciences. He finds a 'well-distributed interdivisional' course at Smith College, in Massachusetts, where undergraduates take a range of modules in American 'history, literature, art or music, and philosophy, education, religion, government, or sociology' (40).

Over the seventy or so years since McDowell was writing, interdisciplinarity has remained central to the theory and practice of American studies. Crisscrossing between academic subjects is built into the daily routine of professors and undergraduates alike. Certain topics and disciplines once part of the mix have, it is true, declined in importance during this period, or even disappeared: it is unlikely, for example, that many contemporary programmes in American studies offer a module in the history of U.S. medicine, as the University of Pennsylvania once did (McDowell 1948, 58). Yet, the attempt to spark conversations between multiple subjects is a key principle that has not been significantly challenged.

Who could fail to be a fan of interdisciplinarity? To state instead that you are in favour of respecting disciplinary boundaries seems tantamount to saying you would prefer to remain in a cramped cell than to have freedom of movement across a city of ever-changing sights. It looks like a vote in favour of narrowness, insularity, conformity. By contrast, much of the enduring appeal of American studies is bound up with its attempts to outwit the system of demarcated disciplines which began to cohere in universities on both sides of the Atlantic during the nineteenth century. It promises the exhilaration of boundary-crossing, even trespass. Exciting possibilities open up for the American studies practitioner: the chance to assemble eclectic bodies of primary material, for example, or the opportunity to learn new skills (so, the literary critic above who sets out initially to read novels about the Viet Nam War might end up also developing expertise as a film scholar, an analyst of painting, even as an anthropologist). American studies offers the prospect as well of belonging to an expanded intellectual sphere. Where university departments in the subject exist, the corridors might be shared by historians and philosophers, and by drama scholars and political scientists. This sense of mixing and multiplicity is still apparent when American studies takes looser institutional forms, such as conferences and journals.

Practitioners of American studies, however, are often liable to make a still stronger claim for the benefits of interdisciplinarity. From this perspective, such an approach to study is valuable not simply because it extends the individual scholar's set of competences or because it fosters a more diverse academic community, so that next to you at the coffee machine you are liable to find cool and interesting people from subjects radically distinct from your own original specialism. Rather, interdisciplinarity is to be embraced because in and of itself it contributes to that pursuit of social justice which, as we saw in the Introduction, has often motivated American studies. Politically speaking, according to this argument, it is endowed with more radical potential than academic practices that are more observant of disciplinary borders.

A version of this political case for interdisciplinarity appears in a valuable introduction to American cultural studies written by the British Americanists Neil Campbell and Alasdair Kean. Early in their book, Campbell and Kean describe America as 'a vast borderland' or, using Mary-Louise Pratt's term, as 'a contact zone', where multiple cultures with varying degrees of power intersect and clash. The interdisciplinary method permits the American studies scholar not only to traverse this complex space of cultural collisions but to understand it as an uneven landscape in which issues of justice and equality are at stake. As Campbell and Kean write:

> Interdisciplinary studies, which interconnects *and* transgresses boundaries as a method of exploration, provides a suitable methodology through which to engage with and critique . . . dominant voices, and to appreciate and listen to other voices, recognising their mutual struggles to be heard. (2016, 13, emphasis in original)

We will return to the political work done by American studies in more detail in Chapter 6. For the moment, however, it is important simply to note this claim that to be interdisciplinary in studying

America is to be aligned with the disempowered and the marginalised in their contest with 'dominant voices'.

AGAINST INTERDISCIPLINARITY

Who 'can speak against such a noble, exciting notion?', asks Thomas Docherty in a punchy journalistic piece on the topic of interdisciplinarity (2009, n.p.). As observed in the previous section, interdisciplinary scholarship seems self-evidently such a good thing in its challenge to the claustrophobia of single-subject areas as to disable any possible reservation or criticism. Yet, as may be guessed, Docherty's question here is a rhetorical one since he is prepared himself to critique interdisciplinarity, finding it deeply problematical in its intellectual procedures. While he does not have American studies particularly in mind, his article cues us to ask searching questions of this field, given the extent to which interdisciplinarity is spun through its DNA. Self-examination of this kind is more valuable than uncritically accepting the virtue – indeed the preeminence – of interdisciplinary practice.

We can begin this interrogation at the point at which we concluded the previous section: that is, with the bold claim by Campbell and Kean that the interdisciplinarity of American studies is attuned to the cause of social justice. For is this unequivocally the case? Rather more than Campbell and Kean allow seems to depend on exactly what motivations underlie people's interdisciplinary crossing between subject areas. After all, weaving the study of literary fiction together with that of film, or putting architecture criticism in conversation with sociology, might not *in itself* fulfil a radical political agenda. Subordinate American 'voices' may indeed be captured by this method; to return to our example at the start of this chapter, a literary critic might think differently of novels about the Viet Nam War written by members of the white social elite after considering, in addition, experimental films and videos by members of minority communities in the United States, such as Trinh T. Minh-ha's *Surname Viet Given Name Nam* (1989), *A Tale of Love* (1995) and *Forgetting Vietnam* (2015). Simply incorporating these 'other voices' in a larger-scale project, however, is not the same as endowing them with power and thereby helping to redress their weakness in the face of 'dominant' cultural forces. Interdisciplinary studies can 'transgress' academic boundaries, to recall one of the verbs used by Campbell and Kean, without this necessarily correlating with political subversion or rebellion. Where there *is* radicalism in the interdisciplinary work carried out within American studies, other factors besides new, distinctive combinations of subjects may also be in play. One of these would be the practice of interrogatory reading of primary materials which the American literature specialist already has to hand when they turn to the study of theatre, say, or painting or sport in the United States.

Interdisciplinarity in American studies has been criticised on other grounds besides its uncertain political effects. For one thing, the bringing together of so many subjects threatens to overwhelm the capacity of an entire university department or faculty, let alone the abilities of the individual scholar. From another perspective, the problem is not so much the sheer volume of material to be processed as its potential *incoherence*, its looseness or high degree of disarticulation. Thoughts of this sort have been expressed from the beginnings of American studies' institutional life up until the present. In the early 1950s, for example, writing in *Mademoiselle* (the self-styled 'magazine for smart young women'), Rachel Mellinger characterised the field as 'a pleasant academic smorgasbord' which offers students almost unlimited choice in objects of study (1954, 92). As a Swedish form of buffet that allows diners to select from many hot and cold dishes set out together, a smorgasbord provides an eating experience hospitable to the most widely varying tastes. Running through Mellinger's article, however, is the question of whether eclectic offerings of this range are as conducive to a serious academic programme as they are to a nice meal out.

While Mellinger turns to culinary metaphor to voice doubts about interdisciplinarity, Docherty, in the article cited previously, has recourse to the world of interior design. Again, it should be stressed that American studies is not specifically targeted in his critique of interdisciplinary practice. However, as a field given over more than most to interdisciplinarity, American studies is implicated in Docherty's charge that 'Just as the 1960s let it all hang out, so we let our disciplines overflow into each other like anarchic lava lamps' (2009, n.p.). Readers unfamiliar with trends in domestic furnishings during the 1960s and 1970s may not have seen a lava lamp in action. This ingenious device brought an impression of slowed-down volcanic eruption into your living room, as heat from a lightbulb hidden in the lamp's base interacted with a mixture of coloured wax and clear liquid contained in the glass vessel above. Blobs of red, orange, purple and other colours would then float up and down in mesmerising fashion, sometimes drifting into each other to form larger globules. Like Mellinger's smorgasbord reference, however, Docherty's figure of the lava lamp is wounding, with its implication that interdisciplinary scholarship consists merely in putting the various subjects in play into random, ever-changing configurations. Aesthetically, the results are pleasing enough; intellectually, though, in Docherty's view, the outcome is disastrous.

Although Mellinger and Docherty both expose what they see as the weaknesses of interdisciplinarity, close inspection of their metaphors uncovers differences between their respective positions. For Mellinger, the issue with American studies is not that the contributing disciplines become fused and forfeit their identities. Just as in the culinary smorgasbord a meatball can still be told apart from a herring, so, for Mellinger, literary criticism, history, sociology and so on are still discernible as distinct subject areas within the American studies ensemble. The problem, however, is their manageability together – the sense, perhaps, that you can have too much of a good thing. By contrast, Docherty sees traditional disciplines losing definition and liquefying when they are put into sustained interaction with each other. It is possible, though, to accept his argument that new intellectual patterns result from interdisciplinarity without conceding the case that these are trivial or compromised. Roland Barthes, the great French theorist of culture, is persuasive here when writing in a 1972 essay on research done by younger scholars that 'Interdisciplinary study consists in creating a new object, which belongs to no one' (Barthes 1989, 72). At its strongest, interdisciplinary work in American studies fulfils this mission, creating a 'new object' of study that incorporates but is not reducible to scholarship on U.S. literature, U.S. music, U.S. governmental systems and the rest. This object is not static or uncontested, of course, liable to be construed the same way by all who have been involved in the field across multiple generations. Thus, while early practitioners sometimes saw themselves as contributing to the interdisciplinary study of 'American myth' or 'the American mind' (a topic taken up in this chapter's next section), contemporary Americanists may conceive of their work across numerous subject areas as uncovering instead something more like American *power* or American *injustice*.

TOTALITY AND FRAGMENTATION IN AMERICAN STUDIES

To look at the second issue of American studies' premier journal in the United States, published in the summer of 1949, is to sense an academic subject that from its inception was very wide-ranging. In this particular instalment of *American Quarterly*, an article on documentary film sits next to one on U.S. poets' engagement with science, while a piece on the 'Ash Can' School of modern American painting shares space with reflections on the culture of Boston after the Civil War. Equivalent eclecticism would be if a journal of 'British studies' was to follow an essay on Morris dancing with, first, an article about Victorian photography, then one about contemporary dialect poetry in Glasgow. This variety in American studies is highly enticing from one perspective, yet potentially disorienting from another. As some observers of the field from its first institutional phase onwards have not been slow to point out, there are few restrictions as to what it might cover. Anything goes, it seems, as long as it either originates in or can in some way be anchored to the United States.

Given this diffusion of topics, it is unsurprising that some of the most influential early work in American studies also exhibits a contrary tendency to marshal the material tightly. The gap between *The Great Gatsby* and a dry nineteenth-century government report on the developing U.S. railroad system, to recall an unlikely pairing from Leo Marx's *The Machine in the Garden*, becomes bridgeable if both things are understood in relation to some fundamental conception of America that is powerful enough to make irrelevant their obvious differences. Some examples of these conceptual structures or schemas can be given from the first-generation scholarship in American studies that was considered in Chapter 2. So, in *The American Adam*, R. W. B. Lewis discloses his book's organising motif in its title: the figure of the 'Adamic hero' – an adventurer 'equivalent to the prince or king in classical drama' (1955, 128) – whom Lewis pursues across a wide variety of American writings. In *The Machine in the Garden* itself, Marx finds a fulcrum in what he calls 'a distinctively American theory of society' that has developed and mutated across several centuries (2000 [1964], 4). By tracing a recurrent clash in the work of American writers between 'rural myth' and 'an awareness of industrialization as a counterforce' (229) – put simply, between 'garden' and 'machine' – Marx is able to bring together and discipline otherwise quite disparate primary materials. Finally, 'the myth of the garden' is fundamental to the design also of Henry Nash Smith's *Virgin Land*, albeit sometimes posed here not against the machine but against 'the myth of the Great American Desert', given the book's geographical focus on the West (1970 [1950], 175).

Each of these texts from early in the life of American studies has its own distinctive preoccupations. Nevertheless, the sense that they share certain conceptual foundations and structural templates has led commentators to group them together with the work of like-minded first-generation Americanists as examples of the so-called 'myth and symbol school' (the description deriving, as we saw in Chapter 2, from *Virgin Land*'s subtitle). The term 'school' is queried by Alan Trachtenberg, wary of the high degree of cohesion this implies. He is more comfortable with 'myth and symbol', however, believing that this part of the label captures the extent to which the first scholars in American studies understood the culture of America 'to consist in myths [. . . that is to say,] constructs whose power over collective intelligence and behavior is uniquely powerful' (1984, 667). Lawrence Buell, the Americanist and ecocritic of our own time, sounds a similar note when he writes that Lewis, Marx, Smith and others of this inaugural wave managed to 'generate something like a method' for American studies by 'isolating', in their particular ways, 'a putatively defining image of American culture and exploring it by recourse to an interweave of literary and cultural analysis' (1999, 13). Variations exist, of course, in the 'image[s] of American culture' settled on by these individual scholars: the machine/garden pairing, for instance, offers a rather different device than the figure of the American Adam for thinking about the United States. Nevertheless, what is at least as noticeable as such differences is this work's shared interest in *totality*, the belief that all of America can be accessed via these key images, myths and symbols.

While not quite 'a Golden Age' in American studies, Buell writes (1999, 14), the myth and symbol school nevertheless represents a moment in the subject's history that was characterised by both high ambition and methodological cohesion. But though it can still be celebrated for its achievements, the movement is also open to substantial critique. One of the most forceful reassessments appeared at a time when the school actually still retained some of its sway over the field. Bruce Kuklick's essay, 'Myth and Symbol in American Studies' launches its attack on a number of fronts. It is, to begin with, deeply resistant to this scholarship's exalting of 'the mental realm' (1972, 437), its prioritising 'of imaginative perception, of the analogy-perceiving, metaphor-making, mytho-poetic power of the human mind' (436–437). Writing at a time when Viet Nam was still burning, and African American and Native American challenges to white rule in the United States remained vigorous, Kuklick is understandably hostile to myth and symbol scholars' relegation of material concerns so as better to focus on the categories of mind and imagination. But he has other lines of critique, too, including the school's claims, without sufficient research, to be uncovering mental constructions widely shared in America (the idea of 'the American Adam', for instance). As Kuklick asserts, 'the imputation of collective beliefs is an extraordinarily complex empirical procedure which ought not to be undertaken lightly' (445).

Subsequent commentators, too, have considered how the myth and symbol school's commitment to telling a unified narrative about America came at the cost of reducing or repressing altogether the exploration of many other stories that did not fit the paradigm. Thus, contemplating the later phase of American studies we still occupy, Buell finds it resembling not a 'school', with that word's suggestions of orderliness and centralisation, but rather a 'debating ground' that offers space to numerous 'semi-competing/semi-overlapping' interests (1999, 14, 15). Buell's sense of living in an 'age of Americanist dissensus' (14) has an echo in phrasing used by Russ Castronovo and Susan Gillman in their introduction to another volume on the state of the field. The heyday of the myth and symbol school, they write, was followed in American studies by a long revisionist period, in which scholarship centred on 'all the hyphenated minority cultures and canons, histories and regions' intersected with 'theoretical work on nations, nationalism, and transnationalism', resulting in 'a healthy lack of consensus' as to the field's object and purpose (2009, 2). As their use of the word 'healthy' in relation to the current moment suggests, Castronovo and Gillman are not nostalgic for the kind of scholarship practised in American studies' first generation.

If this school's emphasis on shared myths and symbols has been seen by later Americanists to be flawed analytically, it has also been contested on *political* grounds. The reference by Castronovo and Gillman to the earlier period's inattention to 'all the hyphenated minority cultures and canons' reminds us of the fact, noted in Chapter 2, that myth and symbol scholarship tends to privilege a white perspective on America (a white *patriarchal and straight* perspective, at that). Taking only one example, Lewis begins *The American Adam* by describing the archetypal hero that is his subject as 'untouched and undefiled by the usual inheritances of race and family' (1955, 5). Yet, he is able to say this only because almost all of the examples he discusses in the book are white – a category that, like so many of his period, he takes to be free of racial markers, almost a *non-race* in relation to which the racialised identities of African American, Asian American and so on become visible. Myth and symbol scholarship is thus in danger of fortifying intellectually that white rule which has traditionally prevailed in America. This is certainly not to imply that the first Americanists were straightforward reactionaries: Marx, for example, recalls in an afterword to a later printing of *The Machine in the Garden* that he viewed himself 'as a socialist' and also as someone already sensitised to 'our society's increasingly reckless assault on the integrity of the natural environment' (2000 [1964], 369). Yet it is difficult to correlate such extracurricular political commitments with the general drift of published myth and symbol scholarship. As Patrick Brantlinger puts it trenchantly, 'the early practitioners of American studies did not conceive of their work as oppositional criticism. Myth was less a term of demystification than celebration' of America (1990, 30).

Compared with that first period in American studies, the field now looks fragmented. This is not a condition to be regretted, since the declining power of the field's early paradigm has for several decades opened up opportunities for greater diversity. Minority voices, previously suppressed or underrepresented, are heard more easily, if far from perfectly. It may be, however, that in our own moment the multiple fragments of American studies still cohere in a sense of common purpose: not any longer to document a key myth or symbol, but rather in a more materially grounded way to explore how power is reproduced and contested in the United States and in U.S. satellites across the world. This is a topic for much more consideration in Chapter 6.

COMPARATIVE AMERICAN STUDIES

The previous section considered how the myth and symbol school, which was once dominant in American studies, lost its status as the paradigm to follow in the face of increasing recognition that it effaced or at least minimised attention to multiple minority cultures and communities in the United States. But if American studies' programme has been transformed by this enhanced sensitivity to social, cultural and ethnic configurations in the United States itself, it has also been significantly modified by a growing interest in U.S. relationships with other parts of the world and how these might be mapped. To say something about the effects of this globalised consciousness on American studies method, we begin with a scene from one of the best-known texts in the U.S. literary canon.

Early in Melville's *Moby-Dick* (1851), Ishmael, the novel's narrator, finds himself sharing a room – a bed, in fact – with the South Sea islander Queequeg as they prepare for a whaling voyage out of Massachusetts. Inexperienced, introspective and white, Ishmael views his companion at first as an instance of pure otherness. Culturally, Queequeg appears to be unrecognisable: he is in the habit of carrying around with him 'a lot of 'balmed [i.e. embalmed] New Zealand heads' (2002 [1851], 32), while even his 'greatest admirer could not have cordially justified his bringing his harpoon into breakfast with him' (40). Visually, too, he seems unassimilable, with the prolific inking of his skin exacerbating the effect of indecipherability: Ishmael speaks of his 'unearthly tattooings' (55). Yet, as Ishmael thinks further about Queequeg, this sense of incomprehensible strangeness eases. *Comparative analysis*, situating Queequeg in relation to a very familiar American icon, allows him to be understood after all. Ishmael reflects that his head 'reminded me of George Washington's head, as seen in the popular busts of him. . . . Queequeg was George Washington cannibalistically developed' (55). Rather than remaining illegible or uninterpretable, the South Sea islander actually brings to mind now the first president of the United States.

Thinking across national and cultural divides proves crucial to Ishmael in an otherwise unmanageable human interaction. Once he is able to make sense of Queequeg by comparing him to Washington, he is drawn into friendship with him: the chapter concludes with them exchanging 'confidential disclosures' in their shared bed, 'a cosy, loving pair' (57). Yet we too, interpreting this moment in *Moby-Dick*, may find it helpful to operate as comparativists in search of meaningful resemblances or analogies. For the description of someone who attempts to understand a cannibal from overseas by aligning him with something very close to home has echoes of passages in the early modern French writer Michel de Montaigne's essay, 'On the Cannibals' (c. 1580). Montaigne strips cannibalistic practices in the 'New World' of some of their alienness when he compares them to uses of torture across Europe in his own period. Any conceited sense of European preeminence in morality is undermined by this comparative tactic, since 'there is more barbarity in eating a man alive than in eating him dead; more barbarity in lacerating by rack and torture a body still fully able to feel things' (2003, 235–236). The particular critique which Montaigne is making of Europe can be set aside on this occasion (very important though it is), since what matters for us here is his essay's resemblance to or foreshadowing of this sequence in *Moby-Dick*. It becomes clear that, notwithstanding its radical idiosyncrasy and innovation, Melville's novel should be read comparatively, situated alongside a set of literary precursors that extends far beyond Montaigne. The text gains in interpretability when positioned next to Shakespeare's plays, for example, or Milton's *Paradise Lost*.

This episode in *Moby-Dick*, in which a comparative cast of mind is beneficial to both narrator and reader, is suggestive for us as we consider the operating procedures of American studies. The field's very name might be taken to imply a parochial, inward-looking stance – what Janice Radway summarises as a project to uncover a U.S. culture that is 'unitary', even 'intensely longed-for' (1999, 8). And yet much of American studies' most productive research actually travels the globe to draw out illuminating comparisons with U.S. culture and society. Before giving some examples of such scholarship, however, it is important to make two further points about method that are prompted by the scene in Melville's novel.

The first is that to say American studies is interested in cross-border comparison only takes us so far. Just as interdisciplinarity in the field is at its weakest when it merely adds one subject area to another, catalogue-style, without considering how possibilities for new thought are opened up by the subjects' intertwining, so a comparative mode is diminished where it merely roams the world looking for objects to juxtapose and thereby 'parades coverage in place of comparison' (Castronovo and Gillman 2009, 3). What is important is not the mere juxtaposition of Exhibit A from the United States and Exhibit B from elsewhere in the world, but, rather, the active and dynamic forms taken by their relationship. John Carlos Rowe makes the point well when he writes that 'Rather than treating such cultural differences as discrete entities . . . this new comparative approach stresses the ways different cultures are transformed by their contact and interaction with each other' (2002, 169). So, in the example given previously, how exactly might we describe the mode of *Moby-Dick*'s interaction with the passages from 'On the Cannibals' to which it can productively be compared? Are we witnessing *revision*, for instance, or *revaluation*, or *critique*, or *parody* . . . or something else? Here, as on all other occasions in American studies when cross-border comparison is at issue, numerous analytical options are available to the scholar.

Secondly, it is apparent that in the analogy drawn by Ishmael between Queequeg and George Washington, the American figure serves to ground the comparison; the text refers to Queequeg as 'George Washington cannibalistically developed', rather than approaching things the other way round and imagining Washington as a presidential development of Queequeg. In comparative American studies, however, the terms of intellectual trade are not uniformly in favour of the United States. America does not always function as the privileged entity in the analysis of such cross-border transactions. As Donald Pease and Robyn Wiegman summarise, American studies given over to a comparative mode 'would no longer move from the U.S. center' (2002, 27).

Comparative American studies can be seen in action by attending for a moment to the prolific work of Paul Giles. Giles's academic career, which has seen him occupy university positions in the

United Kingdom, United States and Australia, affords a glimpse of the globally dispersed sites of American studies research and teaching. In his writing, however, as well as in his institutional affiliations, Giles frequently crosses borders. A comparative method of analysis is apparent across a series of books that begins by mapping transatlantic encounters between American and British literatures, before turning more recently to an exploration of transpacific exchanges between writings of the United States and those of Australia and New Zealand. It is striking how often in this work Giles turns to optical imagery to outline the benefits of comparativism when thinking about American literature (and, indeed, about America more broadly). So, for instance, the method equips the scholar with 'bifocalism' and a 'stereoscopic focus' (2011, 193, 209), or it permits 'perspectival reversals' (2013, 116), or – quoting the poet W. H. Auden – it bestows the 'gift of double focus' (2006, 249). Metaphors of mirrors and prisms also abound. The argument is, of course, that American literary production *looks* different when it is juxtaposed with literatures from beyond the borders of the United States (the reverse is also true). At other points in his writing, however, Giles chooses figures that suggest that a comparative approach to American literature has a more transformative outcome still. An example here comes from the book on U.S. literature's entanglements with Australasia, as Giles reflects that his method is 'slanted more toward juxtaposition, where cultural formations overlap and interfere with each other in surprising ways, thereby giving the map of the subject a new cartographic and conceptual twist' (2013, 18). Such an approach has implications for American studies more broadly, rather than being resonant only for work on literary materials. For if comparative analysis shows that U.S. literature is not autonomous, but bound up instead in relationships with writing from elsewhere, it would seem appropriate to extend this line of inquiry and rigorously challenge ideas of U.S. exceptionalism in other domains, too.

Another example that is not focused on literature enables us to see more readily the political payoff of comparative American studies. This chapter began by considering how research into U.S. responses to the Viet Nam War might demonstrate the interdisciplinarity that is a core activity for Americanists; it is perhaps appropriate to end it by briefly indicating what comparativism can bring to the same topic. In the course of an essay arguing in general terms for a comparative approach in American studies, Rowe makes the specific point that it is vital 'the response to the Vietnam War [not be] studied solely through U.S. texts . . . Vietnamese perspectives must be represented in such studies' (2002, 172). Some of these viewpoints are readily accessible to the Anglophone reader, testifying more powerfully than even the best-intentioned 'U.S. texts' to the human and ecological devastation caused by American activity during the war. Take, for instance, *The Republic of Vietnam, 1955–1975: Vietnamese Perspectives on Nation Building* (2020), a collection of essays edited by Tuong Vu and Sean Fear which aims at an effect of defamiliarisation by dislodging the dominant representations of the conflict that have been laid down by U.S. literature, cinema and veterans' memoir. Or turn, perhaps, to the *Journal of Vietnamese Studies*, founded in 2006, which features articles in English by scholars often with bases in Viet Nam itself. And this is to cite only some of the relevant critical materials available in English. To access other 'Vietnamese perspectives' on the war, however, the Americanist will need to develop the appropriate linguistic competence. Speaking more generally, a fully developed comparative American studies would ask practitioners to develop high-level skills in other languages besides English. Rowe, in fact, is among those figures in the field who have long called for an end to Anglophone dominance in American studies.

SUMMARY

Before it turned to consider more generally the interdisciplinarity at the heart of American studies practice, the chapter started with a specific example. We saw how a project on American responses to the Viet Nam War that begins in tightly focused study of a set of canonised novels might unfurl across disciplinary lines, extending not only to other kinds of writing but to multiple other art forms. This work could also go beyond the humanities by utilising approaches from anthropology and sociology in order to gather much larger samples of primary evidence. At its strongest, a large-scale project such as this is not *multi*disciplinary (simply additive in logic, as film studies and art history, say, are put with literary criticism), but properly *inter*disciplinary (with the encounter between disciplines prompting each to recognise its limitations and, rather than seeking pre-eminence or autonomy, to appreciate what is to be gained by its place in a larger ensemble of subjects).

The chapter then reviewed more abstractly the case for interdisciplinarity in American studies. Claims that this not only infuses the field with energy and innovation but better enables it to contribute to the cause of social justice, were reviewed. So, too, were dissenting arguments that interdisciplinarity, both in American studies and in other academic areas, results in forms of scholarship that lack rigour and coherence.

In the chapter's subsequent sections, two other questions bearing on methodology in American studies were considered. Firstly, myth and symbol scholarship that prevailed in the subject's initial, postwar phase was set against the field's later history: it is not dismissing the power of myth and symbol scholars, who attempted ambitious, indeed totalising accounts of culture in America, to point out the racial and gender biases underlying much of their work. The American studies that comes afterwards presents a more fragmented but also a more liberated landscape. Secondly, attention was given to comparativism in American studies, which transforms the meaning of U.S. artefacts by considering them alongside materials from elsewhere in the world. As Giles argues, 'restoring the kind of expansive comparative matrix' (2013, 61) that has been repressed in exceptionalist understandings of American culture is not only intellectually gainful but politically progressive.

FURTHER READING

Joe Moran's *Interdisciplinarity*, 2nd ed. (Abingdon: Routledge, 2010) is not much concerned with American studies; however, it is highly recommended here as a prompt to thinking historically and critically about a topic of great interest to the field. Also bracing, though needing to be read now with awareness of intellectual and institutional shifts since it was first published, is Stanley Fish's essay, 'Being Interdisciplinary Is So Very Hard to Do' in his collection, *There's No Such Thing as Free Speech, and It's a Good Thing, Too* (New York: Oxford University Press, 1994), 231–242. Closer to home, and returning to a volume already cited in this book, Philip J. Deloria and Alexander I. Olson discuss interdisciplinarity at length in *American Studies: A User's Guide* (Oakland: University of California Press, 2017).

With comparative American studies in mind, Thomas Bender's *A Nation Among Nations: America's Place in World History* (New York: Hill and Wang,

2006) is recommended for its sturdy resistance to ideas of American exceptionalism and its commitment instead to a 'cosmopolitan approach to our national history' (301). In Bender's view, this comparative method is not only intellectually compelling but ethically imperative, since it opens up the past and present of the United States to 'a global human-rights perspective' (300). See also the UK-based journal *Comparative American Studies*, founded in 2003, which publishes work that 'extends scholarly debates about American Studies beyond the geographical boundaries of the United States, repositioning discussions about American culture within an international comparative framework' ('Aims and Scope' 2021, n.p.).

Three anthologies of essays on theory and method in American studies should also be highlighted. *Locating American Studies: The Evolution of a Discipline*, ed. Lucy Maddox (Baltimore, MD: Johns Hopkins University Press, 1999), is as helpful here as it is in regard to topics covered in Chapter 2. *The Futures of American Studies*, ed. Donald E. Pease and Robyn Wiegman (Durham, NC: Duke University Press, 2002) is colossal in scale, but with manageable themed sections (including a set of articles on comparative American studies). *States of Emergency: The Object of American Studies*, ed. Russ Castronovo and Susan Gillman (Chapel Hill: University of North Carolina Press, 2009), is a shorter sample of stimulating reflections on what American studies is now and where it might go in the future.

THE SCALES OF AMERICAN STUDIES

In his essay 'Circles' (1841), the American Transcendentalist Ralph Waldo Emerson, a figure mentioned several times in this book, reflects on the difficulties of establishing and securing boundaries. The world's irrepressible fluidity, Emerson says, is such that 'around every circle another can be drawn' (2003, 225). Even those structures fashioned either by nature or by human activity that seem most stable and enduring cannot maintain their shape for long in the face of this ceaseless flux; as Emerson puts it, 'There is no outside' that will persist, 'no inclosing wall, no circumference' (227). From one vantage point, such a condition is terrifying, since like all other things on earth any intellectual schema or classificatory system we devise 'rushes on all sides outwards to new and larger circles, and that without end' (227). From Emerson's perspective, however, this fragility or permeability of our conceptual designs is cause not for vertigo but for 'enthusiasm' (238), serving as an invitation to fresh creativity. '[I]n short', he concludes, we are forever prompted 'to draw a new circle' (238).

Though Emerson's essay is far-reaching in its philosophical suggestiveness, I turn to it here as a way into thinking about some of the circles that American studies has attempted to draw around itself in its existence as an accredited academic field. All disciplines, of course, face challenges in defining and demarcating themselves. Economists, for instance, debate whether their mathematically grounded subject should extend to incorporate perspectives from the humanities, such as philosophy and psychology; practitioners in medicine have similar conversations about whether the field might be redesigned to give a place to literary

DOI: 10.4324/9781315726748-6

studies. In each of these cases, old circles are liable to give way to new ones. Perhaps to a greater extent still, however, American studies has slipped between very different understandings of its 'outside' or its 'inclosing wall' (to use Emerson's terms). Already in this book, we have seen significant shifts with regard to the number and nature of the academic subjects which it includes. A field principally given over in its first phase to literary criticism and the analysis of other verbal materials has been redrawn by large-scale study of film, TV and visual culture. Debates have also occurred around the incorporation of anthropology, sociology and political science in American studies, given that the subject is usually sited among the humanities.

Emerson's spatial metaphors of wall, circle and circumference, however, are helpful in taking us closer still to the topic of this chapter. For among the most persistent questions American studies has asked itself is where to fix its geographical boundaries or how to delimit the territory with which it is concerned. Our discussion will show that, far from taking the space they analyse to be a constant, practitioners of the subject have frequently debated and modified this. The chapter will review American studies' operation at four different scales, labelled here *subnational*, *hemispheric*, *transpacific* and *global*. Each of these conceptions of the geographical area that the field covers is consequential rather than neutral, having major implications for the kind of scholarly work that will be done and that work's real-world effects.

SUBNATIONAL AMERICAN STUDIES

Given the received wisdom in many parts of the world that 'American', as an adjective, refers exclusively or at least most compellingly to the United States, it might seem uncontentious to define American studies as the study of the U.S. and by extension to take the nation's borders as the subject's circumference. For an alternative perspective, however, consider an essay by Wai Chee Dimock that reflects on the field in the wake of Hurricane Katrina in 2005. Dimock acknowledges at the outset that the 'conflation of nation and field' has the virtues of clarity and economy as a programme for American studies, since it assures the potential researcher that 'to study the United States, we need go no further than the United States' (2009, 145). However, she quickly challenges this seemingly unarguable assertion, arguing that, like any other nation-state, the U.S. is not so much 'a closed space' as 'an open network, with . . . nothing that will keep it defensibly separated from the rest of the world' (146). In light of this insight, it would be absurd if American studies practitioners attempted to bring to their scholarly projects the kind of zeal for strict boundary maintenance that characterises the work of the United States Border Patrol. The field, Dimock writes, 'can bear no resemblance to the territorial form of the nation. The nation is sovereign, or imagines itself to be. The field can have no such pretension' (146).

The distinction which Dimock draws here between the physical scale of the United States, on the one hand, and the intellectual reach of American studies, on the other, is something which we might think of as taking hold in the subject as it has developed during the last three decades. It is true, as later sections of the chapter will demonstrate, that consciousness of the hemispheric, transoceanic or even global dimensions of American studies has intensified in recent times. Nevertheless, to avoid falling into self-congratulation and concluding that by comparison with ourselves the earliest practitioners in the field had no sense of spatial complications and instead took the borders of the United States unproblematically as bounds beyond which they should not trespass, we might turn to two inaugural moments in American studies which give a very different picture. Firstly, the opening issue of *American Quarterly*, house journal of the subject in the U.S., disavowed any hint of parochialism by taking as the subject of its contributions 'various aspects of American world influences' ('Front Matter' 1949, 3). These articles were transatlantic in scope, engaging with topics such as cultural relations between the United States and France or the intertwining of U.S. and Italian literatures. Secondly, Tremaine McDowell, whose pioneering introduction to American studies was discussed in Chapter 4, writes in the book that 'American civilization is studied most effectively by a college or university which is studying at the same time local institutions within the United States and foreign civilizations beyond our national boundaries' (1948, 82). Here, then, is further evidence of spatial self-consciousness in American studies from the very beginning – an understanding that the territory to be covered by the subject will be shifting and extensive, not demarcated in stable fashion by U.S. frontier posts.

Later sections of this chapter will review the most territorially expansive versions of American studies. At this point, however, I want to consider another geographical level that is important in the field. For it is the case that taking the nation-state of the United States as the field's analytic unit activates not only too large but, simultaneously, too *small* a scale. McDowell is insightful here, also. His chapter on the subject's geographical imagination is entitled 'Region, Nation, World', indicating that it is important for the American studies scholar to move nimbly among differently scaled spaces – a point he underlines when stating that 'an American curriculum is most effective when it combines national materials with materials which are both more and less than national' (1948, 82). Not only more than national, then, but also *less*. Having anticipated this chapter's discussion of the more than national research undertaken by American studies, we focus first of all on its less than national engagement – on, that is to say, its inquiries at the level of *the regional*.

Whenever American studies is driven by a concern to interpret the United States in its totality, as we saw happening in some of the work of the myth and symbol school, it is in danger of neglecting significant differences between U.S. regions. Some initial reluctance during our own moment to think in regional terms is quite understandable. For regionalism as an outlook has often been deeply conservative, both ideologically and intellectually. In the case of the American South, for example, materials seemingly as far apart as the collection of scholarly essays *I'll Take My Stand* (1930) and the cinematic romcom *Sweet Home Alabama* (2002) share a tendency to endorse the region's traditional white folkways, without much indication that challenges and alternatives to these exist. The effect is to freeze knowledge of the South at a particular point, as well as to inhibit moves towards political progress. But regionalism in the American context does not have to take such conservative form; it can instead, in Neil Campbell's words, be 'outward-looking', dedicated not to unthinking preservation of the territory under discussion but instead to its 'critical interrogation' (2013, 51). Brief consideration here of approaches to another territory – the American West – should help to show the dynamic and progressive possibilities of regionally focused research.

The revisionist scholar of the American West has first to acknowledge the existence of a large repository of politically regressive images and narratives. Representations of the region from the nineteenth century until near to or even into our own moment have often, to begin with, been male-oriented, indeed masculinist. Where women feature in these materials, they are liable to be restricted to such minor roles as saloon prostitutes or the stoical wives of homesteaders. Instead, from heroic paintings to so-called 'dime novels', and from popular ballads to film westerns, there has been a tendency to prioritise male agency. The landscape itself, ranging from prairie to desert, is presented by many writers, painters and filmmakers as a space to be conquered by men's assertive actions. 'Enter the Man', as the first chapter of Owen Wister's literary western *The Virginian*, puts it – a gendered piece of scene-setting which the novel subsequently develops, for instance when describing the West as 'this great playground of young men' excitedly caught up in 'the romance of American adventure' (1998 [1902], 11ff., 51). Such narratives have been told not only in literature and film but in much intellectual production also. In Chapter 2 we noted that for all its importance as a pioneering exposition of American studies method, Henry Nash Smith's *Virgin Land* is compromised by a pronounced masculinism in its framing of the West and its selection of materials to discuss.

Feminist scholars who turned to the American West as a research topic in the 1970s and 1980s thus faced a difficulty similar to that which, earlier on, had confronted women who lived in the region and responded to it creatively in a variety of forms. This latter group, says Annette Kolodny, 'shared a discomfiting awareness of powerful prior male images that needed to be tamed and refined' (1984, 223). Not just 'tamed and refined', indeed, but *critiqued and undone*. Feminist scholarship of the West during the past half-century has built on and significantly extended those earlier attempts to imagine an alternative gender politics for the region. Kolodny herself played a key part in this enterprise, in particular in her groundbreaking book, *The Land Before Her* (1984). She works here with an expanded array of primary materials, uncovering women's counter-vision of the West not only in 'published texts' of many sorts, together with 'private letters and diaries', but in their designs for 'herb gardens, flower beds, or attractively planted town squares' (12). Cultural studies' openness to analysing artefacts of many sorts combines in Kolodny's work with feminist commitment and enables her to mount a major challenge to the prevailing sexual politics of American West studies. Numerous scholars have followed Kolodny and contributed to writing on the American West that redesigns the field so as to recognise female agency. Women previously missing from verbal and visual archives have been recovered: for an example, see Figure 5.1, which shows Mary Longfellow, a teacher and independent homesteader in nineteenth-century Broken Bow, Nebraska. Revisionary studies of the West have also focused on other groups frequently excluded from or marginalised by earlier scholarship, including environmental activists, sexual dissidents and peoples of colour.

Figure 5.1 Solomon D. Butcher, *Miss Mary Longfellow holding down a claim west of Broken Bow, Nebraska* (undated).

Source: The Library of Congress, Washington, D.C.

Though this research is too prolific and multistranded to lend itself to a brief summary here, a few important texts can still be highlighted. White hegemony in models of the region, for example, is contested in Quintard Taylor's *In Search of the Racial Frontier: African Americans in the American West 1528–1990* (1998) and in a volume co-edited by Taylor with Shirley Ann Wilson Moore, *African American Women Confront the West, 1600–2000* (2008). Queer and trans subjectivities across the American West, meanwhile, are explored in fine-grained studies that include Clare Sears's *Arresting Dress: Cross-Dressing, Law, and Fascination in Nineteenth-Century San Francisco* (2015) and Carol Mason's *Oklahomo: Lessons in Unqueering America* (2016).

To engage in regionally focused work of these kinds is not to be committed to an agenda of insularity. On the contrary, such critical regionalism looks outwards as well as inwards, being continually sensitive to how the localities it takes as its objects of study have been modified by demographic, social, cultural, political and economic inputs from elsewhere. Some of these transforming currents have their origins in other parts of the United States (as with the South's recent reshaping by location there of heavy industry once concentrated in or destined for the states of the 'Rust Belt' further north). But other forces of local transformation come from beyond the borders of the U.S. Returning to the South as our example, recent research has sought to dislodge older, parochial understandings of the region and to explore instead its historic openness to various transnational currents, with these including, of course, the Atlantic slave trade sustained over two centuries, as well as later migrations from the islands of the Caribbean. The South is thus to be understood as belonging not only to national space but to a sprawling geography that has been called the circum-Caribbean. Reframed in this way, New Orleans connects with Haiti and Cuba, as well as with Houston and Chicago. Regional or subnational territories of the United States, as they are engaged now by American studies, emerge as *transnational* also.

HEMISPHERIC AMERICAN STUDIES

American studies in its current phase is unequivocally transnational in scope, pursuing its objects of interest far beyond the official boundaries of the United States. In following this trajectory, it accords with the German sociologist Ulrich Beck, who criticises what he terms the 'container model' of a given nation for imposing 'a *territorial* understanding of society based upon state-constructed and state-controlled borders' (2006, 27, emphasis in original). Making this point, however, gets us only so far, for it remains important to identify several distinct strands of transnational research in American studies and to assess the effects on the field of each of these geographical expansions.

By way of introducing the first of them, I turn to an important, if neglected film, *The Three Burials of Melquiades Estrada* (2005), directed by as well as starring Tommy Lee Jones. The movie bears many marks of the western, which Lee Clark Mitchell describes as 'our most distinctive national narrative form' (2015, 454). Though it deviates from classic instances of the genre in being set in the contemporary moment rather than the middle years of the nineteenth century, it observes nevertheless the genre's formal patterns and thematic preoccupations. Pete Perkins, the central character played by Jones himself, is a cowboy. He and other action-oriented men dominate the screen, ultimately depriving a number of female characters of the dramatic effect which, for a moment, they seem poised to achieve. As the plot unravels, horses, not cars, become the protagonists' main form of transport. And yet . . . despite all of this subservience to a 'national narrative form', *The Three Burials* is also *more than national*, reminding us that full understanding of the culture, politics and economics of the United States is not to be gained by remaining within the country's borders. Migrants from Mexico, including Melquiades Estrada himself, share the story with characters of U.S. affiliation. People, ideas and money are shown crisscrossing the U.S./Mexico frontier ceaselessly and with complex effects. The final scenes even take place on the Mexican side, suggesting at least a temporary dislodging of the United States from pre-eminence in this particular transnational dynamic.

The trajectory of *The Three Burials*, venturing into the border zone so as to grasp more thoroughly the part it plays in shaping life in the U.S. interior, follows a route that has been taken in recent decades by American studies itself. The field now incorporates, to a significant degree, the insights and methods of *border studies*. While, relatively speaking, researchers have paid little attention to the U.S./*Canada* frontier as a site of political, economic and cultural exchange, they have been increasingly drawn towards an exploration of the border with Mexico. The implications of this research are far-reaching. For conservative visions of the unity or homogeneity of the United States start to break down when thought is given to the mingling of races, ethnicities, political orientations, religious affiliations, cultural traditions and languages that occurs in these borderlands and replicates itself across the nation. The work of uncovering and theorising the sociocultural dynamics of the U.S./Mexico frontier fulfils the interdisciplinary premise of American studies in drawing upon and bringing together multiple specialisms, ranging from anthropology to philosophy, psychology to geography, and musicology to literary studies. Key figures include Gloria Anzaldúa, José David Saldívar, Ramón Saldívar and also Edward Casey and Mary Watkins, co-authors of *Up Against the Wall* (2014), a rich text that finds the culture of the border zone to be as liquid as the Rio Grande that flows through it. Anzaldúa's remarkable book, *Borderlands/La Frontera: The New Mestiza* (1987), which mixes prose with poetry, autobiography with political manifesto, and English with Spanish, indicates as well that research in American studies which is attentive to these borderlands might be innovative in form besides content.

Many scholars who have turned to the U.S./Mexico border as a subject of urgent inquiry have not rested there, however, but have engaged in work that is still more spatially mobile. Here the developing interests of the contemporary Americanist José David Saldívar might be taken as exemplary of expanded geographical coverage in American studies more generally. In an early, groundbreaking study, *Border Matters*, Saldívar is especially interested in writings from either side of the U.S./Mexico frontier, presenting this bilingual archive as 'a paradigm of crossings, intercultural exchanges, circulations, resistances, and negotiations' (1997, ix) and as an enactment of 'traversing and mixing, syncretizing and hybridizing' (107). Already, such border-crossing research contributes, as Saldívar puts it, to 'the "worlding" of American studies' (xiii), revealing the insufficiency of 'our monocultural national categories' (129) and helping instead 'to instill a new transnational literacy in the U.S. academy' (xiii). However, one of Saldívar's subsequent books, *Trans-Americanity*, travels more widely still. In its most expansive mood, indeed, it imagines American studies to be equivalent to *global studies*, with the researcher required to venture far and wide in order to assess as fully as possible the profound effects which the United States has on the politics, economics and culture of other nations. The U.S. 'belongs', Saldívar says, 'through its new imperialism to the whole world' (2012, 187). But while observing how people working in American studies might thereby be driven to explore spaces such as 'the Global South' and 'the Afro-Asian-Pacific' (xvii), his particular focus remains on 'Greater Mexico' (xvii) and, beyond this, on territories he labels 'hemispheric' and 'inter-American' (191), meaning all of North, Central and South America, together with the islands of the Caribbean.

Hemispheric scholarship thus includes work on the border zone between the United States and Mexico, but also spirals outwards from this. As well as encouraging practitioners of American studies to extend their reach, this transcontinental research prompts them to ask unsettling questions about the very name of the field to which they contribute. In Chapter 1, we saw that the earliest known use of the term 'America' made no reference to the space occupied by the present-day United States. The world map which Waldseemüller and Ringmann produced in early modern France features the word on the *southern* part of the American continent, positioned across the land now occupied by Chile and Argentina. Later usage, however, increasingly promoted the narrow identification of 'America' with the United States, thus stripping the term of the continental implications it had at the time of its coining. 'American' has had a similar history, with the adjective, like the noun, frequently taken as referring only to U.S. matters. Nowhere, of course, has this reductionism been practised more keenly than in the United States itself. So, for example, Theodore Dreiser could call a novel *An American Tragedy* (1925) safe in the knowledge that his readers would expect from the title a sad story set in the U.S., not in Peru or Nicaragua. Likewise, few viewers of David O. Russell's film *American Hustle* (2013) would have been surprised to find it centred on con artists in New York and New Jersey, rather than in Rio de Janeiro or Buenos Aires.

Attempts from within the United States to reinflate the meaning of 'America' and 'American', so that the terms are presumed once more to apply to a continent rather than being reserved for the U.S., have been modest and sporadic. The people making this case, indeed, have sometimes been contrarians or eccentrics, rather than figures central to U.S. culture. Take the quirky example of James D. Law (1865–1928), a polymath born in Scotland and based in Pennsylvania, who combined pioneering work on the technologies of film and photography with expertise in the poetry of Robert Burns. At the turn of the twentieth century, Law complained about verbal imperialism on the part of his adopted nation, asserting that 'We of the United States, in justice to Canadians and Mexicans, have no right to use the title "Americans" when referring to matters pertaining exclusively to ourselves' (1903, 111n.). Seeking alternatives to 'America' and 'American' that would avoid such linguistic appropriation, Law proposed 'Usonia' and 'Usonian', deriving the noun and adjective from 'the initials of "United States of North America"' (112n.). Had these suggestions taken off, film audiences in 2011 would have flocked to see *Captain Usonia: The First Avenger*, while rock fans in 2004 would have been listening to Green Day's *Usonian Idiot*. Unsurprisingly, however, given their phonetic strangeness and the challenge they posed to long-established verbal custom, Law's coinages did not find favour with a mass audience. Though the great modernist architect Frank Lloyd Wright applied the adjectival form 'Usonian' to sixty or so houses he designed in the United States from the mid-1930s onwards – buildings he intended to embody an authentically national architecture, breaking away from the building styles of Europe – this registered more as an eccentric preference than as a trailblazing initiative for others to follow. Then, as now, the normative power of 'America' and 'American' as descriptors of the U.S. proved very hard to contest.

More recently, however, a concerted effort has been made from within American studies itself to undo the equation of 'America' and the United States. One of the most important interventions came from Janice Radway in her 1998 Presidential Address to the American Studies Association, entitled 'What's in a Name?' Radway reminds us early on that, if Anglophone attempts in the United States to revive the expansive associations of 'America' have been underwhelming, members of other language communities have made this case assertively. Among her key examples is the Cuban poet and revolutionist José Martí's polemical essay 'Nuestra América' (translated into English as 'Our America'), which appeared in 1891 in New York's Spanish-language press and takes 'America' as comprising the ethnically and linguistically diverse peoples of the continent at large, rather than simply the U.S. population. In the face of such arguments, Radway suggests that choosing 'American studies' as the name for a discipline that focuses in the main on the United States is not only misleading but imperialistic. Because of its politically compromised status, she says, there may be better names available for the field – and she goes on to consider three of the possibilities: 'United States Studies', 'Inter-American Studies' and 'Intercultural Studies' (1999, 18–21). In the end, each of these labels having been seen to carry its own problems, she concludes that 'the name "American studies" will have to be retained' (17). 'American studies' it is, then. However, the great value of Radway's work and that of many like-minded Americanists who have followed her during the past two decades is that it prompts us to be self-conscious about the subject's naming and, despite the conventional 'America'/U.S. pairing, to be attentive to larger geographies important to factor into any adequate analysis of the social and cultural life of the United States. More of these relevant geographies are considered in the remaining parts of this chapter.

TRANSPACIFIC AMERICAN STUDIES

'The Pacific is my home ocean', declares the novelist John Steinbeck in *Travels with Charley*, the offbeat road narrative he wrote after journeying across the United States in the company of his pet poodle. He continues: 'I knew it first, grew up on its shore, collected marine animals along the coast. I know its moods, its color, its nature' (1961, 161). The 'strong breath of the Pacific' is so pungent for Steinbeck, indeed, that he detects it not only on California's coastline where he lived but also 'very far inland', smelling 'the sea rocks and the kelp' and 'the sharpness of iodine' even as he and his dog travelled through the interior of the United States (161).

American studies, however, has proved far less sensitive than this to the currents of the Pacific. Steinbeck's heightened awareness of how the Pacific shapes experience both in communities along the shore and in the hinterland has, for the most part, not been replicated by scholars in the field. American studies' 'home ocean', historically, has been the *Atlantic*. An impulse to gaze eastwards from the United States to Europe, in particular but not exclusively towards Britain, oriented work in the field for decades. Earlier in this chapter, we saw American studies committing itself to a transnational outlook from the moment of its inception in the middle of the twentieth century; this transnationalism, however, was for a long time mainly Atlantic in direction, rather than looking also to the Pacific. A glance again at articles published in the founding issue of *American Quarterly* in 1949 is handy in indicating which of these two oceans would be navigated most frequently by the subject in the period of its institutionalisation and expansion. The essays' titles alone are revealing, with 'American Influences on Contemporary Italian Literature' followed by 'On What It Is to Be French', Henry Nash Smith's 'The Salzburg Seminar' (considered in Chapter 2) and 'The New World and Sir Walter Ralegh'.

American studies' long-running hesitation about looking westwards from the United States and taking the measure of the Pacific is curious, as well as limiting. For simply to consult the timeline at the end of this book is to see that the United States has long been implicated in military, political, economic and cultural engagements with parts of the vast region labelled the Pacific Basin. Consider, for instance, the flexing of U.S. imperialism in Hawaii and the Philippines very late in the nineteenth century or the nation's subsequent descent into wars in Japan, Korea and Viet Nam. Think, also, of the purposing of Guam, an island in Micronesia, as a centre of U.S. military activity, or of successive export drives that have carried into Pacific countries a wide range of U.S. products from aircraft and motor vehicles to soya beans and Hollywood movies. Directions of transpacific travel, however, have been plural and fluid, rather than unilinear. Countering incursions into their worlds by U.S. marines, missionaries and merchants, people from nations of the Pacific have made the reverse journey in large numbers. These migrant itineraries have had discrepant outcomes. While immigrants from China, for example, experienced atrocity with massacres in Los Angeles in 1871 and at Rock Springs, Colorado in 1885, they have proved resilient and adaptive in forging livelihoods everywhere in the United States from Seattle to Boston. Money has migrated, also, sometimes reversing older vectors of power – as with the significant inroads made in U.S. entertainment corporations by finance capital from China and Japan. Ideas, too, have proved potent when travelling across the Pacific to the United States, with examples including the effects on the nation's poetry of Chinese ideograms and Japanese haikus, or the redesign of Hollywood action and adventure films in light of the stylistics of popular Hong Kong cinema. Transpacific itineraries from and to the United States, then, have been crucial to the nation's formation – and American studies unfortunately restricted itself by a long-running tendency to suppress exploration of these.

In thinking about transpacific dynamics, as with the consideration of any sort of cross-border exchange, 'we need to listen to a wide range of "travel stories"' (Clifford 1997, 38). Who or what is travelling the ocean, in each instance, and with what consequences? Viet Thanh Nguyen and Janet Hoskins do not claim to have produced an exhaustive programme for transpacific study, but they are nevertheless ambitious in identifying an array of topics and figures to consider. At the macro level, researchers should engage with such concerns as imperialism, nationalism, capitalism and the fate of labour; simultaneously, in finer-grained work, they should examine the trajectories of multiple sorts of transpacific traveller, including 'refugees, immigrants, exiles, tourists, adoptees, war brides, undocumented migrants, trafficked people, laborers, managers, and students' (Nguyen and Hoskins 2014, 3). While figures belonging to these different groups all travel across the Pacific, they differ greatly in degrees of power and freedom. Researchers contributing to what has been called the 'transpacific turn' in American studies thus need to be alert to these profound material variations.

Transpacific scholars should also be sensitive to their own institutional locations, some of which are more privileged than others. To counter these significant disparities in the realm of research itself, Nguyen and Hoskins look hopefully towards 'a different kind of transpacific partnership . . . between academics on both sides of the Pacific and in the Pacific' (3–4). It is vital not to regard this orientation towards the Pacific simply as a shiny new toy for the exclusive use of Americanists: after all, much valuable work on the region will be produced by researchers from Japan or Taiwan or Samoa whose projects may touch only slightly or not at all on the United States. While being aware of the risk of academic colonialism, however, American studies should welcome the transpacific turn for its invigoration of the field and for the challenge it poses to any nostalgia which practitioners may still have for the Atlantic and the 'Old World'.

To conclude this section, we return briefly to the point Steinbeck made about the Pacific's continuing power over him even during his travels far inland. Transpacific American studies, too, should cultivate sensitivity to the ocean's multiple appearances and significances in non-coastal settings. A small-scale model for this kind of work is offered by Yunte Huang in an essay that has the subtitle 'Living Transpacifically'. Huang recalls leaving Beijing, the site of his first university, to begin further study in Tuscaloosa, Alabama. Even in this far from oceanic setting, he is still caught up in currents that derive from across the Pacific, being driven to search his new university's library first 'for classical Chinese porn novels' and then for 'another kind of material that is also banned in China: documents related to the Tiananmen Square massacre in 1989' (2014, 253). Shortly after, he gives further evidence of 'the uneven flows of global, transpacific cultural capital', this time remembering how in Beijing he had 'read with hunger' pirated copies of *Moby-Dick* and *Huckleberry Finn* (255). Beijing and Tuscaloosa are alike in the essay in being geographically distant from the Pacific, yet still profoundly shaped for Huang by the varied cargoes which the ocean brings. What he smells in these inland places, however, is not the kelp and iodine referenced by Steinbeck, but the even more pungent odours of culture, politics and power – topics of great interest to a transpacific American studies.

GLOBAL AMERICAN STUDIES

'Around every circle another can be drawn', says Emerson in the essay with which this chapter began. Finally, then, we should consider American studies at its most spatially expansive, going beyond regional, national, hemispheric and transpacific frames of reference and assuming a scale that is properly *global*. An initial sense of what American studies at this geographical level looks like can be gained by turning not to a book of academic commentary, but to Max Brooks's apocalyptic novel, *World War Z* (2006). Possessing one of the most striking of all literary subtitles – *An Oral History of the Zombie War* – *World War Z* is highly mobile in its narrative, tracking a virally transmitted plague of zombies across the globe. Locations are multiple and dispersed, extending from Finland to China, Japan to Brazil, and Greenland to the West Indies. The section of the novel entitled 'Home Front USA' (Brooks 2019 [2006], 137ff.), it is true, economises on travel, focusing more narrowly on how the gathering threat of the zombies forces the civilian and military leaderships of the United States into temporary retreat behind the Rockies or in Honolulu. More generally, however, the U.S. is displaced from the novel's centre, functioning like the many other places referenced here as a temporary resting place or staging post for narrative. *World War Z* frequently jolts the reader from the geographical scale of the nation into that of the globe, with humanity at large described as facing extinction at the hands – or teeth – of the zombies. The novel's premise is that demarcations between countries have drastically loosened and that what matters now about a nation such as the United States is not its territorial integrity but its enmeshing in lines of international transmission, along which flow everything from survival equipment to the zombies themselves.

Brooks's novel offers a vivid parallel in fiction to work done recently by practitioners of American studies who are committed to a planet-wide version of the subject. While such research cannot hope to startle as much as a book about the living dead roaming the world, it nevertheless surprises the reader by positioning the United States in unexpected constellations or networks with other countries, many of them far-flung. As two proponents of a 'globalised' American studies argue, the U.S. should no longer be thought of in privileged terms, as a fulcrum on which the world turns, but instead considered more modestly as 'a node in the global circuit' (Edwards and Gaonkar 2010, 26). *Circuits* in the plural, we might say, as researchers may follow and assess the flows of many things from across the world into, through and out of the United States: the immigrant populations that Edwards and Gaonkar have most strongly in mind, but also cultural forms or political ideas or finance capital. Not every Americanist, of course, operates at this most expansive of geographical scales – important work is still generated from inside more local frames of reference. However, the call by some commentators for a truly global rethinking of American studies has been acted upon by a number of scholars, and a brief consideration of the research of one of the most prominent of these may be helpful.

Wai Chee Dimock, cited earlier in this chapter for her thoughts on reimagining American studies following Hurricane Katrina, has sought throughout her recent work to pursue across the world topics that sometimes seem of quite narrow U.S. import. Her descriptions of the field available to Americanists fight shy of words that give a sense of boundedness or containment (*nation*, above all), preferring instead terms that evoke the open and the fluid. In *Through Other Continents*, for example, she argues that American literature is not 'a discrete entity', but a 'complex tangle of relations . . . a crisscrossing set of pathways, open-ended and ever multiplying, weaving in and out of other geographies, other languages and cultures' (2006, 4). In a more recent book, *Weak Planet*, the metaphors that Dimock uses differ slightly, but still communicate a vision of American studies as a restless, uncontained enterprise. Here, she describes U.S. literature as 'a field multiplane and continually crowdsourced. . . . Improvised from the ground up, with emerging vectors at every turn and input bearers always on hand, a field like this will never have enough finality to effect closure' (2020, 5). These 'vectors', 'inputs' and 'pathways', it should be stressed, are in Dimock's account geographically mobile, potentially travelling to and from any part of the world to distribute or modify the cultural and social productions of the United States. Two of the many rich case studies she offers may be taken as illustrative of her method. Firstly, *Weak Planet* shows how the tragedy of Melville's *Moby-Dick* is defused by fresh 'inputs' or 'user-amended sequels' (2020, 70) from the Trinidadian Marxist theorist C. L. R. James and the Indian novelist Amitav Ghosh. Secondly, in the Katrina essay, Dimock shifts this destructive hurricane out of an exclusively U.S. frame of reference and situates it alongside crises of rising water levels in the Netherlands and the Arctic Circle, evoking in the process 'crosscurrents affecting the entire planet, a seascape turbulent and borderless' (2009, 152).

I will return in Chapter 6 to a crucial aspect of Dimock's project: namely, its energising by a sense of environmental emergency. Her work contributes, as we shall see, to attempts to think through the scope and purpose of American studies at a time of heightened, planet-wide anxiety regarding climate change and catastrophically dwindling biodiversity. Here, however, I want to raise two other matters which have implications not only for Dimock's research but for a globalised version of American studies more broadly.

The first of these is the question of power's uneven distribution across the world and how this is factored into scholarly work.

In *World War Z*, even as a sense of crisis shared by all humanity threatens to make irrelevant the divisions between one country and another, evidence remains of some nations' comparative advantages. The United States, the novel suggests, is still well-equipped in military, technological and economic resources. So, for example, a French army diver whose campaign against the zombies was waged in the catacombs of Paris laments that he and his comrades had to resort to primitive forms of protection as they 'didn't have the American battle uniforms' (Brooks 2019 [2006], 313). Yet, such blatant acknowledgement of unequal power across borders is sometimes lacking in Dimock's writing and, perhaps, in global American studies more generally. Where, for instance, she characterises the 'connective tissues' that bind the United States to the rest of the world as 'input channels, kinship networks, routes of transit, and forms of attachment' (2006, 3), she rather sets aside the issue of who has the greatest control of such inputs and transits. Many of her studies begin with an artefact from the U.S. before spooling outwards to references from elsewhere: a chapter in *Through Other Continents* is typical in this regard in announcing that discussion of the American Beat poet Gary Snyder will open up consideration of 'a kinship arc' extending, among other texts, to 'a Sanskrit epic' from India and a sixteenth-century Chinese novel (2006, 166). The effect, certainly, is to redefine U.S. cultural production, viewing it now as a global rather than narrowly national thing – such is its continuing openness to additions and revisions from elsewhere. Always to begin analysis of this kind with the U.S. material, however, rather than with material sourced from across the world, risks maintaining a sense of America's priority and pre-eminence. It will be crucial, then, for a globalised American studies to consider how *power* – not just an idea or a text – travels along the routes and vectors which Dimock so attractively evokes. As Eric Lott says: 'US culture's global sitings must be thought in and through the balance of power – the conflictual relations of gain, reversal, exploitation, wars of position – that defines them' (2008, 117).

Secondly, it is important to consider more generally the political implications of this version of American studies. From one perspective, it represents the most modest of available models of the discipline, resisting any thought of U.S. exceptionalism and demonstrating the extent to which the nation – conspicuous and potent, to be sure, but not overmighty – is embedded in the world. Seen from another angle, however, global American studies is not humble as a discipline but on the contrary *overbearing*, aspiring at an academic level to that superpower status which the United States continues to exert in military and economic terms. For if, to take only one of Dimock's examples, research into the post-war U.S. poet Robert Lowell leads the Americanist into consideration of Ancient Greek number theory and the physics of Newton and Einstein (2006, 123–141), then potentially there is no limit to American studies' geographical reach (to the subject's temporal grasp, too). The responsibility facing contemporary practitioners of American studies, then, is to renew the field by embedding a planet-wide outlook in their work, but without this taking on the character of an academic land grab on a global scale. The challenge is well-put by Trinh T. Minh-ha, the filmmaker and theorist mentioned in Chapter 4. In any 'space of creative (re)invention', she says, 'the desire to re-circulate domination is constantly lurking' and must be guarded against (1991, 188).

SUMMARY

This chapter has considered debates about the territorial range of American studies that have been staged since the field's emergence. Given the long-established custom of taking 'America' to signify the United States narrowly, rather than referring to the Americas at large, it might have seemed obvious for the new subject to make the limits of its research coincide with the borders of the U.S. itself. We saw, however, that this suggestion was immediately challenged by Americanists and that lively consideration of the appropriate geographical framing of American studies has continued into our own moment. For some scholars, conceptions of the field along national lines are insufficiently receptive to regional variations within the United States, not least in the West and the South. For others, the national model is much too parochial, neglecting the extent to which U.S. culture and society are constructed through encounters with many other parts of the world. This transnational turn in American studies should not be viewed in a monolithic fashion, but instead acknowledged as having multiple strands, including border, hemispheric and transpacific variants.

Finally, the chapter discussed American studies when it is taken to its greatest transnational extent, reaching right across the globe. Questions remain about the implications of this development, which removes the United States from the centre of the world system and connects it by many threads to far-flung nations. Is this a move that helpfully downsizes the work done by Americanists or, on the contrary, inflates it imperially by bringing more and more parts of the world into its orbit? The debate raises broader questions about American studies' ideological positions and effects – and the field's politics is our topic in Chapter 6.

FURTHER READING

The South and the West have been particular subjects of regionally focused work in American studies. For good, substantial introductions to these strands of research, see *A Companion to the American South*, ed. John B. Boles (Malden, MA: Blackwell, 2004) and *A Companion to the Literature and Culture of the American West*, ed. Nicolas S. Witschi (Chichester: Wiley-Blackwell, 2011)

Readers interested in American studies' transnational engagements might begin by consulting work on the frontier between the United States and Mexico, including a book referenced earlier: José David Saldívar's *Border Matters: Remapping American Cultural Studies* (Berkeley: University of California Press, 1997). Scholarship that ranges further into Central and South America, along with the Caribbean, is well-represented by the essays included in *Hemispheric American Studies*, ed. Caroline F. Levander and Robert S. Levine (New Brunswick, NJ: Rutgers University Press, 2008). Important collections on the recent transpacific turn include Janet Hoskins and Viet Thanh Nguyen (ed.), *Transpacific Studies: Framing an Emerging Field* (Honolulu: University of Hawai'i Press, 2014) and Yuan Shu and Donald E. Pease (ed.), *American Studies as Transnational Practice: Turning toward the Transpacific* (Hanover, NH: Dartmouth College Press, 2015). American studies on a still more expansive, global scale is showcased by Wai Chee Dimock in important books cited earlier: *Through Other Continents: American Literature across Deep Time* (Princeton, NJ: Princeton University Press, 2006) and *Weak Planet: Literature and Assisted Survival* (Chicago: University of Chicago Press, 2020). See also the wide-ranging essays collected in *Re-Framing the Transnational Turn in American Studies*, ed. Winfried Fluck, Donald E. Pease and John Carlos Rowe (Dartmouth, NH: Dartmouth College Press, 2011).

Finally, the important work of literary scholar Paul Giles, which was considered in Chapter 4, suggests in itself some of American studies' shifting frames of geographical reference. His early books, including *Virtual Americas: Transnational Fictions and the Transatlantic Imaginary* (Durham, NC: Duke University

Press, 2002), are especially concerned with the United States' cultural dialogues with Britain. More recently, however, a transpacific focus organises Giles's *Antipodean America: Australasia and the Constitution of U.S. Literature* (Oxford: Oxford University Press, 2013); while he traverses larger geographies still in *The Global Remapping of American Literature* (Princeton, NJ: Princeton University Press, 2011). All of these titles are warmly recommended. However, an especially appealing way into spatial concerns in both Giles's work specifically and American studies at large is *American World Literature: An Introduction* (Chichester: Wiley-Blackwell, 2019).

6

THE POLITICS OF AMERICAN STUDIES

EDNA PONTELLIER'S SWIM

As a very small gesture towards redressing American studies' historic lack of attention to sport or to recreation more broadly (something that was noted when reviewing sociology's place in the field in Chapter 3), I begin here by considering a description of athletic activity taken from U.S. literature. The hope is that, as well as being of interest in itself, the episode will help to open up this chapter's topic of the politics of American studies. The scene occurs in Chapter 10 of Kate Chopin's novel set in Louisiana, *The Awakening* (1899). In this part of the text, the white middle-class protagonist Edna Pontellier, holidaying on Grand Isle adjoining the Gulf of Mexico while her businessman husband has stayed behind in New Orleans, has her first moments as an independent swimmer. Throughout the summer, 'Edna had attempted . . . to learn to swim', receiving 'instructions from both the men and women; in some instances from the children'. Previously the combined expertise and encouragement of all these tutors had failed to remove the sense of 'ungovernable dread [that] hung about her' when swimming. Now, however, Edna experiences a 'feeling of exultation' in the water, a sudden sense of possessing 'some power of significant import' (Chopin 1986 [1899], 73).

Politically speaking, how might Americanists respond to this episode of Edna's swim? The scene lends itself to feminist celebration, of course, as one in which a significantly constrained female protagonist is able to carve out a space of freedom, however fleetingly. Later in the novel, Edna will further transgress

DOI: 10.4324/9781315726748-7

the limits applied to bourgeois femininity in the United States of this period, choosing variously to smoke, to walk alone in the New Orleans streets and – Virginia Woolf-style – to seek a room of her own away from the stultifying family home. Perhaps, however, the unsocialised realm of the water in this sequence offers greater possibilities still for liberation, particularly when Edna turns away from the shore while swimming and looks 'seaward to gather in an impression of space and solitude' (74). As well as aligning the moment with countless other American dramatisations of female figures aspiring to escape from gendered constraints, the optimistically inclined reader might find parallels with a larger set of intimations of freedom in U.S. culture. From among many examples that could be chosen, consider just Mark Twain's Huckleberry Finn feeling 'powerful lazy and comfortable' when lying by himself on an island in the Mississippi (2014 [1884], 44) or Walt Whitman's sense of unfettered possibility at the start of 'Song of the Open Road' (1856), asserting that he is 'Healthy, free, the world before me,/The long brown path before me leading me wherever I choose' (1982, 297).

American studies' stance with regard to U.S. culture and society, however, is frequently one of suspicion and interrogation, rather than affirmation. Admittedly, across its history as an academic area, there have been exceptions to this tendency towards political critique – we will see the most prominent of these in the chapter's next section, which considers how during the Cold War from the late 1940s American studies sometimes *fortified* rather than analysed that pro-U.S. sentiment which government and media mobilised against the Soviet Union and its allies. But the field's interrogatory impulse is strong – as will be apparent if we develop our reading of this scene from *The Awakening*. For while Edna has exhilarating feelings of liberation and escape as she swims, these can be shown to derive from the restriction and exploitation experienced by others. Some brief remarks follow on her class and racial privileges in the novel, together with comment on how the swimming scene might also be considered through that ecopolitical lens which is now an important part of the interpretive resources of American studies.

Reading the class politics of Edna's swim is helped by referring to an important non-fictional text that, like *The Awakening*, was published in the United States in 1899. *The Theory of the Leisure Class*, by the Norwegian-American sociologist Thorstein Veblen, debunks boosterish claims that the U.S. is an equal society and attempts to map in detail the patterns of behaviour and thought associated with that upper-middle-class group referenced in its title. For Veblen, the economic power of the leisure class is evidenced by two of its practices in particular: what he calls *conspicuous consumption* and *conspicuous leisure*. His attention specifically to the leisure pursuits enjoyed by *wives* belonging to this wealthy social category offers us a way of thinking darkly about Edna's swim. Rather than an activity to be celebrated as liberating, it emerges instead from this perspective as something that is only made possible by an oppressive, unequal system. Veblen writes that the 'leisure rendered by the wife . . . is, of course, not a simple manifestation of idleness or indolence' (2007 [1899], 57). This squares with our example from *The Awakening*, since Edna is not simply lying on a beach, but engaged in strenuous swimming, almost to the point of exhaustion. However, Veblen goes on, the leisured wife's display of activity in such circumstances proves 'on analysis to serve little or no ulterior end beyond showing that she does not and need not occupy herself with anything that is gainful or that is of substantial use' (57). Again, this captures Edna perfectly – and of course she is only excused from the imperative of 'gainful' enterprise and licensed to spend the summer instead holidaying on Grand Isle and learning how to swim because of the prior capitalist success of her businessman husband back in New Orleans. The very comfort of the Pontelliers implies, in the grimly competitive economics of the United States, the disadvantage and even the poverty of others.

Edna is free to swim not only because of her class positioning but due to her racial categorisation. Sporting and recreational opportunities in the United States during this period were far from colour blind. In a fascinating book that fulfils American studies' interdisciplinary remit as it moves adeptly between literary criticism, popular culture analysis and sociology, William Gleason considers U.S. 'play reformers' of the late nineteenth and early twentieth centuries who attempted 'to conceptualize leisure as a new sphere for self-development, as a way to reconnect Americans to [their] creative, intelligent, and vigorous selves' (1999, 112). Gleason adds, however, that in this culture of play the categories of Americans who 'might be so lifted and enlarged to feel that power proved all too often distressingly small' (16–17). Racial exclusions prevailed (as did prohibitions on the grounds of class). These do not, of course, apply to Edna when she wishes to swim. While her husband is set apart from America's Anglo-Saxon Protestant mainstream by virtue of his Creole status, meaning he has French and Catholic heritage, Edna herself comes from a Presbyterian family in Kentucky; her whiteness is reinforced, indeed, by the detail that her father served as a colonel in the Confederate Army during the Civil War. The racial privilege that she and the rest of her holidaying party enjoy on Grand Isle can be uncovered, however, not only in their right to use a desirable beach at a time when peoples of colour in the South faced restrictions or inferior facilities. Such advantages of whiteness are also inscribed in their staying on Grand Isle in the first place. For we understand Edna to be swimming among African American ghosts, as well as through 'the vast expanse of water' (Chopin 1986 [1899], 74), as soon as it is remembered that during slavery the island had been a site of sugar and cotton plantations. After slavery's abolition in 1865, this white dominance was not so much curtailed as expressed in other forms: a local historian notes, disturbingly, that 'former plantation houses and Negro cabins were . . . utilized as tourist accommodations' (Swanson 1975, 161).

For the most part, the narrator of *The Awakening* seems as inattentive as Edna and her vacationing friends to traces of racialised inequality. An Americanist, however, putting the novel into caustic dialogue with materials from historical studies of the South, can activate considerations of slavery and of the Jim Crow segregation which followed shortly after its abolishing. In the case of Chopin's novel, a practitioner of American studies might also work forwards in time, wondering what the description of the swimming conditions enjoyed by Edna looks like when brought face to face with accounts of environmental disasters in Grand Isle during our own era.

The sea that Edna swims in is described in prose that is appropriately watery. Instead of including multiple, precise details of the sea's texture and volume, the narrative offers a series of environmental impressions traceable to Edna's consciousness. So, for example: 'The whole light of the moon had fallen upon the world like the mystery and the softness of sleep' (73). Yet what is seen and smelt in this encounter with the sea off Grand Isle in the late 1890s may still conjure up in the mind of a time-travelling Americanist some very different sensory data from the same site early in the twenty-first century. The account of Edna's swim records that 'There were strange, rare odors abroad' (73). None of these is sinister: the smells of 'weeds', 'damp, new-plowed earth' and so on. However, from April 2010 onwards, any 'strange, rare odors' to be smelt on Grand Isle were most likely to be those of oil washing ashore in large quantities after the explosion of Transocean's Deepwater Horizon drilling rig in the Gulf, which killed eleven crew members and ruined the region's ecologies and economies. The smell lingers: 'Residents say oil still washes on shore as tar balls', according to a newspaper report from as recently as April 2020 (Douglas 2020, n.p.). In 2010, Grand Isle was still recovering from the colossal damage caused by Hurricane Katrina in August 2005. Hundreds of the island's buildings were destroyed by the wind (for an example, see

Figure 6.1 Information Centre at Grand Isle East State Park, destroyed by Hurricane Katrina (photograph: Marvin Neuman/FEMA, 2005).

Source: U.S. National Archives.

Figure 6.1) – and by the flood waters caused by a storm surge that, as in New Orleans itself, overwhelmed the system of protective levees. Seen through the prism of Hurricane Katrina and Deepwater Horizon, then, Edna's swim looks less like an idyll in its own moment of time than an instant in the much longer history of an ecosystem that is proving increasingly fragile.

Though small in scale, this reading of a short section of *The Awakening* has, I hope, given some indication of how American studies might be done politically. Work in the subject has, in fact, no choice but to be political. If the ideological commitments of people engaged in the field vary, not least according to their particular locations in time and space, what they write and teach still impacts in one way or another on struggles for justice, liberation and equality both in the United States and in zones elsewhere in the world that are touched by U.S. power. In the rest of the chapter, we discuss several phases in the shifting political consciousness of American studies.

Consideration is given first of all to whether the subject took on a patriotic inflection during the Cold War and participated in the United States' cultural and intellectual sorties against the Soviet bloc. The section that comes after, however, examines various insurgent and liberationist turns taken by American studies from the late 1960s up until our own period. While much of the early impetus for this reframing of the field was supplied by feminist, African American and Native American activisms, vital contributions have since been made by scholars and campaigners speaking from diverse locations in Latinx, Asian American, LGBTQ, disability and other communities. Squarely in the sights of this multistranded revisionary initiative is a regressive politics identified as spilling over from mainstream life in the United States into the institutional arrangements, the subject areas and even the methods of American studies itself. The chapter then returns to a topic noted briefly in Chapter 5 and considers American studies' influence by and contribution to an ongoing consciousness of environmental crisis. How green is this field? To what extent or in what ways does it still matter in what Robert Levine has sombrely called our 'Age of Extinction' (2009, 161ff.)? A final, brief section then considers the adversarialism with regard to the United States that now prevails in American studies.

AMERICAN STUDIES AND THE COLD WAR

What do these three U.S. cultural artefacts have in common, despite their different forms? Firstly, Herman Melville's novel, *Moby-Dick* (1851); secondly, Charles Ives's musical composition for brass, strings and woodwind, *The Unanswered Question* (1908, revised 1930–35); thirdly, Jackson Pollock's non-figurative painting, *Number 8* (1949). One answer might be that they are all works which challenged or even outraged prevailing artistic tastes: Melville's text trashes narrative coherence, constantly deviating from its tale about a whaling expedition into ruminations on biology and theology, history and culture; Ives's piece is an early contribution to modernist music, its dissonances departing from classical melody; while Pollock's artwork is distinctive in its compositional mode as well as its abstract patterning, being created by the artist energetically dripping and swirling paints onto a huge canvas stretched out on the floor. Convincing as that response would be, another answer is that they were all called up by the United States in the Cold War campaign it waged against the Soviet Union in the four decades following World War II. The very idiosyncrasy of these and many other artistic productions of the U.S., it was proposed, stood as evidence of the opportunities for individual fulfilment open to Americans. The Soviet system, by contrast, was characterised by U.S. polemicists as promoting mass conformism and shutting down its citizens' possibilities of self-realisation.

Historians have documented in fascinating detail the many ways in which the CIA and other parts of successive U.S. governments, together with corporate and philanthropic organisations, weaponised literature, music and visual art during the Cold War. This story of war by novel and poem, or concerto and collage, is as intriguing as many spy thrillers. Covert funding streams were sometimes set up, permitting U.S. painting or music to be showcased across the world without signs of heavy-handed intervention by the White House. Elaborate cross-border networks of publishers and translators were established by the United States, so that the nation's literary classics might more easily reach hearts and minds around the globe. American cultural producers of many kinds found their loyalties torn or even compromised. The classical composer and conductor Leonard Bernstein, for example, well-known for his leftist politics, nevertheless led the New York Philharmonic Orchestra in 1959 on a successful, U.S.-boosting tour that included on its itinerary the Soviet Union and some of its satellite nations. Three years earlier, the African American jazz trumpeter and bandleader Dizzy Gillespie had performed in the Balkan countries, the Middle East and India, with the U. S. government of the time happy to exploit his creative talents for propaganda abroad even as it sustained a social order at home in which Gillespie's racial community was positioned as second-class.

The most pressing issue for us here is to consider in what ways American studies itself, particularly as practised in the United States itself, was mobilised alongside these arts and artists for the purposes of Cold War campaigning. Given that the field's foundational premise is America's interest and value as an object of study, its potential usefulness in patriotic intellectual struggle against the Soviet system is apparent. As already indicated, American studies' later reckoning with its trajectory often includes expressions of regret or even anger at its presumed complicity in the boosting of the United States during this era. Some harsh verdicts handed down by Americanists of recent decades against their ancestors in the field can be run together at this point. Patrick Brantlinger, quoted in Chapter 4 for his abrasive assessment of American studies' early interest in myths and symbols, argues that the subject's entire drift at the time of the Cold War was 'far less oppositional or critical than nationalist and celebratory', amounting in fact to 'an academic cultural chauvinism' (1990, 27). Michael Denning argues similarly that, in its main institutional bases at least, American studies was 'captured by the discourse of national character and American exceptionalism' (1997, 447). Efforts made during this period to identify key American symbols or archetypes – R. W. B. Lewis's *American* Adam, say, as discussed in Chapter 2 – certainly lend credibility to the charges of Denning, Brantlinger and others that American studies shared with the Cold War White House an emphasis on the distinctiveness of the culture of the United States. Even scholarly ventures abroad by this generation of Americanists – as to the Salzburg seminars discussed in Chapter 2 – have proved liable to sceptical retrospective assessment. Andrew Gross speaks interestingly of an *anticommunist internationalism* (2011, 84), which links these figures in American studies to all of the U.S. musicians, writers and the like who were simultaneously waving the Stars and Stripes across the world. This particular travel is to be distinguished from the more recent transnational practices in American studies – considered in Chapter 5 – that generally have as their goal not so much the consolidation of U.S. power as its *undoing*.

Yet, as Philip Deloria and Alexander Olson argue, to consider mid-century American studies as 'a cultural arm of Cold War statecraft' is simplistic (2017, 93). While any academic field in a given moment will have its dominant political tendencies, this point should not be taken to imply ideological uniformity among its practitioners. Differences, even clashes are to be expected – and such was the case with American studies at the time of the Cold War. Through his own research into this era, Denning himself has played an important part in identifying Americanists who were given to dissent, rather than to facile pro-U.S. pieties. Though his book *The Cultural Front* (1997) acknowledges the pull of patriotic thinking on the period's mainstream American studies, he considers at length the oppositional currents which flowed at its edges or through non-academic settings. The figures he focuses on explored (and participated in) labour struggles, women's movements, African American resistances, and much more. If these ideas had their widest circulation in the Great Depression of the 1930s, they nevertheless had a life also after World War II, offering American studies not only new subjects to consider, but an alternative politics to follow.

To emphasise further the field's political unevenness during the Cold War, we might briefly return to mainstream American studies scholarship itself and suggest that this is actually more complicated than damning assessments of its openness to pro-U.S. mobilisation would allow. It is important not to overstate the case: as we have seen elsewhere in this book, the myth and symbol school often puts centre stage the kind of straight white male who also figures prominently in U.S. Cold War propaganda. Nevertheless, some of its scholarly work fits awkwardly with a patriotic agenda. Analyses of *shared* myths, symbols and narratives do not immediately seem usable by government agencies which aimed at the time to convince people around the world that the United States was the home of sturdy *individuals*. The point here is not so much to assess the truth or otherwise of hypotheses made within American studies about overarching mental structures (the machine in the garden, and so on); instead, we simply note that emphasising that Americans have thoughts in common makes them not so different, after all, from those people of the Soviet bloc who were pictured by U.S. propagandists as prone to groupthink. Here again, then, is reason for caution with regard to narratives that find Cold War American studies operating only as part of the U.S. state.

LIBERATING AMERICAN STUDIES

Many people's lives in the United States late in the 1960s and early in the 1970s proceeded according to long-established rhythms. But in much of the U.S. during this period, there was ferment: political, cultural, psychological. Traditional institutions were challenged; old identities were contested and new ones asserted; familiar intellectual frameworks were radically critiqued, even torn down. The war in Viet Nam continued until the Paris Peace Accords were signed in 1973, devastating Viet Nam's population and ecosystem, and causing painful losses and profound social fractures on the U.S. side. African American activists demanded justice and restitution for centuries of dystopian horror, advancing their claims through strategies that extended from Christian-influenced Civil Rights protest through the self-reliant ethic of the Nation of Islam to the revolutionary campaign of the Black Panthers. Inspired by Black radicalism, many Native American activists were drawn to an equivalent 'Red Power' and combined long-term grassroots organising for social, economic and environmental justice with spectacular acts of dissent, not least the occupation of Alcatraz Island near San Francisco in 1969–71 and the seizure of the replica of the *Mayflower* in Boston in 1970 so as to disrupt unreflective commemoration of white arrival in Native America during the seventeenth century. And if African American, Native American and other minority racial and ethnic identities were sites of fierce struggle in the United States at this time, so too were gender and sexual subjectivities. Second-wave feminism challenged the oppressive patriarchal logic of everyday life in the U.S., addressing its manifestations everywhere from workplace dynamics to mainstream cinema's 'male gaze', and from reproductive rights to the design of university and school syllabuses. Gay, lesbian and trans activists also engaged on multiple terrains, publicly celebrating their sexualities at the first gay pride march in New York City in 1970, but also contesting many forms of violence, exclusion and hostile or caricaturing representation (again including the Hollywood screen).

Given these and other activisms critical or subversive of the U.S. status quo, it is unsurprising that insurgents also directed attention towards the institutions, contents and methods of American studies itself. Here, the subject's relative youth and its non-traditional interdisciplinarity did not save it from scathing critique, both from dissenting academics already teaching and researching it and from current and prospective students. Gene Wise, whose influential 'Paradigm Dramas' essay on configurations of American studies was discussed in Chapter 3, reported from the end of the 1970s on a widespread suspicion that the field had deteriorated into 'an overly timid and elitist white Protestant male enterprise which tended to reinforce the dominant culture rather than critically analyzing it' (1979, 185). Writing just over two decades later, Günter Lenz is, if anything, more acerbic still; he records that by the late 1960s 'American studies were in a deep crisis. They were declared intellectually bankrupt, politically reactionary, a handmaiden of American imperialism during the Cold War era' (2002, 461). Previous discussion in this chapter suggests that the last two parts of this triplet, at least, are something of a caricature of the field as it developed in the decades following World War II. As we saw, practitioners of American studies were not ideologically homogeneous and the scholarship they produced was not always aligned with the drift of Cold War U.S. patriotism. But however questionable such accounts of American studies are, they fairly sum up a body of strong opinion at the time, a marked-out position from which radical criticism could be directed against the subject's design and method. This dissent is, in reality, not so hard to understand. For a politically engaged student at that moment, going straight from a campus rally against the Viet Nam War to a seminar on the niceties of the 'New England mind' in seventeenth-century New England must have been to risk cognitive dissonance, the feeling that American studies was perhaps no longer the most intellectually dynamic and socially purposeful of disciplines.

In higher education on both sides of the Atlantic, much of this insurgent, counter-cultural energy found expression away from the formal structures of American studies. So, for example, many programmes of women's studies were founded, drawing their course contents from other locations in addition to the United States. Forms of 'ethnic studies' appeared in the U.S. from the very late 1960s and then multiplied, spreading out from bolder universities and colleges to reshape even the more staid institutions. Understandably, these fields did not extend their coverage to all ethnicities – the white American of Swedish descent is ethnically marked, after all – but sought instead to repair long-running neglect of the histories and cultures of minority racial communities in the United States. Early impetus went into establishing programmes of African American studies and Native American studies, but scholarly work around racial and ethnic identities resulted – at different rates of progress – in institutionalised attention to other minority formations, including courses in Latinx studies, Jewish American studies, Arab American studies, Asian American studies, and Oceania and Pacific Islander studies. Setting aside here the point that these are themselves large fields that sometimes face questions about their own coherence, it is more important to note that, like women's studies, ethnic studies has had a transformative and lasting effect on intellectual engagement with the United States.

Despite the institutional autonomy at times of these programmes of research and teaching, the concern which they have with the history and construction of diverse communities and subjectivities in the United States has utterly reshaped American studies itself across the last half-century. The fact that some scholars' professional titles may identify them as belonging specifically to programmes of 'African American studies' or to 'women's studies', say, has proved no restriction on their potential to help reconfigure American studies. As vitally important 'input bearers', to borrow Wai Chee Dimock's term from another context (2020, 5), specialists in the study of minority and marginalised identities in the U.S. have been instrumental in the modification of every element of American studies – from research directions and syllabus contents to pedagogical styles and hiring policies. To look now at publishers' lists and course booklets in American studies is, almost without exception, to find a field that is committed to the recovery and exploration of histories of the traditionally unacknowledged, overlooked or caricatured in the United States. In addition to the identity groups identified above, these now include LGBTQ and disability communities. One effect of this reorientation of American studies in recent decades has been to recapture the insurgent force which the subject had on its initial entry into the traditional academic landscape – to make it once more 'a disobedient discipline', in Paul Lauter's striking phrase (2002, 505).

All of this is unequivocally a good and deeply enriching thing. To conclude this part of the chapter, however, it is worth reflecting on two questions raised by the remodelling of American studies in the light of heightened interest in identity formations. The first of these raises the issue of possible *co-optation* or *incorporation* – the worry that African American studies, Native American studies, women's studies, and so on will be drawn into the baggy design of American studies itself with little heed being paid by the latter to the subversive energy and activist commitment that powered their emergence in the first place. Just as merely adding disciplines to one another in the American studies ensemble does not significantly change how things are done unless they are enabled to cross-pollinate in an interdisciplinary fashion, so simply to include in the field strands which are devoted to minority identities is relatively unadventurous. The opportunity needs to be there for these strands to modify and redirect the field at large. Janice Radway was alert to this danger in her Presidential Address to the American Studies Association in 1998, warning the subject against offering only 'an additive intellectual politics, a politics of inclusion, a move that [leaves] intact the assumed privilege of territorial paradigms and the priority of the nationalist community' (1999, 9). The risk Radway alluded to twenty years ago remains pertinent, even as research around racial and ethnic identities, gender and sexual subjectivities, and other marginalised positions in the United States has become part of the common sense, the everyday functioning, of American studies itself. Not for nothing are calls being made at the present time of writing to 'decolonise the curriculum'.

Secondly, it is noticeable that the heightened interest of American studies in identity formations does not always extend to identities of *class*, thereby replicating in the field itself class's occlusion or concealment in much political and social discourse in the United States at large. Some pieces of evidence – not definitive, certainly, but not without weight either – might be introduced to support this claim. First, Neil Campbell's and Alasdair Kean's highly successful primer in the subject, *American Cultural Studies* (fourth edition, 2016). It is noticeable that this volume does not have a chapter dedicated to class to fit alongside chapters given over to ethnicity and immigration, African Americans, religion, gender and sexuality, youth and other topics. The text is a fine resource (highlighted, indeed, in several of the 'Further reading' sections here), but the choice to relegate class to a term in the index rather than make it a more fundamental part of the book's architecture is troubling. Second, chosen entirely at random, the current options in American studies available at the University of Wyoming. The provision looks rich and engaging, with advertised courses including 'Gender, Women, and Migration', 'Latina/o Studies: U.S. Women of Color', 'Pop Music and Sexualities', 'American Civilization: Black Pop Culture' and 'Cultural Diversity in America' ('American Studies Courses' 2021, n.p.). Looking towards this chapter's next section, there are also environmentally engaged modules: 'Cultures of Nature' and 'Environmental Politics'. Other than in the course entitled 'Social Justice in the 21st Century', however, there is no obvious foregrounding of class as a concern of Wyoming's programme. And Wyoming is not, to be sure, an anomaly or outlier in this regard. It is with some justice, then, that Lauter says of practitioners in American studies: 'We have, alas, significantly contributed to the processes of obscuring certain class realities at the center of American experience' (2002, 492). Karl Marx, indeed, has been much less central to the field's recent development than major theorists of race, gender, sexuality and nation.

There is certainly no desire here to dislodge American studies' liberating engagement with racial, ethnic, gender, sexual and other identities, as this has widened and deepened over several decades, and to install class instead as the field's governing concern. Instead, the challenge facing us is consistently to think through class's entanglements with all of these other dimensions of our being in society. Questions of class should be active in all research and teaching done in American studies – including, to anticipate the chapter's next section, the work in the field which takes *the environment* as its initiating topic.

ECOPOLITICAL AMERICAN STUDIES

In Chapter 5, the geographical restlessness of Max Brooks's novel of zombie apocalypse, *World War Z*, was taken as equivalent to or emblematic of American studies now when it imagines itself operating on a truly global scale. But though mention was made of many of the widely dispersed locations that the text cuts between, one of its most significant sites went unremarked. It is important to consider it now, however, because more than any other of the novel's settings it prompts the reader to think about the planet as a whole. The section in question centres on an Australian astronaut, Terry Knox, who found himself orbiting the earth in a space station while the zombie pandemic took its course below. Occasionally he references specific countries (the United States, Saudi Arabia, Pakistan); for the most part, however, his recollections are shaped so as to evoke the sheer irrelevance of the idea of *the national* in the face of a planet-wide emergency. Knox remembers gazing 'through the view port down on our fragile little biosphere'. Fires could be seen burning across the earth ('a billion of them'), their dense smoke eventually obscuring his view. As he summarises: 'It was like looking down on an alien planet, or on Earth during the last great mass extinction' (Brooks 2019 [2006], 260).

This sense or apprehension of 'extinction' is one with which many people now are familiar. Even cursory watchers of news bulletins, to say nothing of Extinction Rebellion activists, will have learned of already catastrophic changes in the earth's environmental health. Global warming is marked by disturbing symptoms everywhere, ranging from melting glaciers at the Poles through rising sea levels in the Pacific and Indian Oceans that threaten many low-lying communities to unsupportable levels of heat and drought. Mining, deforestation and industrialised farming continue to destroy diverse and fragile habitats. Thousands of animal and plant species are driven to extinction every year. In such conditions of worldwide ecological collapse, to continue to operate through a national framework risks appearing at best indulgent, at worst grossly irresponsible for blocking engagement with the planetary that is now the only scale that matters. As Lawrence Buell, a pioneering figure in U.S. ecocriticism, puts it: 'To think "environmentally" or "ecologically" requires thinking "against" or beyond "nationness"' (2007, 227). American studies itself, of course, is implicated in this crisis of relevance, vulnerable like any other programme of national or area study to the charge that it does not answer the needs now of 'our fragile little biosphere'.

In the face of environmental despoliation, which endangers the survival prospects of both humans and non-human nature, there are certainly more pressing things to do than worry about a particular academic discipline. Nevertheless, it is imperative to continue thinking about American studies even in these circumstances. For, without overstating the field's activist potential relative to other and more direct forms of environmental intervention, it seems it may have a useful role to play in green campaigning. One way to start thinking about what the subject can contribute is to introduce Buell's notion of 'ecoglobalist affect'. What he means by this is 'an emotion-laden preoccupation with a finite, near-at-hand physical environment defined, at least in part, by an imagined inextricable link between that specific site and a context of planetary reach' (2007, 232). Among the examples from U.S. literature that Buell uses to illustrate the concept is the Native American writer Leslie Marmon Silko's novel *Ceremony* (1977), where 'a particular site' on Laguna Pueblo land in New Mexico enters 'force fields of planetary scope' (Buell 2007, 233) when it is used for extracting uranium for the atomic bombs dropped on Hiroshima and Nagasaki in 1945.

Though Buell speaks of this opening-up of a globalised environmental consciousness as emotionally driven and takes his examples from fiction and poetry, we can identify a similar process at work in reflective writing that contributes to an environmentally engaged American studies. Consider, for example, the effect of zooming-out from the microscopically localised to the planetary in an essay by Wai Chee Dimock on the nineteenth-century U.S. Transcendentalist Henry David Thoreau. Chapter 5 noted that Dimock's recent, globally framed work is especially concerned with questions of environmental damage and repair – and in this article, she starts with Thoreau's description of hearing the cry of a loon (a large aquatic bird) in *Walden* (1854). Rather like our own reading earlier of *The Awakening*, which flashed forward from Edna Pontellier's swim in a pristine Gulf of Mexico to the oil-saturated water of the same site in 2010, Dimock moves from the loon's presence in the mid-nineteenth century to documenting its poignant absence later as a result of environmental degradation (2020, 53). This is a transition not only in time but in space, for the essay opens out from the extinct loon in Massachusetts to acknowledge threats to biodiversity on a global as well as broader U.S. scale, referring to 'humpback whales, prairie chickens, sea turtles, and coral reefs – all endangered species today' (55). Dimock's article is evidence of how an environmentally conscious American studies begins to answer the demands for a global framing of the field which were considered in Chapter 5.

It is important, though, that adjustments in scale of this kind are not rushed. The damaged local topographies with which environmentally engaged work in American studies typically begins are sites for investigation and intervention, as well as being thresholds to larger spaces. This point can be illustrated by considering another recent essay in the field, which begins not on land, like Dimock's work on Thoreau, but at sea (it is also, coincidentally, an instance of the transpacific American studies that was reviewed in Chapter 5). Alice Te Punga Somerville's topic is what has been called 'the Great Pacific Garbage Patch': 'a large stretch of rather concentrated plastic debris' which is moved by 'the regular system of tides and currents' that flow between Japan and the West Coast of the United States (2017, 320). The scale of this mobile mass of non-biodegradable material is staggering – 'bigger than Texas', Somerville writes (320). Her essay goes on to explore the Garbage Patch at multiple scales. Most immediately, it is identified as devastating to marine ecologies, with damage following to the economic and social systems of the many island and coastal communities they help to sustain. The accumulated 'microplastic' has barely visible yet destructive effects on 'coral, tiny oceanic organisms, or the breathing parts of living fish' (331). 'Marine life is gently suffocated' (320). This last phrase, in particular, brings to mind Rob Nixon's important idea of 'slow violence' done to the environment – a 'calamitous' process, Nixon writes, that requires from us an adjustment of perspective, since unlike visible acts of harm it is 'a violence that is neither spectacular nor instantaneous but rather incremental and accretive' (2011, 2). The 'slow-motion toxicity' Nixon refers to (3) is also apt as a description of the Garbage Patch as this massive pollutant drifts to and fro in the Pacific.

Like Nixon, Somerville aims to identify agents of causation for the environmental deterioration she documents (so, too, does Dimock, for the loon did not die out in Massachusetts for reasons of biological predetermination). Though the United States is certainly not the sole polluter of the Pacific, its imprint on this mass of plastic is strongest, not only because of the nation's geographical proximity but because of its hyperdeveloped cultures of consumption and disposability. As her essay goes on, Somerville also performs the shift of geographical scales noted above. Without losing sight of the Garbage Patch's horrifying materiality in the northern Pacific, she also approaches it *metaphorically*, taking it as emblematic of many forms of environmental degradation that as a powerful nation the United States has historically visited upon sites across the ocean. To be specific: 'weapons testing, military activity, and exploitative resource extraction' – together with tourism (329). In common with Buell, Dimock and other Americanists whose research and teaching put degraded ecosystems centre stage, Somerville clearly adopts what Vermonja Alston calls 'the broader sense of the term "environment"', which permits 'a questioning of relations of power, agency, and responsibility to human and non-human' spheres (2020, n.p.). To this list, we might add a concern with the question of justice for those on the receiving end of U.S. ecocide. These are, of course, themes also engaged by practitioners of American studies considered in other parts of this chapter – even if *their* starting point in exploring them might be a U.S. novel or film, rather than a dried-up riverbed in Colorado or oil-poisoned water in South Dakota.

CODA: RESOURCES OF HOPE

Anyone reading books in American studies, or attending American studies conferences, soon encounters expressions of an adversarial view of the United States. The reasons for this political antipathy are not hard to discern (lots of them, indeed, have been set out in this book). For many Americanists, the object of their study, extending all the way back to the earliest interventions by English, French and Spanish colonists in the space that would later become the United States, presents a horrifying spectacle: close to *dystopian*, in fact. From such a perspective, the American past resembles that 'pile of debris', the accumulation of 'wreckage upon wreckage', which in an essay written in 1940 the German Marxist philosopher and critic Walter Benjamin described as coming into the view of 'the angel of history' (2007, 258, 257). So, in a very brief, selective chronicle: the genocide of Native Americans; African American slavery and the racist structures that followed on its abolition; violence and prejudice towards diverse immigrant populations, including Chinese, Japanese and Latinx communities; brutal campaigns by the forces of capital against organised labour, as in the Colorado coalfields in 1913–14; imperial ventures overseas, dislodging legitimate local rulers from Queen Lili'uokalani in Hawaii in 1893 to Salvador Allende, president of Chile, in 1973; the sowing of countless killing fields abroad through military action; the engineered despoliation of the environment. And so on . . . indefinitely. It is a record that would appear to give American studies little reason for political optimism. Nor is much consolation necessarily to be had in the cultural materials that also preoccupy Americanists, for these may be shown to be complicit in the oppressive historical forces quickly sketched here or, at best, to offer only partial resistance.

The more recent past of the United States – the *present*, even – is not noticeably more promising. While a list as long as that in the previous paragraph is not necessary here, some disturbing images and stories come quickly to mind. Consider, for example, the ongoing attrition of Black lives or, in 2017–18, federal authorities' incarceration of young migrant children away from their parents in the border zone with Mexico. Or think about the distressing fact that Barack Obama, whose election as U.S. President in November 2008 sparked joy both at home and beyond, proved so prolific when in office in launching civilian-killing drone attacks in Pakistan, Somalia and Yemen.

Confronted by such evidence of violence and injustice, it is unsurprising if the position of many Americanists towards the United States tends towards the abrasively critical. The fact that, in the current moment of drones, racist cops and exploitative corporations, the field often resembles an *anti*-American studies is thus not so much a misstep as a necessity.

Nevertheless, the very negativity of these critiques of the United States implies, as its positive, the desire for a radically transformed nation. Americanists might also profitably scan the materials they work with for what the Welsh socialist thinker and cultural critic Raymond Williams called in a book of 1989 'resources of hope'. This interpretive effort can still be made even where those materials appear politically unpromising or compromised. A valuable blueprint for such work is supplied by the great U.S. Marxist scholar Fredric Jameson, who proposes that 'a *functional* method for describing cultural texts is articulated with an *anticipatory* one' (1981, 296, emphases in original). What Jameson is asking us to do here is to look for 'Utopian impulses' (296), for hints of different and better futures, in the very texts that may at the same time be serving the interests of oppressive power. While American studies is necessarily adept in 'functional' reading (exploring how an unjust and unequal system in the United States is reproduced), its political consciousness might be expanded by placing greater emphasis on 'anticipatory' interpretation (seeking alternative forks in the road that the nation might profitably take). To return to the example from *The Awakening* with which we started this chapter, Edna's swim is genuinely liberating and speaks, if only momentarily and from a place of social privilege, of desire for an alternative world. Just the work of reconstructing the U.S. so that this transformed space is available to all needs to be done.

SUMMARY

The politics of American studies has been under review throughout this book, even when the chapters may have appeared interested in other things. This chapter, however, formalised that concern and enabled us to consider more directly the field's political tendencies. The picture that has emerged here is complicated, presenting American studies as a site not of ideological consensus, but dispute and mutation. During the Cold War, to begin with, it was not simply a cheerleader for the liberal values of the United States in its struggle with the Soviet Union: firstly, because of the continuing circulation within the field of politically subversive traditions; secondly, because of some resistance in myth and symbol scholarship itself to patriotic badging. Likewise, for all of the liberating effects of American studies' incorporation post-1960s of identity-focused work – redesigning programmes of research and teaching to make them less the exclusive province of straight white males – ambiguities emerged in our discussion. A particularly troubling question is whether the iconoclastic force that brought African American studies, Native American studies, Latinx studies, women's studies, queer theory, disability studies and so on into being in the first place can be sustained when they are incorporated into a multistranded programme such as American studies itself.

The chapter then assessed the version of American studies shaped principally by contemporary environmentalism. We saw that this typically operates in supple fashion across multiple scales, from the global through the national to the regional – indeed to *the less than regional*, since much important work in this vein begins by exploring the degradation of very specific landscapes (not least landscapes crucial to Indigenous communities).

FURTHER READING

An excellent summary of American studies' trajectory in the United States, with particular emphasis on its political orientations in the Cold War and immediately afterwards, can be found in Philip J. Deloria and Alexander I. Olson, *American Studies: A User's Guide* (Oakland: University of California Press, 2017), pp. 79–112. For a rich account of a politically dissenting version of American studies that developed before World War II and, sometimes in underground form, remained inspirational to many Americanists during the Cold War, see Michael Denning, *The Cultural Front: The Laboring of American Culture in the Twentieth Century* (London: Verso, 1997).

The critical literature on the histories, cultures and activisms of ethnic minorities and identity formations in the United States is huge and resistant to easy excerpting here. However, the chapters on 'American culture and identity', 'Ethnicity and immigration', 'African Americans' and 'Gender and sexuality' in Neil Campbell and Alasdair Kean, *American Cultural Studies: An Introduction to American Culture*, 4th ed. (Abingdon: Routledge, 2016), are fine starting points. For two bracing reflections on the perils as well as gains of incorporating identity-oriented study in programmes of higher education, not least in American studies itself, see Robyn Wiegman, *Object Lessons* (Durham, NC: Duke University Press, 2012) and Roderick A. Ferguson, *The Reorder of Things: The University and Its Pedagogies of Minority Difference* (Minneapolis: University of Minnesota Press, 2012).

The literature of environmentally engaged American studies is similarly rich. See, for example, Lawrence Buell, *Writing for an Endangered World: Literature, Culture, and Environment in the U.S. and Beyond* (Cambridge, MA: Belknap Press of Harvard University Press, 2001). Writings by Rebecca Solnit are enthusiastically recommended for their combining of intellectual weight and activist urgency: from among many titles, see *Storming the Gates of Paradise: Landscapes for Politics* (Berkeley: University of California Press, 2007) and *Savage Dreams: A Journey into the Hidden Wars of the American West* (Berkeley: University of California Press, 2014).

CONCLUSION

Why do American studies *now*? What case can be made for the subject as a site of intellectual activity that remains meaningful and important in our own moment? No academic field, after all, is guaranteed endless life or enduring health. Disciplines sometimes wane as conceptual paradigms shift, as higher education models change, or as the social needs to which those disciplines were once felt to answer evolve. Subjects that were formerly prominent in university curricula may find themselves either rendered obsolete or miniaturised to mere tributaries within new disciplinary configurations. Think, for example, of Ancient Greek and Latin, or rhetoric, or logic – all standalone subjects once, but suffering this fate of being downsized and incorporated in stronger disciplines. Thus, any account of the worth of American studies now cannot get by on documenting its intellectual achievements over the last seventy or eighty years, but instead needs to argue for its ongoing vibrancy and relevance, its importance even, in the world as it is.

One way of demonstrating the usefulness of American studies may be to employ its mix of approaches in discussing recent, tumultuous events in the United States. I am writing this early in 2021. On 6 January, following President Trump's refusal to concede electoral defeat by Joe Biden in November 2020, and notwithstanding the utter failure of his campaign's subsequent efforts to have the results of ballots altered or annulled by the courts, a crowd of his supporters broke into the U.S. Capitol in Washington, D.C., as a joint session of Congress was about to confirm Biden as President-elect. As a result of the confusing, frightening events that followed over the course of several hours, five people lost their lives.

DOI: 10.4324/9781315726748-8

The costumes, props and words utilised by these protesters give us, I hope, sufficient material to illustrate the effectiveness of American studies as a multistranded interpretive practice. In *their* example intended to show American studies' deftness in engaging with a wide range of things and concepts, Philip Deloria and Alexander Olson turn quirkily to the case of toilet roll dispensers in the United States (2017, 268–293). This apparently unpromising topic – 'something so mundane it would not seem to have much to say' (268) – actually allows them to move 'back and forth across analytical registers' (269), broaching issues of labour, class, industry, aesthetics and much else besides. Given this precedent, the far more spectacular happenings at the Capitol should be fertile ground for an American studies project. In analysing these events, an interdisciplinary combination of history, visual culture studies, literary criticism and anthropology proves productive.

Knowledge of the American past, to begin with, is helpful in positioning the 6 January attack in a history of insurrectionary actions against forms of power viewed as oppressive by those protesting. While the American colonies' campaign of resistance to British rule during the 1770s was evidently one of the protesters' historical examples, more galvanising still were tales of the South's secession from the United States in 1860–1. Widely circulated photographs showed people in the vestibules and corridors of the Capitol carrying not only the Stars and Stripes but also the flag of the rebellious Confederacy that confronted the Union during the American Civil War. We considered in the Introduction how the U.S. flag has had variable meanings for African Americans, conjuring up ideas of liberation for some but connotations of violent threat for many more. The Confederacy's flag is less open to plural interpretation, however, with its blatant associations with white supremacism. Its display by the Capitol seditionists, at a time still charged by memories of the killing of George Floyd and many other African Americans by law enforcement officers, represented a clear attempt to renew racist terror (a message reinforced by other protesters whose clothing carried slogans alluding favourably to Nazi genocide).

If knowledge of American sedition across centuries is helpful in contextualising the raid on the Capitol, so too is awareness of conspiratorial visions in U.S. political history. The insurgents of 6 January were a motley group, comprising representatives of many positions on the far right of the American political spectrum. Prominent among them, though, were adherents of the QAnon conspiracy theory, which, according to one helpful summary, alleges that 'the world is run by a cabal of Satan-worshipping pedophiles' (Roose 2021, n.p.). Though this theory is global in its range, claiming that Pope Francis and the Dalai Lama are among the cabal's members, its principal focus remains American: noted Democrats such as Barack Obama and Hillary Clinton, together with celebrity progressives including Tom Hanks and Oprah Winfrey, are taken to be the plot's masterminds. In this comic book version of apocalypse, Trump stands as an agent of goodness, recruited by U.S. generals 'in order to break up this criminal conspiracy . . . and bring its members to justice' (Roose 2021, n.p.).

QAnon is so lurid in its contents and so totalising in the allegations it makes as, at first glance, to seem unprecedented. But while it is undeniably distinctive by virtue of being circulated on new social media platforms, it has other features that render it not anomalous at all, but, on the contrary, affiliated to a durable tradition in U.S. political discourse. Here it is instructive to turn to cultural historian Richard Hofstadter's classic study, *The Paranoid Style in American Politics*, first published in 1965. Hofstadter writes that this paranoid style is given to hypothesising 'a vast and sinister conspiracy, a gigantic and yet subtle machinery of influence set in motion to undermine and destroy a way of life' (2008 [1965], 29). Hyperbole is its key rhetorical mode: American political paranoids think in 'apocalyptic terms' and claim to be uncovering a conspiracy which is 'set in motion by demonic forces of almost transcendent power' (29). Though Hofstadter's text is open to criticism for its conflation of disparate groups in American history as equivalent instances of the paranoid style, and for its underplaying of paranoia's potential insights in a U.S. political sphere often given up to uncritical reproduction of the status quo, it is still an essential resource in helping us to grasp the fevered thinking, the millennial fervour even, of a movement such as QAnon.

Yet it is not only expertise in American history that is vital in analysing the raid on the Capitol. Other sorts of scholarship are insightful, too, suggesting the value of that compounding of knowledges that characterises American studies. The Confederate flag, for example, especially in its garish juxtaposition with the nationalist iconography of paintings on the Capitol's walls, lends itself to analysis informed not simply by historical awareness but by sensitivity to visual culture. So, too, do some of the protesters' choices of costume and paraphernalia. Particularly apt for discussion here is how Jake Angeli, the thirty-something self-styled 'QAnon Shaman' from Arizona, chose to present himself during the insurrection. As images prominent in media coverage showed, Angeli came dressed for the occasion rather differently to those of his comrades who opted instead either for paramilitary clothing or for everyday leisurewear. In the decorous words of the *New York Times*, 'Mr. Angeli's outfit was one of the most recognizable from the breach, pushing him from obscure fame on the right-wing fringes to dinner-table conversations across the United States' (Wright 2021, n.p.).

Angeli's costuming and body decoration, together with the props he carried, present us with an abundance of signs to interpret. The horns adorning his head and some of the tattoos are European rather than American in derivation, gesturing towards the Vikings and by extension to fantasies of a dominant Nordic race untroubled by the need to share power with peoples of colour. Other aspects of his clothing, however, appear more bound up with U.S. tradition. His fur hat, for instance, resembles the distinctive headgear worn by the early nineteenth-century American frontiersman Davy Crockett, which again hints at a narrative of white authority over the claims of other races. Oddly, however, Angeli's visual style also contains traces of the iconography of a *non-white* American community. I have in mind here his bare chest and face paint, which may evoke most strongly resistance by Native Americans to the white man's systematic devastation of their world. Yet, to be precise, what is summoned up in this instance is not so much the history of Native Americans themselves as a long tradition of whites 'playing Indian', in Philip Deloria's phrase. Deloria explores how, from the era of protest against British colonial rule to post-war counter-cultures, white Americans have sometimes found it strategically advantageous to display selected tokens of Indianness – a case in point being when members of the Tammany Society in late eighteenth-century New York City paraded down Fifth Avenue in 'paint and fur and feathers' (1998, 56). Minus the feathers, this describes Angeli in the Capitol, too (note by the way that, extending such tactical appropriation, he sometimes calls himself Yellowstone Wolf).

Such behaviours, however, should not be taken naively as signifying multiracial alliance. Rather, the adoption of elements of Native American costume, decoration and weaponry expresses a sense that Native Americanness itself is merely ornamental, something that the white supremacist can pick up and discard according to the occasion. As Deloria writes, playing Indian tends to be narcissistic rather than outward-looking in motivation, premised on 'being indigenous, free, white, and male' (146).

The example considered in the last few paragraphs suggests the continuing vitality of interdisciplinary research into American culture and society. While historical scholarship in itself can tell us much about precedents in the United States for both the insurrectionary violence and the paranoid theorising of Trump's crowd, it still takes us only so far in unpacking this assault on the Capitol. Owing to its intermixture of disciplines, American studies permits us to range more widely and to consider not just the content of the protest, but also its *form*: the flags, say, or the costuming choices, or the verbal styles. Anthropology, another contributing discipline in American studies (as we saw in Chapter 3), can also be effective in this piece of research, enabling fine-grained study of such phenomena as the various right-wing groups which comprised the crowd. How, for example, should we understand the structure, the doctrine and the rituals of the neo-fascist Proud Boys, in comparison to the folkways of the QAnon conspiracists?

As well as bringing this blend of knowledges to a discussion of the Capitol incursion, an American studies approach is beneficial by virtue of being politically galvanising. The politics of American studies is, of course, not a simple or singular matter: in the course of this book, we have traced the field's ideological mutations, acknowledging moments when it has taken on a conservative rather than radical character. Much of the subject's current momentum, however, is in the direction of progressivism. Even when the trigger for their work is something as apparently depoliticised as maritime painting in nineteenth-century Maine or foodways in twentieth-century Louisiana, contemporary practitioners of American studies are likely to have as an underlying concern the exploration of injustice, inequality and power imbalance in the United States. Indeed, not just the 'exploration' of these things, but, more actively, their *attempted redress*. It would heap too much responsibility on the field to claim that it can directly shape and deliver social outcomes: even the best-attended conference of Americanists, after all, is limited in its capacity for praxis when compared with a mass political movement able to orchestrate street marches, occupy social media platforms and run election candidates. Nevertheless, scholarship in the subject may still supply and fortify radical campaigns that, of necessity, are carried out principally on other terrains. In the specific instance of the Capitol raid, American studies performs a valuable function for progressive politics where it traces the ideological lineage of the protesters, unpicks their iconography and critiques their rhetoric.

Taking these recent events in the United States as a topic for discussion has, I hope, helped to bring out the usefulness of American studies now. The field's disciplinary mix enables us to think expansively about what happened in Washington, D.C., drawing upon the combined resources of history, anthropology, art criticism and literary study rather than operating within a single interpretive framework. At a time of intensifying 'culture wars' in the United States, when fierce ideological battles are waged over the meanings of narratives and images and symbols, American studies, with its defining interest in the cultural, seems in fact more indispensable than ever to the task of making sense of the country it takes as its principal object. In modest and circumscribed ways, it also contributes, as we have seen, to a liberated American politics. A question remains, nevertheless, as to why all this should matter beyond the borders of the United States itself. Why should we consider American studies a *globally* important field, rather than one merely of parochial interest to U.S. citizens themselves?

An answer to this question might start with reference to a lengthy profile in the *New Yorker* of Thomas Friedman, star columnist for the *New York Times* and someone who, with great commercial and critical success, has written frequently about the United States' place in the world now. Though he is associated with U.S. boosterism, promoting the nation's great merits, Friedman denies at one point in the article that he dreams of its global dominance: 'I'm not out to conquer the world', he says, 'It's a much more inward-looking patriotism' (Parker 2008, n.p.). In the very next sentence, however, he declares: 'I want everyone to become an American'. This manifesto is breathtakingly bold – and to be resisted. For one thing, what, precisely, is it to be 'American'? Friedman's aspiration for everyone is attractive enough if 'American' means, for instance, the early Quakers in New England who mobilised against slavery, or the U.S. women in the nineteenth century who fought tirelessly for the vote, or the queer activists who took on the New York City police during the Stonewall riots of 1969. The prospect is much less enticing, however, if 'American' signifies the 'robber barons' of late-nineteenth-century U.S. capitalism, or the lynching mobs of the South, or the architects of mass destruction during two wars waged against Iraq. But even after 'American' has been glossed in this way, there remains the question of just how desirable it is to fashion all the globe's inhabitants according to the pattern of a single nation. Much more attractive and enriching than such homogenisation or unanimity across borders is a global order characterised instead by *polycentrism*. 'Within a polycentric vision', as Ella Shohat and Robert Stam write, 'the world has many dynamic cultural locations, many possible vantage points' (2014, 48).

Challenges of this kind to the dominance of any single nation, not least the United States, are greatly to be welcomed. Returning to two theorists cited in Chapter 5, Brian Edwards and Dilip Parameshwar Gaonkar similarly downsize the U.S., conceptually speaking, when they propose that we think of it now as 'a cosmopolitan node, or a turnstile in the global flows' (2010, 9). No longer viewed as a fixed point around which everything else moves, rather like Jerusalem when early modern mapmakers situated it at the centre of the world, it should be understood more modestly as temporary host to 'a proliferating set of trajectories, national, subnational, and regional, that make up the present global matrix' (26). Nevertheless, even while throwing cold water on excitable assertions of the supremacy of the United States, Edwards and Gaonkar still feel compelled to describe it as 'arguably the most important of nodes in the global circuitry' (26). Though by now we may be living in 'the Chinese Century', succeeding the 'American Century' anointed by publisher Henry Luce in 1941 (as discussed in Chapter 2), the U.S. continues to reach far across the world. Its economic agency and its cultural force remain colossal; so, too, does its environmental footprint, even in the face of terrifying evidence of climate change and species loss. Examples of political vision and strategy are still dispersed from the United States, also, ranging from the toxic white populism of Trump to the progressive model of Black Lives Matter. As Paul Giles summarises: 'America is the phenomenon which all local cultures must seek to come to terms with in relation to culture, politics, and power' (2010, 63).

None of these vectors of influence is irreversible or unilinear, of course. Communities elsewhere in the world are not powerless when confronted by imports from the United States: rather, they may *indigenise* these, creatively repurposing them for local conditions (as when UK grime artists braid hip hop influences with garage, dancehall, jungle and other musical traditions). Nations also export to the United States in their turn – everything from Scottish whisky and French literary theory to South Korean cinema and Russian ice hockey players. All of this multistranded activity, however, ceaselessly flowing in and out of the U.S., indicates that wherever our location on the globe this is still a nation which it is crucial to reckon with. Such accounting is liable, at least at times, to be interrogatory and critical, distancing people from the United States rather than binding them to it in the way Friedman hopes. But whatever its tone or its outcome, analysis of the U.S. is as pressing as ever.

In advancing the cause of American studies, however, it is important not to be shrill. The risk of hyperbole is ever-present, as when Edwards and Gaonkar go so far as to claim that critical interest in the United States suffuses the globe. 'Now everyone can and does know America', they write, 'everyone is an Americanist' (2010, 39). This is unconvincing. Firstly, citizens of Durban and Damascus, or Dublin and Dakar, are not universally oriented towards or preoccupied by the U.S. Secondly, taking an interest from afar in Kendrick Lamar's latest track, say, or the newest Hollywood superhero movie is not exactly being 'an Americanist', which implies operating self-consciously within the conceptual paradigms and interpretive protocols of American studies itself. Any temptation to think of American studies as *the* key area of intellectual work in the contemporary world-system should be firmly resisted, since, as noted in Chapter 5, arguments along those lines are imperialistic, achieving for the United States on the plane of ideas that global pre-eminence which on other terrains it effects by McDonald's and nuclear missiles. Trying to make the case without stridency, we might say that current power dynamics continue to make viable a U.S.-focused discipline.

Though Edwards and Gaonkar exaggerate when estimating how many 'Americanists' are operating worldwide, there is still merit in their argument that the practice of American studies now is democratised both within and beyond the United States. Researchers in the field, they show, are not confined to dedicated university departments, but, instead, are likely to carry out their work from widely varying settings. This adaptability of the subject's practitioners is important, for recent years have seen the closure of a number of American studies departments and centres on both sides of the Atlantic. Such retrenchment is of course cause for concern, especially where it forms part of a more extensive scaling-back of the humanities. It should not, however, be taken as indicating the enfeeblement of American studies itself: institutional realignment is hardly synonymous with intellectual crisis. From its earliest days, indeed, when scholars in the field frequently operated out of university departments of English or history, American studies has been adept in finding viable workspaces. As John Carlos Rowe observed almost twenty years ago, during an earlier wave of cutbacks to dedicated American studies provision, 'The absence of formal programs . . . need not indicate a lack of vitality' in the subject, since its future strength depended not on plentiful institutional padding of its own but on forging 'educational coalitions with ethnic, women's, gender and sexual, and cultural studies and critical theory' (2002, 177). All of the coalitions cited by Rowe in 2002 remain productive for American studies in our own moment (though we should add other important intellectual alliances that have emerged subsequently, notably contacts with environmental studies). Rowe's confidence about the health of the field, too, is justifiable at the present time. I hope in this book not only to have shown the accomplishments to date of American studies but to have set out grounds for its survival, indeed its prospering.

GLOSSARY

Abstract Expressionism: 'There is no clumsier label in art history than "Abstract Expressionism"' (Hughes 1997, 467). Yet the term persists as an attempt to capture the non-figurative style of a group of mid-twentieth-century U.S. painters and sculptors otherwise divergent both formally and temperamentally. Abstract Expressionists included Willem de Kooning, Jackson Pollock and Mark Rothko.

American Revolutionary War: sometimes called 'the American Revolution' or 'the American War of Independence', this was the armed struggle by thirteen British colonies to free themselves from rule by London. After growing political tensions, hostilities broke out in 1775. War was formally concluded by the signing in 1783 of the Treaty of Paris, which ratified the United States as a sovereign nation.

antebellum: referring, in the U.S. context, to the period before the Civil War of 1861–5. The term is a Latin composite, with *ante* meaning 'before' and *bellum* 'war'.

Black Lives Matter (BLM): non-hierarchical movement for racial justice in the United States and beyond, founded in 2013 by three African American women: Patrisse Cullors, Alicia Garza and Opal Tometi. A particular galvanising force was the acquittal of neighbourhood watch coordinator George Zimmerman for the killing, in Sanford, Florida, of unarmed Black teenager Trayvon Martin. Racist law enforcement remains a key target of BLM. Yet, as the movement's website makes clear, it aims at broader social transformation by 'creating space for Black imagination and innovation, and centering Black joy' ('About' 2020, n.p.).

canon: originally used in theological contexts where it signifies 'books of holy scripture which religious leaders accept as genuine' (Baldick 2015, 51), 'canon' as a term in literary studies refers to a body of fiction, poetry, drama and other writing deemed worthy of serious engagement by scholars. Recent decades, however, have seen the idea of the literary canon interrogated for its prescriptive and exclusionary qualities.

Cold War: period of mainly non-military confrontation between the United States and the Soviet Union, extending from just after World War II until the Soviet Union's collapse in 1991. The Cold War was fought worldwide, with both sides employing political, economic and cultural weapons to try to win the hearts and minds of populations.

Confederacy: shorthand for the Confederate States of America – that grouping of southern, slaveholding states that seceded from the United States in 1861, precipitating the four-year Civil War. The Confederate forces were defeated by the Union Army of the U.S. government after a conflict that, according to the most careful scholarly estimate, caused approximately 752,000 deaths (Hacker 2011, 338). One of the war's major outcomes was the abolition of slavery by the Thirteenth Amendment to the Constitution, ratified in 1865.

'dime novels': cheaply priced, action-driven novels produced from the 1860s onwards to meet the demands of an emerging mass readership in the United States. Fiction of this kind spanned a number of genres; however, as we saw in Chapter 2 when considering Henry Nash Smith's *Virgin Land*, westerns were especially popular.

ethnography: systematic study of the lifeworld and rituals of a particular community or people. While ethnography, as a major strand of anthropology, has often focused on pre-modern societies, it may be used as a research tool with regard to any organised or rule-bound group (e.g. contemporary American football fans at a game).

exceptionalism: in this context, the notion of America's uniquely privileged status, its freedom from the constraints and downturns facing other polities. Though the idea's roots can be traced back to seventeenth-century New England, with the Puritans' utopian visions of a new society (see Chapter 1), the term is applied most often to the United States itself post-independence. In Donald Pease's valuable summary: 'American exceptionalism includes a complex assemblage of theological and secular assumptions out of which Americans have developed the lasting belief in America as the fulfillment of the national ideal to which other nations aspire' (2009, 7).

field-imaginary: a term, especially associated with Donald Pease, that is used to describe the organising vision of American studies. Pease supplies a helpful gloss: 'the field's fundamental syntax – its tacit assumptions, convictions, primal words, and the charged relations binding them together' (1994, 11).

iconophobia: mistrust or even hatred of images.

Indigenous Environmental Network (IEN): grassroots movement established by Indigenous peoples in the United States in 1990, with the aims of countering environmental despoliation and economic injustice.

interdisciplinarity: attempt to re-energise traditional fields of academic study, or *disciplines*, by challenging their autonomy and bringing them into 'new configurations and alliances' (Moran 2010, 1). While interdisciplinarity is a feature of many subject areas, it is strikingly foregrounded in American studies.

Iroquois: confederacy of Native American peoples, associated especially with the Great Lakes region on either side of the present-day border between the United States and Canada.

Jim Crow: the system of race relations prevailing in the American South from the late nineteenth century until the 1960s, characterised by the segregation of white and Black in schools, universities, hospitals, restaurants, trains, buses and other public services. The term comes from a debased characterisation of an African American in the song 'Jump Jim Crow', performed in blackface by the white entertainer Thomas Dartmouth Rice (1808–60).

Latinx: term given to people in the United States of Central or South American heritages. While *Latino* (male) and *Latina* (female) are also still in common usage to describe members of this community, 'Latinx' has the advantage of being gender-neutral.

literary nationalism: the aspiration, especially as expressed in the mid-nineteenth century by such figures as Ralph Waldo Emerson, Margaret Fuller, Herman Melville and Walt Whitman, for the United States to be original in its literary production, thereby mimicking in the sphere of writing the *political* autonomy from Europe which it had achieved through success in the American Revolutionary War.

Louisiana Purchase: commercial transaction in 1803, whereby, for a price of fifteen million dollars, the United States acquired from France some two million square kilometres of the American mainland. The newly acquired territory encompassed many of the present-day Midwestern and Western states, and in effect doubled the landmass of the United States.

myth and symbol school: name given to a dominant tendency in American studies following World War II, which sought to identify and examine intellectual or imaginative schemas shared across America. This school's achievements, together with its significant blind spots, are considered in Chapters 2, 4 and 6.

New Criticism: a critical approach dominant in literary studies in the middle part of the twentieth century, particularly in the United States. New Critics tended to characterise the literary text as a self-referring verbal structure and were unwelcoming to alternative interpretive modes interested in history, say, or in writers' social contexts. As Chapter 2 notes, reading of this sort was unsympathetic to the more worldly literary criticism done within American studies.

9/11: shorthand term for the coordinated wave of terrorist attacks against U.S. targets on 11 September 2001. Hijackers loyal to Al-Qaeda, a radical Islamic grouping, seized control of four passenger aircraft; two were flown into the World Trade Center in New York City (causing both towers to collapse), a third into the Pentagon in Washington, D.C., while the fourth crashed in Pennsylvania. Almost 3000 people were killed. The consequences of 9/11 have been felt in domains ranging from geopolitical dynamics to psychological health and can be said to be still playing out.

Occupy Wall Street: major grassroots protest against economic injustice, inaugurated in September 2011 in New York City's financial quarter. For an excellent account of the movement's tactics and outcomes, see Massey and Snyder (2012).

pastoral: literary mode reaching as far back as Greek poetry of the third century BCE that idealises rural life as against the supposed disharmony and inauthenticity of urban conditions. The classic study of the pastoral tradition in American literature is Leo Marx's *The Machine in the Garden* (1964), discussed in Chapter 2.

poststructuralism: radical theoretical movement, dating from the mid-1960s, that challenges the underpinnings and assumptions of many academic disciplines, including philosophy, psychoanalysis, history and literary studies. Poststructuralists undo binary oppositions, explore rather than arrest the play of meanings in a text and resist notions of totality in favour of open-endedness.

precariat: this term brings together *precarious* and *proletariat* in the attempt to grasp a form of labour characteristic of contemporary capitalist economies. The *Oxford English Dictionary* traces its emergence to the late 1980s and takes it as referring to 'People whose employment, income, and living standard are insecure or precarious; such people considered collectively as a social class'.

Puritanism: a radical theology that emerged in England in the later sixteenth century, founded on the belief that further reforms were needed to *purify* Protestantism of residual Catholic influences.

While Puritans had significant effects on English life, particularly in the rule of Oliver Cromwell in 1653–8 following the Civil War, their most sustained success was in the north-eastern portion of the present-day United States. From the early seventeenth century onwards, waves of Puritan migrants seeking hospitable terrain for their forms of belief and worship arrived in America and established a social order that monitored not only people's religious observance but many aspects of their everyday lives.

scrimshaw: a folk art particularly associated with sailors of America's north-east coast, and described by Herman Melville in *Moby-Dick* as consisting in part of 'lively sketches of whales and whaling-scenes, graven by the fishermen themselves on Sperm Whale-teeth' (2002 [1851], 221).

Transcendentalism: loosely describable as an American version of European romanticism, this flourished in the United States in the middle third of the nineteenth century and challenged the period's mainstream thought by promoting the value of individual vision and heightened interaction with the natural world. Important Transcendentalist thinkers and writers include Emerson, Whitman and Henry David Thoreau. The movement was not exclusively male, however: among the women who played an active role were early feminists Margaret Fuller and Sophia Ripley (in 1841 Ripley co-founded Brook Farm in Massachusetts – intended as a communal experiment in living according to Transcendentalist principles).

transnational: term applied to economic, political, cultural and other exchanges across national boundaries. The word is preferred here to the similar *international* because of its stronger connotations of interactivity and dynamism.

TIMELINE

1507	'America', the name inspired by that of Florentine merchant Amerigo Vespucci, appears for the first time on a map in Europe
1542	publication in Spain of Alvar Núñez Cabeza de Vaca's *La relación*, describing a journey into present-day Texas, New Mexico and Arizona
1565	founding by Spanish expeditionaries of a settlement at St. Augustine, Florida
1585	beginnings of ultimately abortive attempt to establish an English colony at Roanoke Island, now in North Carolina
1607	founding of first permanent English settlement in America, in Jamestown, Virginia
1619	'20 and odd Negroes', from present-day Angola, forcibly transported to Jamestown on a Dutch ship, inaugurating the American trade in Black bodies
1620	the 'Pilgrim Fathers' accelerate Puritan settlement in present-day New England, establishing a community at Plymouth, Massachusetts
1636	founding of Harvard College (later University) in Cambridge, Massachusetts
1636–7	Pequot War in Connecticut between Pequot Native Americans and English settlers
1641	slavery declared legal in Massachusetts
1675–6	King Philip's War in Massachusetts pits a coalition of Native Americans against English settlers

1692–3	trials in Salem, Massachusetts, result in the execution of fourteen women and six men for alleged witchcraft
1712	major slave revolt in New York, one of many such acts of Black resistance
1733	founding of Georgia, extending the British colonial presence southwards
1754–63	French and Indian War, in which Native Americans align themselves with either French or British forces which were contending for colonial dominance in North America
1763	Sir Jeffery Amherst initiates biological warfare against Native Americans, through the use of smallpox-infected blankets
1765–7	the Stamp Act and Townshend Duties, authorised by the British government in London, outrage British colonists in North America for imposing additional tax burdens
1773	Boston Tea Party in Massachusetts, as colonists destroy imported, tax-carrying tea
1775	outbreak of the American Revolutionary War: fighting between settlers and British colonial forces occurs in Lexington and Concord, Massachusetts
1776	signing by revolutionaries of the American Declaration of Independence: the final document, to appease southern colonies, omits the critique of slavery which Thomas Jefferson included in an earlier draft
1778	first of approximately 370 land treaties is signed between Native American peoples and the U.S. government: *every one of them will be violated by the latter*
1783	independence of the United States, following its victory in the Revolutionary War, is conceded by Britain with the signing of the Treaty of Paris
1789	George Washington elected first U.S. President
1803	the Louisiana Purchase sees the United States massively expand its territory by buying from France a huge parcel of land extending from the Mississippi to the Rockies

1808	legislation prohibiting the importing of enslaved persons comes into force in the United States
1812–14	the War of 1812, over maritime and trading disputes, between the United States and Britain
1817–18	First Seminole War, as Native Americans in Georgia and Florida resist the seizure of their lands for cotton production
1820	the Missouri Compromise admits Missouri into the United States as a slaveholding state but prohibits slavery in Louisiana Purchase lands further north
1830	President Andrew Jackson signs the Indian Removal Act, relocating southern Native Americans from their ancestral territories to less fertile lands west of the Mississippi
1831	Nat Turner leads a major slave rebellion in Virginia
1838–9	'Trail of Tears': the forced march westwards of 16,000 Cherokee, resulting in catastrophic fatalities as well as territorial dispossession
1845	Texas, an independent republic after seceding from Mexico in 1836, is annexed by the United States
1846–8	U.S. acquisition of California and the present-day south-western states, following war with Mexico
1849	California Gold Rush
1850	Fugitive Slave legislation passed in Washington, D.C., requiring the immediate return of runaway enslaved persons to their owners (wherever in the United States they are found)
1857	Supreme Court's decision in the case of *Dred Scott v. Sandford* denies the right of citizenship to African Americans
1859	white abolitionist John Brown leads an armed raid on the federal arsenal at Harpers Ferry, Virginia, hoping to incite and enable a mass uprising of slaves
1861	outbreak of the American Civil War, following secession from the Union of eleven slaveholding states in the South (the Confederacy)
1863	President Abraham Lincoln issues the Emancipation Proclamation, asserting that 'all persons held as

	slaves' within the seceding states 'henceforward shall be free'
1864	Sand Creek Massacre, in which a white militia slaughters members of the Cheyenne nation occupying gold-rich ancestral lands in Colorado
1865	ending of the Civil War, with the Confederate forces' surrender; abolition of slavery by the Thirteenth Amendment to the U.S. Constitution; assassination of President Lincoln by Confederate supporter John Wilkes Booth
1869	ceremony at Promontory Point, Utah commemorates the coast-to-coast unification of the American rail network
1870	John D. Rockefeller and associates establish Standard Oil, which monopolises the oil industry in the United States for four decades
1872	hunters begin the mass slaughter of buffalo, devastating the ecology, economy and culture of the Plains Indians
1876	defeat of the U.S. cavalry, led by General George Custer, by a coalition of Native American forces at the Battle of the Little Bighorn, Montana
1877	withdrawal of U.S. military forces from the South denotes an end to Reconstruction – the federally driven attempt, post-Civil War, to address the region's racial inequalities and injustices
1890	killing by tribal police officers of the Lakota Sioux leader Sitting Bull at Standing Rock Indian Reservation, South Dakota; massacre by U.S. troops of several hundred Lakota men, women and children at Wounded Knee, South Dakota
1893	U.S. forces engineer the overthrow of Queen Lili'uokalani, the last independent monarch of Hawaii, which would later become a state of the United States
1896	U.S. Supreme Court judgement in the case of *Plessy v. Ferguson* upholds the legality of racially segregated public facilities

1898	Spanish-American War in the Caribbean and Pacific
1899–1902	Philippine-American War during which Filipino rebels, having initially welcomed U.S. assistance in overthrowing Spanish rule, turn against the Americans themselves as a new force of colonial occupation
1910	early phase of the Great Migration – a mass movement by African Americans away from the racially oppressive and economically disadvantaging South
1913	automobile entrepreneur Henry Ford introduces a moving assembly line to his factory at Highland Park, Detroit
1917	the United States enters the First World War in support of Britain and its allies, overturning its declaration of neutrality in 1914; beginnings of the first 'Red Scare', a backlash against radical political activity that extends in this phase until 1920
1918	Jamaican activist Marcus Garvey founds the U.S. section of the Universal Negro Improvement Association, aimed at facilitating Black emigration to Africa
1920	start of Prohibition, outlawing the manufacture, transportation and sale of alcohol (not officially annulled until 1933)
1921	Immigration Quota Act restricts the numbers of new arrivals in the United States
1927	execution of Italian immigrant anarchists Nicola Sacco and Bartolomeo Vanzetti
1929	Wall Street Crash, wiping billions of dollars off the value of U.S. stocks and helping to precipitate the Great Depression of the 1930s
1930	Nation of Islam established in Detroit, Michigan, by Wallace D. Fard
1933	Franklin D. Roosevelt becomes U.S. President and initiates the New Deal – a package of large-scale public investments aimed at reviving the economy
1941	the United States enters the Second World War on the side of the Allies, following the Japanese bombing of its naval base at Pearl Harbor, Hawaii

1945	the United States drops atomic bombs on the Japanese cities of Hiroshima and Nagasaki, leading to Japan's surrender
1947	investigation by the House Committee on Un-American Activities into alleged communist infiltration of the Hollywood film industry
1950	Senator Joseph McCarthy pours accelerant onto a second 'Red Scare' by alleging widespread communist penetration of the U.S. State Department
1950–3	the Korean War, aligning the United States with South Korea against the Chinese- and Soviet-supported North
1953	Julius and Ethel Rosenberg executed after being convicted of conspiring to pass atomic secrets to the Soviet Union
1954	Supreme Court decision in the case of *Brown v. Board of Education of Topeka* (Kansas) prohibits racial segregation in U.S. schools
1955	year-long bus boycott in Montgomery leads to the outlawing of racially segregated transport facilities
1961	Bay of Pigs fiasco, as newly elected U.S. President John F. Kennedy authorises a botched attempt by Cuban exiles to invade Communist-administered Cuba; Kennedy sends U.S. troops and equipment to Viet Nam to help prop up the South's regime against insurgents and the communist forces of North Viet Nam
1962	Cuban Missile Crisis, bringing the nuclear powers of the United States and the Soviet Union into a tense standoff over Soviet military build-up in Cuba
1963	Dr. Martin Luther King, Jr. delivers his 'I Have a Dream' speech at the March on Washington; President Kennedy is assassinated in Dallas, Texas
1964	Civil Rights Act prohibits discrimination in hiring policy and in access to public facilities on grounds of race, religion, national origin and sex; as war intensifies in Viet Nam, Congress passes the Gulf of Tonkin Resolution to grant enhanced powers of intervention to the U.S. President

1965	assassination of radical African American leader Malcolm X
1966	Black Panther Party for Self-Defense founded in Oakland, California, beginning as a movement against aggressive policing of the Black community but broadening into an insurgent campaign for African American liberation
1967	500,000 U.S. troops stationed in Viet Nam
1968	assassination of Martin Luther King by a fugitive white felon in Memphis, Tennessee precipitates unrest in more than 100 U.S. cities; assassination of U.S. politician Robert Kennedy, brother of the late President; massacre at My Lai in Viet Nam, as U.S. forces kill over 500 unarmed civilians
1969	first landing on the moon by U.S. astronauts
1970	National Guardsmen fire on anti-war protesters at Kent State University, Ohio, killing four students and injuring nine
1973	President Richard Nixon signs the Paris Peace Accords, putting an end to direct U.S. involvement in Viet Nam; occupation by Native American activists of Wounded Knee on South Dakota's Pine Ridge Indian Reservation; Supreme Court decision in the case of *Roe v. Wade* affirms the constitutionality of women's right to obtain an abortion
1974	Nixon resigns as President when facing impeachment by Congress for his knowledge of a break-in at the Democratic National Headquarters in the Watergate complex, Washington, D.C.
1976–7	Alex Haley's non-fiction book *Roots*, followed by its adaptation as a TV mini-series, has a major impact on modern Americans' awareness of the history of slavery
1981	first cases of AIDS reported in the United States – President Ronald Reagan's administration will later be criticised for its inadequate response to this health emergency
1986	Iran–Contra affair: the Reagan administration illicitly sells arms to Iran to obtain funds for the right-wing Contra rebels in Nicaragua

1991	U.S. forces lead a military coalition in the First Gulf War, ending Iraq's occupation of Kuwait
1992	Los Angeles riots, following the court acquittal of police officers who had been filmed in 1991 beating the African American Rodney King
1993	mass fatalities during federal authorities' raid on the headquarters, near Waco in Texas, of the Branch Dravidians religious sect
1995	Timothy McVeigh and Terry Nichols, motivated by libertarian, anti-government beliefs, blow up the Alfred P. Murrah Federal Building in Oklahoma City, killing 168 men, women and children
1996	arrest of the anarchist Theodore Kaczynski, known as the 'Unabomber', after a 17-year campaign of bombing university and commercial targets
1998	impeachment of President Bill Clinton, on charges of lying under oath and obstruction of justice, fails to remove him from office
2000	disputed Presidential election is decided by the Supreme Court in favour of Republican George W. Bush, rather than his Democrat rival Al Gore
2001	Al-Qaeda suicide attacks by passenger jets on the World Trade Center in New York City and the Pentagon in Washington, D.C., causing almost 3,000 deaths; retaliatory invasion of Afghanistan launched by President Bush
2003	U.S. forces spearhead a military coalition that, without UN sanction, invades Iraq and overthrows the regime of Saddam Hussein
2005	Hurricane Katrina devastates New Orleans and neighbouring parts of the Gulf Coast
2008	collapse of Wall Street investment bank Lehman Brothers signals a major national – and international – financial crisis
2009	Barack Obama sworn in as first African American President of the United States
2010	package of health care reforms – 'Obamacare' – passes through Congress

2011	U.S. forces kill Al-Qaeda leader Osama Bin Laden in a raid in northern Pakistan; 'Occupy Wall Street' protests, beginning in New York City, target corporate profiteering and economic inequality
2013	Patrisse Cullors, Alicia Garza and Opal Tometi found Black Lives Matter in response to the acquittal of the person accused of killing unarmed African American teenager Trayvon Martin in Sanford, Florida
2014	major Black Lives Matter protests following the killing by police officers of Michael Brown in Ferguson, Missouri, and Eric Garner in New York City
2017	inauguration of businessman and reality TV star Donald Trump as forty-fifth U.S. President
2020	Trump survives in office after impeachment for abuse of power and obstruction of Congress; a white police officer's killing of African American George Floyd in Minneapolis galvanises anti-racist activism across the United States and beyond; COVID-19 pandemic has grievous effects on the U.S., causing the deaths of over 300,000 Americans by the year's end
2021	Joe Biden is sworn in as President – with Kamala Harris as the first African American and Asian American Vice-President – following an electoral victory bitterly disputed by Trump and his followers, some of whom storm the Capitol in Washington, D.C. two weeks before the inauguration; Trump, post-presidency, survives a second impeachment; Congress passes Biden's $1.9 trillion financial aid bill

REFERENCES

'About'. 2020. Black Lives Matter. https://blacklivesmatter.com/about/.
'About us.' 2018. British Association for American Studies. www.baas.ac.uk/about-us/.
Adorno, Theodor W. and Max Horkheimer. 2002 [1947]. *Dialectic of Enlightenment: Philosophical Fragments*, ed. Gunzelin Schmid Noerr, trans. Edmund Jephcott. Stanford: Stanford University Press.
'Aims and Scope.' 2021. *Comparative American Studies: An International Journal*. www.tandfonline.com/action/journalInformation?show=aimsScope&journalCode=ycas20.
Alston, Vermonja J. 2020. 'Environment.' In *Keywords for American Cultural Studies*, 3rd ed., ed. Bruce Burgett and Glenn Hendler, n.p. Hybrid print/online edition. New York: New York University Press. https://nyupress.org/9781479822942/keywords-for-american-cultural-studies-third-edition/.
'American Studies Courses.' 2021. University of Wyoming. www.uwyo.edu/ams/course-offerings/.
Antsyferova, Olga. 2006. 'American Studies in Russia.' *European Journal of American Studies*, 1 (1), n.p. https://journals.openedition.org/ejas/366.
'Areas of Concentration.' 2020. American Studies, Yale University. https://americanstudies.yale.edu/undergraduate/areas-concentration.
Atwood, Margaret. 2011. 'The Road to Ustopia.' *The Guardian*, 14 October. www.theguardian.com/books/2011/oct/14/margaret-atwood-road-to-ustopia.
Auerbach, Jonathan. 2006. 'American Studies and Film, Blindness and Insight.' *American Quarterly*, 58 (1), 31–50.
'BAAS2020 University of Liverpool Draft Schedule.' 2020. University of Liverpool. www.liverpool.ac.uk/media/livacuk/schoolofhearts/documents/english/Website,BAAS,2020,Provisional,Programme.pdf.
Baldick, Chris. 2015. *The Oxford Dictionary of Literary Terms*, 4th ed. Oxford: Oxford University Press.

Barthes, Roland. 1989. *The Rustle of Language*, trans. Richard Howard. Berkeley: University of California Press.

Baudrillard, Jean. 2010 [1988]. *America*, trans. Chris Turner. London: Verso.

Beck, Ulrich. 2006. *The Cosmopolitan Vision*, trans. Ciaran Cronin. Cambridge: Polity.

Beeman, Richard. 2010. *The Penguin Guide to the United States Constitution: A Fully Annotated Declaration of Independence, U.S. Constitution and Amendments, and Selections from 'The Federalist Papers'*. London: Penguin.

Bender, Thomas. 2006. *A Nation Among Nations: America's Place in World History*. New York: Hill and Wang.

Benjamin, Walter. 2007. *Illuminations: Essays and Reflections*, ed. Hannah Arendt, trans. Harry Zohn. New York: Schocken Books.

Blackburn, Simon. 2016. *The Oxford Dictionary of Philosophy*, 3rd ed. Oxford: Oxford University Press.

Brantlinger, Patrick. 1990. *Crusoe's Footprints: Cultural Studies in Britain and America*. New York: Routledge.

Brooks, Max. 2019 [2006]. *World War Z: An Oral History of the Zombie War*. London: Duckworth.

Buell, Lawrence. 1999. '"Commentary" on Henry Nash Smith, "Can "American Studies" Develop a Method?"' In *Locating American Studies: The Evolution of a Discipline*, ed. Lucy Maddox, 13–16. Baltimore, MD: Johns Hopkins University Press.

———. 2007. 'Ecoglobalist Affects: The Emergence of U.S. Environmental Imagination on a Planetary Scale.' In *Shades of the Planet: American Literature as World Literature*, ed. Wai Chee Dimock and Lawrence Buell, 227–248. Princeton, NJ: Princeton University Press.

———. 2013. 'The Necessary Fragmentation of the (U.S.) Literary-Cultural Imaginary.' In *The Imaginary and Its Worlds: American Studies after the Transnational Turn*, ed. Laura Bieger, Ramón Saldívar and Johannes Voelz, 23–41. Hanover, NH: Dartmouth College Press.

Butts, Francis T. 1982. 'The Myth of Perry Miller.' *The American Historical Review*, 87 (3), 665–694.

Campbell, Neil. 2008. *The Rhizomatic West: Representing the American West in a Transnational, Global, Media Age*. Lincoln: University of Nebraska Press.

———. 2013. *Post-Westerns: Cinema, Region, West*. Lincoln: University of Nebraska Press.

Campbell, Neil and Alasdair Kean. 2016. *American Cultural Studies: An Introduction to American Culture*, 4th ed. Abingdon: Routledge.

Castronovo, Russ and Susan Gillman. 2009. 'Introduction: The Study of the American Problems.' In *States of Emergency: The Object of American Studies*, ed. Russ Castronovo and Susan Gillman, 1–16. Chapel Hill: University of North Carolina Press.

Chion, Michel. 1994. *Audio-Vision: Sound on Screen*, ed. and trans. Claudia Gorbman. New York: Columbia University Press.

Chopin, Kate. 1986. *The Awakening and Selected Stories*, ed. Sandra M. Gilbert. New York: Penguin.

Clifford, James. 1997. *Routes: Travel and Translation in the Late Twentieth Century*. Cambridge, MA: Harvard University Press.

Coates, Peter. 2006. 'The Human and Natural Environment.' In *A New Introduction to American Studies*, ed. Howard Temperley and Christopher Bigsby, 7–28. Harlow: Pearson Education.

Cooper, Anna Julia Cooper. 1902. 'The Ethics of the Negro Question.' https://dh.howard.edu/cgi/viewcontent.cgi?article=1018&context=ajc_addresses.

Danforth, Samuel. 2006 [1671]. 'A Brief Recognition of New-Englands Errand into the Wilderness', ed. Paul Royster. https://digitalcommons.unl.edu/cgi/viewcontent.cgi?article=1038&context=libraryscience.

Deloria, Philip J. 1998. *Playing Indian*. New Haven, CT: Yale University Press.

Deloria, Philip J. and Alexander I. Olson. 2017. *American Studies: A User's Guide*. Oakland: University of California Press.

Denning, Michael. 1997. *The Cultural Front: The Laboring of American Culture in the Twentieth Century*. London: Verso.

Dimock, Wai Chee. 2006. *Through Other Continents: American Literature across Deep Time*. Princeton, NJ: Princeton University Press.

———. 2009. 'World History according to Katrina.' In *States of Emergency: The Object of American Studies*, ed. Russ Castronovo and Susan Gillman, 143–160. Chapel Hill: University of North Carolina Press.

———. 2020. *Weak Planet: Literature and Assisted Survival*. Chicago: University of Chicago Press.

Docherty, Thomas. 2009. 'Our Cowed Leaders Must Stand Up for Academic Freedom.' *Times Higher Education*, 9 April. www.timeshighereducation.com/comment/leader/our-cowed-leaders-must-stand-upfor-academic-freedom/406098.article.

Donne, John. 2008. *The Major Works*, ed. John Carey. Oxford: Oxford University Press.

Douglas, Erin. 2020. 'A Decade after Deepwater Horizon, Way of Life for Louisiana's Coastal Communities Threatened.' *Houston Chronicle*, 17 April. www.houstonchronicle.com/business/article/A-decade-after-Deepwater-Horizon-way-of-life.

Douglass, Frederick. 1999. *Selected Speeches and Writings*, ed. Philip S. Foner and Yuval Taylor. Chicago: Lawrence Hill Books.

Edwards, Brian T. and Dilip Parameshwar Gaonkar. 2010. 'Introduction: Globalizing American Studies.' In *Globalizing American Studies*, ed. Brian T. Edwards and Dilip Parameshwar Gaonkar, 1–44. Chicago: University of Chicago Press.

Emerson, Ralph Waldo. 2003. *Nature and Selected Essays*, ed. Larzer Ziff. New York: Penguin.

Faulkner, William. 2015 [1951]. *Requiem for a Nun*. London: Vintage.

Franklin, Benjamin. 2015. *The Autobiography and Other Writings*, ed. Jill Lepore. New York: Alfred A. Knopf.

'Front Matter.' 1949. *American Quarterly*, 1 (1), 1–3.

Fuller, Margaret. 1978. *Essays on American Life and Letters*, ed. Joel Myerson. Lanham, MD: Rowman & Littlefield.

'General Session in American Studies.' 2020 [1947]. Salzburg Global Seminar. www.salzburgglobal.org/multi-year-series/general.html?pageId=6772.

'Geology.' 2018. Grand Canyon National Park. www.nps.gov/grca/learn/nature/grca-geology.htm.

Giles, Paul. 2006. *Atlantic Republic: The American Tradition in English Literature*. New York: Oxford University Press.

———. 2010. *Transnationalism in Practice: Essays on American Studies, Literature and Religion*. Edinburgh: Edinburgh University Press.

———. 2011. *The Global Remapping of American Literature*. Princeton, NJ: Princeton University Press.

———. 2013. *Antipodean America: Australasia and the Constitution of U.S. Literature*. New York: Oxford University Press.

Glaude, Eddie S. Jr. 2014. *African American Religion: A Very Short Introduction*. Oxford: Oxford University Press.

Gleason, William A. 1999. *The Leisure Ethic: Work and Play in American Literature, 1840–1940*. Stanford: Stanford University Press.

Gray, Jonathan and Amanda D. Lotz. 2019. *Television Studies*, 2nd ed. Cambridge: Polity Press.

Gross, Andrew M. 2011. '"Death Is So Permanent. Drive Carefully": European Ruins and American Studies circa 1948.' In *Re-Framing the Transnational Turn in American Studies*, ed. Winfried Fluck, Donald E. Pease and John Carlos Rowe, 72–96. Dartmouth, NH: Dartmouth College Press.

Gruesz, Kirsten Silva. 2014. 'America.' In *Keywords for American Cultural Studies*, 2nd ed., ed. Bruce Burgett and Glenn Hendler, 21–26. New York: New York University Press.

Gunn, Giles (ed.). 1994. *Early American Writing*. New York: Penguin.

Hacker, David J. 2011. 'A Census-Based Account of the Civil War Dead.' *Civil War History*, 57 (4), 307–348.

Hansson, Sven Ove. 2008. 'Philosophy and Other Disciplines.' *Metaphilosophy*, 39 (4/5), 472–483.

Ho, Karen. 2009. *Liquidated: An Ethnography of Wall Street*. Durham, NC: Duke University Press.

Hofstadter, Richard. 2008 [1965]. *The Paranoid Style in American Politics*. New York: Vintage.

Hoxworth, Kellen. 2020. 'Football Fantasies: Neoliberal Habitus, Racial Governmentality, and National Spectacle.' *American Quarterly*, 72 (1), 155–179.

Huang, Yunte. 2014. 'Conclusion: Living Transpacifically.' In *Transpacific Studies: Framing an Emerging Field*, ed. Janet Hoskins and Viet Thanh Nguyen, 250–256. Honolulu: University of Hawai'i Press.

Hughes, Robert. 1997. *American Visions: The Epic History of Art in America*. London: Harvill Press.

Indigenous Environmental Network. 2020. www.ienearth.org/.

Jameson, Fredric. 1981. *The Political Unconscious: Narrative as a Socially Symbolic Act*. London: Methuen.

Kaag, John. 2016. *American Philosophy: A Love Story*. New York: Farrar, Straus and Giroux.

Kerouac, Jack. 2000 [1957]. *On the Road*. London: Penguin.

Kolodny, Annette. 1984. *The Land Before Her: Fantasy and Experience of the American Frontiers, 1630–1860*. Chapel Hill: University of North Carolina Press.

Kuklick, Bruce. 1972. 'Myth and Symbol in American Studies.' *American Quarterly*, 24 (4), 435–450.

Lauter, Paul. 2002. 'American Studies, American Politics, and the Reinvention of Class.' In *The Futures of American Studies*, ed. Donald E. Pease and Robyn Wiegman, 486–509. Durham, NC: Duke University Press.

Law, James D. 1903. *Here and There in Two Hemispheres*. Lancaster, PA: The Home Publishing Company.

Lenz, Günter H. Lenz. 2002. 'Toward a Dialogics of International American Cultural Studies: Transnationality, Border Discourses, and Public Culture(s).' In *The Futures of American Studies*, ed. Donald E. Pease and Robyn Wiegman, 461–485. Durham, NC: Duke University Press.

Lester, Toby. 2009. 'A New Geography.' In *A New Literary History of America*, ed. Greil Marcus and Werner Sollors, 1–6. Cambridge, MA: Belknap Press of Harvard University Press.

Levine, Robert S. 2009. 'American Studies in an Age of Extinction.' In *States of Emergency: The Object of American Studies*, ed. Russ Castronovo and Susan Gillman, 161–182. Chapel Hill: University of North Carolina Press.

Lewis, R. W. B. 1955. *The American Adam: Innocence, Tragedy, and Tradition in the Nineteenth Century*. Chicago: University of Chicago Press.

Lott, Eric. 2008. 'National Treasure, Global Value, and American Literary Studies.' *American Literary History*, 20 (1–2), 108–123.

Luce, Henry R. 1999 [1941]. 'The American Century.' *Diplomatic History*, 23 (2), 159–171.

Maddison, Angus. 2007. *Contours of the World Economy, 1–2030 AD: Essays in Macro-Economic History*. Oxford: Oxford University Press.

Malcolm X. 1989. *Malcolm X Speaks*, ed. George Breitman. Atlanta: Pathfinder Press.

Marx, Karl. 1994. *Selected Writings*, ed. Lawrence H. Simon. Indianapolis: Hackett Publishing Company.

Marx, Leo. 2000 [1964]. *The Machine in the Garden: Technology and the Pastoral Ideal of America*. Reissue, with new Afterword. New York: Oxford University Press.

Massey, Jonathan and Brett Snyder. 2012. 'Occupying Wall Street: Places and Spaces of Activism.' *Places Journal*, n.p. https://placesjournal.org/article/occupying-wall-street-places-and-spaces-of-political-action/.

Mather, Cotton. 1855 [1702]. *Magnalia Christi Americana; or, The Ecclesiastical History of New-England; from its First Planting, in the Year 1620, unto the Year of Our Lord 1698*, ed. Thomas Robbins. Hartford, CT: Silas Andrus and Son.

Matthiessen, F. O. 1968 [1941]. *American Renaissance: Art and Expression in the Age of Emerson and Whitman*. New York: Oxford University Press.

McDowell, Tremaine. 1948. *American Studies*. Minneapolis: University of Minnesota Press.

Mead, Margaret. 1947. 'The Salzburg Seminar in American Civilization.' Report to the Harvard Student Council. www.salzburgglobal.org/fileadmin/user_upload/Documents/General_SGS_Documents/1947_MeadArticle.pdf.

———. 1951. 'Anthropologist and Historian: Their Common Problems.' *American Quarterly*, 3 (1), 3–13.

Mellinger, Rachel. 1954. 'American Culture: The High and the Low-Down.' *Mademoiselle*, 40 (December), 92–93, 115–117.

Melville, Herman. 2002 [1851]. *Moby-Dick*, ed. Hershel Parker and Harrison Hayford, 2nd ed. New York: Norton.

———. 2016. *Billy Budd, Bartleby, and Other Stories*, ed. Peter Coviello. New York: Penguin.

Miller, Perry. 1939. *The New England Mind: The Seventeenth Century*. New York: Macmillan.

———. 1956. *Errand into the Wilderness*. Cambridge, MA: Belknap Press of Harvard University Press.

Minh-ha, Trinh T. 1991. *When the Moon Waxes Red: Representation, Gender and Cultural Politics*. New York: Routledge.

Mitchell, Lee Clark. 2015. '"Is There Actually Any Jiménez?": Believing as Seeing in *The Three Burials of Melquiades Estrada*.' *Quarterly Review of Film and Video*, 32 (5), 446–455.

Mitchell, W. J. T. 1986. *Iconology: Image, Text, Ideology*. Chicago: University of Chicago Press.

Montaigne, Michel de. 2003. *The Complete Essays*, ed. and trans. M. A. Screech. London: Penguin.

Moran, Joe. 2010. *Interdisciplinarity*, 2nd ed. Abingdon: Routledge.

Muir, Hugh. 2020. 'Cornel West: "George Floyd's Public Lynching Pulled the Cover Off Who We Really Are".' *The Guardian*, 19 October. www.theguardian.com/us-news/2020/oct/19/cornel-west-george-floyds-public-lynching-pulled-the-cover-off-who-we-really-are.

Murphey, Murray G. 2001. 'Perry Miller and American Studies.' *American Studies*, 42 (2), 5–18.

Nguyen, Viet Thanh and Janet Hoskins. 2014. 'Introduction: Transpacific Studies: Critical Perspectives on an Emerging Field.' In *Transpacific Studies: Framing an Emerging Field*, ed. Janet Hoskins and Viet Thanh Nguyen, 1–38. Honolulu: University of Hawai'i Press.

Nixon, Rob. 2011. *Slow Violence and the Environmentalism of the Poor*. Cambridge, MA: Harvard University Press.

Obama, Barack. 2020. *A Promised Land*. New York: Crown.

Parker, Ian. 2008. 'The Bright Side: The Relentless Optimism of Thomas Friedman.' *The New Yorker*, 3 November. www.newyorker.com/magazine/2008/11/10/the-bright-side.

Parks, Gordon. 2005. *A Hungry Heart: A Memoir*. New York: Washington Square Press.

Parrington, Vernon Louis. 1930. *Main Currents in American Thought: An Interpretation of American Literature from the Beginnings to 1920*. 3 vols. New York: Harcourt, Brace and Company.

Pease, Donald E. 1994. 'New Americanists: Revisionary Interventions into the Canon.' In *Revisionary Interventions into the Americanist Canon*, ed. Donald E. Pease, 1–37. Durham, NC: Duke University Press.

———. 2009. *The New American Exceptionalism*. Minneapolis: University of Minnesota Press.

Pease, Donald E. and Robyn Wiegman. 2002. 'Futures.' In *The Futures of American Studies*, ed. Donald E. Pease and Robyn Wiegman, 1–42. Durham, NC: Duke University Press.

Powdermaker, Hortense. 1950. *Hollywood, the Dream Factory: An Anthropologist Looks at the Movies*. New York: Little, Brown and Company.

Pyne, Stephen. 1999. *How the Canyon Became Grand*. New York: Penguin.

Radway, Janice. 1999. '"What's in a Name?": Presidential Address to the American Studies Association, 20 November, 1998.' *American Quarterly*, 51 (1), 1–32.

Ricks, Christopher and William L. Vance (ed.). 1992. *The Faber Book of America*. London: Faber and Faber.

Roose, Kevin. 2021. 'What Is QAnon, the Viral Pro-Trump Conspiracy Theory?' *The New York Times*, 17 January. www.nytimes.com/article/what-is-qanon.html.

Rowe, John Carlos. 2002. 'Postnationalism, Globalism, and the New American Studies.' In *The Futures of American Studies*, ed. Donald E. Pease and Robyn Wiegman, 167–182. Durham, NC: Duke University Press.

Saldívar, José David. 1997. *Border Matters: Remapping American Cultural Studies*. Berkeley: University of California Press.

———. 2012. *Trans-Americanity: Subaltern Modernities, Global Coloniality, and the Cultures of Greater Mexico*. Durham, NC: Duke University Press.

Salter, Michael. 2019. 'Brett Kavanaugh's Nomination and the Moral Context of Trauma Science.' *Journal of Trauma & Dissociation*, 20 (2), 135–139.

Shockley, Martin Staples. 1946. 'American Literature in American Education.' *College English*, 8 (1), 23–30.

Shohat, Ella and Robert Stam. 2014. *Unthinking Eurocentrism: Multiculturalism and the Media*, 2nd ed. Abingdon: Routledge.

Shrivastava, B. K. 1987. 'American Studies in India.' *American Studies International*, 25 (2), 41–55.

Smith, Henry Nash. 1949. 'The Salzburg Seminar.' *American Quarterly*, 1 (1), 30–37.

———. 1957. 'Can "American Studies" Develop a Method?' *American Quarterly*, 9 (2), 197–208.

———. 1970 [1950]. *Virgin Land: The American West as Symbol and Myth*. Reissue, with new Preface. Cambridge, MA: Harvard University Press.

Smith, John. 2006 [1616]. *A Description of New England*, ed. Paul Royster. https://digitalcommons.unl.edu/cgi/viewcontent.cgi?article=1003&context=etas.

Sollors, Werner. 2000. 'Introduction.' In *The Multilingual Anthology of American Literature: A Reader of Original Texts with English Translations*, ed. Marc Shell and Werner Sollors, 1–11. New York: New York University Press.

Somerville, Alice Te Punga. 2017. 'The Great Pacific Garbage Patch as Metaphor: The (American) Pacific You Can't See.' In *Archipelagic American Studies*, ed. Brian Russell Roberts and Michelle Ann Stephens, 320–338. Durham, NC: Duke University Press.

Spiller, Robert E. 1949. 'Review of Tremaine McDowell, *American Studies*.' *American Quarterly*, 1 (2), 166–169.

Steinbeck, John. 1961. *Travels with Charley: In Search of America*. London: Heinemann.

Swanson, Betsy. 1975. *Historic Jefferson Parish: From Shore to Shore*. Gretna, LA: Pelican.

Tafuri, Manfredo. 1976. *Architecture and Utopia: Design and Capitalist Development*, trans. Barbara Luigia La Penta. Cambridge, MA: The MIT Press.

Thoreau, Henry David. 1997 [1854]. *Walden*, ed. Stephen Fender. Oxford: Oxford University Press.

Trachtenberg, Alan. 1984. 'Myth and Symbol.' *Massachusetts Review*, 25 (4), 667–673.

Twain, Mark. 2014 [1884]. *Adventures of Huckleberry Finn*. New York: Penguin.

'Undergraduate Courses.' 2020. American Studies, Yale University. https://americanstudies.yale.edu/undergraduate-program/courses.

Vanderbilt, Kermit. 1986. *American Literature and the Academy: The Roots, Growth, and Maturity of a Profession*. Philadelphia: University of Pennsylvania Press.

Veblen, Thorstein. 2007 [1899]. *The Theory of the Leisure Class*, ed. Martha Banta. Oxford: Oxford University Press.

Vespucci, Amerigo. 1894. *The Letters of Amerigo Vespucci and Other Documents Illustrative of His Career*, ed. and trans. Clements R. Markham. New York: Burt Franklin.

Wacquant, Loïc. 2004. *Body & Soul: Notebooks of an Apprentice Boxer*. New York: Oxford University Press.

The White House. 2017. 'The Inaugural Address: Remarks of President Donald J. Trump – As Prepared for Delivery, Friday, January 20, 1917, Washington, D.C.' www.whitehouse.gov/briefings-statements/the-inaugural-address/.

———. 2020. 'Executive Order on Protecting American Monuments, Memorials, and Statues, and Combating Recent Criminal Violence.' 26 June. www.whitehouse.gov/presidential-actions/executive-order-protecting-american-monuments-memorials-statues-combating-recent-criminal-violence/

Whitman, Walt. 1982. *Poetry and Prose*. New York: The Library of America.

Winthrop, John. 2015 [1630]. 'A Model of Christian Charity.' The Winthrop Society. www.winthropsociety.com/doc_charity.php.

Wise, Gene. 1979. '"Paradigm Dramas" in American Studies: A Cultural and Institutional History of the Movement.' *American Quarterly*, 31 (3), 293–337.

Wister, Owen. 1998 [1902]. *The Virginian*, ed. Robert Shulman. New York: Oxford University Press.

Wright, Richard. 1935. 'Between the World and Me.' *Partisan Review*, 2 (8), 19–20.

Wright, Will. 2021. 'Trump Loyalists Arrested and Charged With Involvement in Capitol Siege.' *The New York Times*, 9 January. www.nytimes.com/2021/01/09/us/politics/capitol-riot-charges.html.

Yokota, Kariann Akemi. 2010. 'Bodies of Knowledge: The Exchange of Intellectuals and Intellectual Exchange between Scotland and America in the Post-Revolutionary Period.' In *Globalizing American Studies*, ed. Brian T. Edwards and Dilip Parameshwar Gaonkar, 84–114. Chicago: University of Chicago Press.

INDEX

9/11 (September 11, 2001) 8, 172, 181

Abstract Expressionism 62, 77, 168
Acoma Pueblo 77-78, 80
Adorno, Theodor 81
African Americans 14, 67, 72-73, 87-88, 108-109, 143, 146, 168-169, 171; African American studies 149-151, 157-158; history of 4-5, 8, 69-71, 123, 147, 155-156, 160, 174-182; representations of 1-10, 44, 66-67, 95; and U.S. nationalism 4-5, 9, 29-30, 145
Alston, Vermonja 155
America: definitions of 7-8, 15-20, 35-36, 126-128
The American Adam (Lewis) 53-54, 72, 106-109, 145
'The American Century' (Luce) 38-40, 58-59, 165
American Declaration of Independence 9, 175
American football 41, 88, 169
American Gothic (Parks) 1-4, 6, 10
American Gothic (Wood) 2-4
American Indian Movement (AIM) 67; *see also* Native Americans
American Landscape (Sheeler) 53-54
American Quarterly 75-76, 106, 119, 129
American Renaissance (Matthiessen) 65-67
American Revolutionary War 28, 37, 68, 171, 175
American Studies Association (ASA) 60, 75, 127, 150
Anderson, Paul Thomas 81
Angeli, Jake 162
anthropology 47, 56, 72, 169; and American studies 12, 49, 84-87, 93, 95, 98-99, 101, 114, 118, 125, 160, 163-164
Anzaldúa, Gloria 125
architecture 84, 99, 127; and American studies 63, 77-79, 93-95, 101, 103
Asian Americans 109, 126, 143, 156, 182; study of 67, 149
Atwood, Margaret 23
Auden, W. H. 113
Auerbach, Jonathan 75-76, 80-81
The Awakening (Chopin) 138-143, 153, 157

'The Ballot or the Bullet' (Malcolm X) 5
Barthes, Roland 105
baseball 7, 85
Baudrillard, Jean 29
Beidler, Philip 98
Beloved (Morrison) 6
Benjamin, Walter 155

Bernstein, Leonard 144-145
'Between the World and Me' (Wright) 6
Biden, Joe 159, 182
Bierstadt, Albert 75
Billy Budd, Sailor (Melville) 62
Blackburn, Simon 15
Black Lives Matter (BLM) 69-70, 166, 168-169, 182; *see also* African Americans
Black Panthers 147, 180
Body & Soul (Wacquant) 87-88
borders 20, 73, 123, 130, 133, 144, 156, 165, 170; and American studies 7, 13, 67, 102, 112-113, 118-119, 124-126, 134-135; border studies 124-126, 136; U.S./Mexico 124-126, 136, 156, 176
Borderlands/La Frontera (Anzaldúa) 125
The Bostonians (James) 71
Brantlinger, Patrick 109, 145
'A Brief Recognition of New-Englands Errand into the Wilderness' (Danforth) 23
Britain 30, 34-35, 37-39, 106, 160, 175-176, 178; and American studies 57, 60, 64, 76, 80, 102, 113, 128-129, 136-137
British Association for American Studies (BAAS) 57, 60, 64, 76
Brooklyn Bridge (Trachtenberg) 53, 75
Brooks, Max 131-132, 134, 151-152
Buell, Lawrence 21, 23, 107-108, 152-153, 155, 158
Burns, Ken 98-99

Campbell, Neil 16, 102-104, 150-151, 158; studies of the American West 50, 80-82, 120
'Can "American Studies" Develop a Method?' (Smith) 48, 60
canon 42, 49, 52-53, 65, 77, 81, 98, 108-110, 114, 169; critique of 67-68; modifications to 53, 67-68; *see also* literature

Casey, Edward 125
Castronovo, Russ 108-109, 112, 116
Ceremony (Silko) 153
Chion, Michel 83
Chopin, Kate 138-143
Christianity 22-23, 74-75, 147; *see also* Puritans; religion
cinema *see* film
'Circles' (Emerson) 117-118, 131
Civil Rights 67, 147, 179
Civil War 33-34, 69, 106, 141, 160, 168-169, 176-177
Clark, William 31, 33
class 172; and American studies 6-8, 28, 49, 76, 78, 87, 95, 138-141, 150-151, 160
Coates, Peter 91
Cold War 144-145, 169; and American studies 13-14, 139, 143, 145-148, 157-158
Cole, Thomas 75
colonialism 18, 37, 41, 162; *see also* empire; history
Columbus, Christopher 18
comparativism: in American studies 13, 96, 110-116
Confederacy 69, 141, 160-162, 169, 176-177; *see also* Civil War
Constitution, U.S. 29, 89-90, 169, 177
Cooper, Anna Julia 4-5
Cooper, James Fenimore 49, 52, 88
Coppola, Francis Ford 71-72
Crane, Hart 53
cultural studies 8, 122, 167; and American studies 16, 68, 91-92, 102, 128, 136, 150-151, 158
Curtis, Edward 77-78, 80

Danforth, Samuel 23
Deepwater Horizon 142-143
De las Casas, Bartolomé 18
Deleuze, Gilles 82
Deloria, Philip J. 16, 98, 115, 146, 158, 160, 162-163
Denning, Michael 46, 145-146, 158
Derrida, Jacques 82

A Description of New England (Smith) 25, 26-28
Dickinson, Emily 66
'dime novels' 51, 68, 121, 169
Dimock, Wai Chee 118-119, 132-136, 149, 153-155
Docherty, Thomas 103-105
Donne, John 21
Douglass, Frederick 5, 66-67, 71, 73
Dunbar, Paul Laurence 44
dystopia 23, 46, 147, 155; *see also* utopia

Eakins, Thomas 66
economics 11, 24, 39-40, 43-44, 48, 61, 123-126, 129, 134-135, 165, 173; and American studies 62, 72, 82, 92-93; economic prospectuses of the 'New World' 25-30; and injustice 10, 57, 88, 140, 147, 154, 170, 172, 178, 182
ecopolitics 78, 89, 147, 165, 167, 170; and American studies 14, 81, 91-92, 109, 122, 133, 139, 141-143, 151-156, 158; 'ecoglobalist affects' (Buell) 153; *see also* Massachusetts; New England
Edwards, Brian T. 60, 132, 165-167
Edwards, Jonathan 72-73
Eggers, Dave 68
Emerson, Ralph Waldo 35, 52, 65-66, 73, 117-118, 131, 171, 173; *see also* literary nationalism; Transcendentalism
empire 20-21; U.S. imperialism 126-130, 148, 156, 166
environment *see* ecopolitics
Errand into The Wilderness (Miller) 24, 40-41, 47
'The Ethics of the Negro Question' (Cooper) 4-5
ethnicity 82, 88, 110, 125, 128, 147, 158; ethnic studies 149-151, 167
ethnography 80, 82, 86-87, 98, 169 *see also* anthropology

Europe 18-20, 22, 25, 36, 39, 76, 111, 162, 173-174; and American studies 55-58, 60, 85, 128-129; U.S. relationships with 28-31, 38, 64-65, 72, 127, 171
Evans, Walker 53, 75
exceptionalism 13, 23, 113, 115-116, 134, 145, 170

Faulkner, William 68-69
feminism 31, 65, 147, 173; and American studies 14, 51, 67, 71, 121-123, 138-139, 143, 146, 149-150, 157-158, 167
film 6, 88, 95, 114, 120-121, 124, 126, 130, 147, 166; and American studies 8, 12, 50, 57, 63, 68, 75-77, 79-84, 93, 98, 101, 103, 118
Fiske, Nathan 35
Fitzgerald, F. Scott 51, 53, 106
Floyd, George 69, 160, 182
food 27, 39, 62, 163
Ford, Christine Blasey 90
Ford, John 57
Franklin, Aretha 83
Franklin, Benjamin 28-30, 37, 83
Franklin, Thomas E. 8
Friedman, Thomas 164-166
Frost, Mark 82
Fuller, Margaret 35, 65, 171, 173
Full Metal Jacket (Kubrick) 98

gangsta rap 83
Gaonkar, Dilip Parameshwar 60, 132, 165-167
gender 82, 88, 90, 121, 139, 147, 167; and American studies 87, 95, 115, 121-122, 150-151, 158; *see also* feminism; LGBTQ; masculinity
geography 61, 80; and American studies 7, 13, 49, 52-53, 67, 72, 81, 91-94, 107, 118-137, 151-155; early geographical study of America 10, 17-18, 21-22, 25, 27, 31-37; *see also* maps

geology 27, 92
Get Out (Peele) 6
Ghosh, Amitav 133
Giles, Paul 112-113, 115, 136-137, 166
Gillespie, Dizzy 145
Gillman, Susan 108-109, 112, 116
Girders and Workers (Hine) 79
Glaude, Eddie S., Jr. 75
Gleason, William 140-141
global American studies: global coverage 7, 13, 19-20, 108, 110, 113, 116, 118-119, 124-126, 129, 131-137, 146, 152-154, 158; internationally dispersed sites of study 55-60, 112-113, 164
globalisation 123, 131, 161, 165-166
The Godfather trilogy (Coppola) 71-72
'God's Controversy with New-England' (Wigglesworth) 23
Gothic 2-4, 6, 42
Grand Canyon 91-92
The Grapes of Wrath (Ford) 57
The Grapes of Wrath (Steinbeck) 74
Gray, Jonathan 82-83
Great Depression 57, 74, 93, 146, 178
The Great Gatsby (Fitzgerald) 51, 53, 106
The Green Berets 98
Gross, Andrew 145-146
Gruesz, Kirsten Silva 20

Hale, Salma 33-34
Harvard University 30, 45, 55-57, 65, 174
Hawthorne, Nathaniel 52, 66
hemispheric American studies 118-119, 123-128, 131, 135-136
Herr, Michael 97
heteronormativity 14, 54, 59, 109, 146, 157
Hine, Lewis 79
hip hop 7, 83, 166; *see also* music
history 171-172; American colonial 19-23, 25, 47-48, 155, 162, 168;
American intellectual 37, 41, 47, 54, 59, 72-75, 144-145; and American studies 8, 12, 45, 49, 55, 62, 64, 68-72, 75-76, 80-81, 85, 92-94, 101, 105, 160, 164; *of* American studies 16-17, 36, 41, 45-46, 75, 107-108, 139, 145-151, 167; U.S. 31-37, 60, 74, 89, 94, 115-116, 147-148, 155-156, 160-162; *see also* literature
History of the Indies (de las Casas) 18
Ho, Karen 86-87
Hofstadter, Richard 161
Hollywood 6, 62, 81-82, 86, 90, 129-130, 148, 166, 179; *see also* film
Horkheimer, Max 81
horror 81, 147; *see also* Gothic
Hoskins, Janet 130, 136
Huang, Yunte 131
Huckleberry Finn (Twain) 48, 82, 139
Hughes, Robert 4, 77, 94, 168
humanities 117, 167; and American studies 12, 63-75, 77-85, 89, 93, 98-99, 101, 114, 118
Hurricane Katrina 68, 118, 132-133, 142-143, 181
Hutchinson, Anne 48

identity 14, 65, 80, 84, 149-150, 157-158; *see also* class; ethnicity; gender; LBBTQ; race
I'll Take My Stand (Twelve Southerners) 120
imperialism *see* empire
'Indian Notebooks' (Thoreau) 34
Indigenous communities *see* Native Americans
Indigenous Environmental Network 89, 170
In Dubious Battle (Steinbeck) 74
industry 68, 123, 160, 177; *see also* *The Machine in the Garden* (Marx); pastoral
'Information to Those Who Would Remove to America' (Franklin) 28-30

interdisciplinarity 73, 78, 103-105, 115, 170; and American studies 8, 11-12, 36, 44-45, 49, 53, 55, 59, 62, 64, 66, 74, 80-81, 85, 94, 96-106, 113-115, 125, 140, 148, 150, 160-164
Iroquois 62, 170; *see also* Native Americans
Ives, Charles 144

James, C. L. R. 133
James, Henry 71
Jameson, Fredric 156-157
Jarmusch, Jim 81
Jefferson, Thomas 31, 71, 78-79, 175
Jim Crow 69, 141, 170-171
Johansson, Scarlett 88
Johnson, Denis 97
Jones, Tommy Lee 124
justice 43, 67, 147, 168, 170, 172, 177, 181; and American studies 9, 57, 89, 102-103, 105-106, 115, 143, 151, 155-156, 163-164

Kaag, John 72, 94
Kaepernick, Colin 88
Kavanaugh, Brett 90
Kean, Alasdair 16, 102-104, 150-151, 158
Kellogg, Ray 98
Kerouac, Jack 61
King, Rodney 5, 181
Kolodny, Annette 51, 121-122
Kubrick, Stanley 98
Kuklick, Bruce 108

labour 3, 6-7, 9, 29, 55, 74, 79, 130, 146, 156, 160, 172; *see also* class
The Land Before Her (Kolodny) 121-122
landscape 6, 52-53, 65, 76, 79, 91, 121, 158; *see also* geography
Lauter, Paul 150-151
Latinx 14, 143, 171; study of 67, 149, 151, 156
law 160, 168, 178-179; and American studies 89-90

Law, James D. 127
Lee, Spike 5
leisure 39; *see also* sport; *The Theory of the Leisure Class* (Veblen)
Lenz, Günter 148
Lester, Toby 19
Levine, Robert 136, 143
Lewis, Meriwether 31, 33
Lewis, R. W. B. 53-54, 72, 74, 106-107, 109, 145
LGBTQ 14, 48, 123, 143, 147-149, 165
Lin, Maya 100
literature 6, 37, 87, 89, 117-118, 121, 144, 169, 172; literary criticism and American studies 10, 12, 31, 34-36, 41-45, 47-55, 58, 62-68, 75-76, 79-84, 88, 90, 92-94, 96-98, 100-101, 103-105, 107, 110-114, 118-119, 125, 129, 133-143, 160, 164, 171-172; literary nationalism 35, 64-65, 72, 171; literature and the environment 153-154, 158
Longfellow, Mary 122
Lossing, Benson J. 33
Lott, Eric 134
Lotz, Amanda 82-83
Louisiana 138-143, 163; *see also* Hurricane Katrina
Louisiana Purchase 31-33, 171, 175-176
Lowell, Robert 135
Luce, Henry 38-40, 58-60, 165
Lynch, David 82

The Machine in the Garden (Marx) 45, 51-54, 68, 75, 106-107, 109, 147, 172
Maddison, Angus 39
Magnalia Christi Americana (Mather) 22
Mailer, Norman 97
Main Currents in American Thought (Parrington) 41-45, 59
Malcolm X 5-6, 180
Malcolm X (Lee) 5

maps 165; of America 17-20, 31-34, 36-37, 126, 174
Martí, José 127-128
Marx, Karl 9, 151
Marx, Leo 45-46, 51-54, 59, 64, 68, 75, 106-107, 109, 172
masculinity 3, 97, 121, 124, 147, 163; masculinism in American studies 14, 44, 51, 54, 59, 66-67, 121-122, 146, 148, 157; *see also* feminism
Mason, Bobbie Ann 97
Massachusetts 22-23, 31, 35, 43, 46, 101, 110, 173-175; ecology of 25, 27, 73, 86, 153-154; *see also* New England
Mather, Cotton 22, 43
Matthiessen, F. O. 65-67
McDowell, Tremaine 100-101, 119-120
Mead, Margaret 56-58, 84-85, 95; *see also* anthropology
medicine 10, 62, 101, 117-118
Mellinger, Rachel 104-105
Melville, Herman 6-7, 35, 42, 52, 62, 66, 110-112, 131, 133, 144, 171, 173
Midwest, American 31, 171
migration 22, 27-29, 46, 71, 80, 123-124, 129-130, 132, 151, 156, 158, 173, 178
Miller, Perry 24, 40-41, 45-49, 51-54, 59, 74; *see also* Puritanism
Milton, John 111
mind: as category in American studies 46-48, 72, 74, 105-106, 108, 148
Mississippi, the 91, 139, 175-176
Mitchell, Lee Clark 124
Mitchell, W. J. T. 76
Moby-Dick (Melville) 42, 110-112, 131, 133, 144, 173
'A Model of Christian Charity' (Winthrop) 23
modernism 52, 55, 127, 144
Montaigne, Michel de 111
Moran, Joe 68, 115, 170; *see also* interdisciplinarity

Moran, Thomas 92
Morrison, Toni 6
Morse, Jedidiah 31
multidisciplinarity 112, 114, 150; *see also* interdisciplinarity
multilingualism 67, 114, 125
music 95, 144, 146, 151, 166; and American studies 63, 81, 83-84, 93, 98-99, 101, 105, 125
'My Slave Experience in Maryland' (Douglass) 5
'Myth and Symbol in American Studies' (Kuklick) 108
myth and symbol school 59, 81, 145-147, 157; aims and objects of 53-54, 105-108, 115, 120, 171; critiques of 54, 59, 108-110, 115, 120, 146

nation 29-31, 33, 35, 38-41, 52, 56-57, 86, 88, 127, 129-130, 144-145, 151, 155-157, 165-166, 173; and American studies 7, 12-14, 52, 57-59, 72-73, 96, 108, 111, 115-116, 118-120, 123-126, 131-135, 145, 150, 152, 166; U.S. nationhood 30, 34, 37, 91, 168, 175; U.S. nationalism 4-6, 8-9, 13-15, 19-20, 34, 130, 145, 150, 158, 161-162, 164-165, 170; *see also* borders; Cold War; exceptionalism; global American studies; literature; white
Nation of Islam 147, 178
Native Americans 25, 88, 149-150, 157, 170; activism of 14, 108, 143, 147, 162, 180; cultures of 50-51, 77, 153, 158; history of 20, 30, 33-34, 69, 77, 80, 85-86, 155, 174-177; white imitation of 162-163
New Criticism 44, 48, 171
New England 6-7, 10, 22-24, 40, 43, 46-48, 53, 77, 148, 165, 170, 174; ecology of 25, 27-28, 91
The New England Mind (Miller) 45-48, 51-52, 54, 74

New Mexico 74, 77-78, 94, 153, 174
New Orleans 62, 68, 123, 140, 143, 181
'New World' 20-21, 25, 28, 30, 51, 111, 129; *see also* Puritans; utopia
New York City 61, 76, 101, 126-127, 148, 162, 165, 175, 182; architecture of 75, 79; commercial life of 49, 86-87, 172, 181-182
New York Times 162, 164
Nguyen, Viet Thanh 97, 130, 136
Nixon, Rob 154
Novick, Lynn 98
Number 8 (Pollock) 144

Obama, Barack 5, 156, 161, 181
O'Brien, Tim 97
Occupy Wall Street 89, 172, 182
'Of the Cannibals' (Montaigne) 111
O'Keeffe, Georgia 94
Olson, Alexander I. 16, 98, 115, 146, 158, 160
On the Road (Kerouac) 61
O'Sullivan, Timothy 92

Pacific Ocean 17, 86, 149, 152; and American studies 13, 113, 118, 126, 128-131, 135-137, 154-155; U.S. history in 129-130, 155, 178
painting 2-3, 75, 104, 144, 162-163, 168; of the American West 50, 92, 94, 121; and American studies 12, 50, 52-55, 62, 64, 66, 68, 77, 84, 101, 106; *see also* Abstract Expressionism; visual arts
'"Paradigm Dramas" in American Studies' (Wise) 84-85, 148
paradise 28; *see also* utopia
Paradise Lost (Milton) 111
'The Paradise of Bachelors and the Tartarus of Maids' (Melville) 6-7
The Paranoid Style in American Politics (Hofstadter) 161
Paris, Treaty of 30, 168, 175
Parks, Gordon 2, 4, 6-10, 29

Parrington, V. L. 41-45, 48, 59, 64-65
pastoral 45, 51-52, 75, 91, 172
Pattee, Fred Lewis 35
Pearl Harbor 38, 178
Pease, Donald E. 12, 112, 116, 136, 170
Peele, Jordan 6
philosophy 9-10, 15, 117, 172; and American studies 12, 45, 49, 63, 72-75, 81, 93-94, 101-102, 125
photography 1-10, 29, 68, 92-93, 95, 99, 160; and American studies 7-8, 33, 50, 52-53, 63, 75-80, 84; as documentary 6-8, 9-10, 52, 79-80; and film 6; and painting 2-4
Pike, Albert 69-70
Pocahontas 25-26
Poe, Edgar Allan 42
poetry 19, 29, 35, 44, 51, 55, 90, 100, 113, 127, 130, 144, 153, 169, 172; and American studies 8, 53, 55, 66, 68, 75, 94, 106, 125, 134-135; imagining America in 6, 17, 21, 23, 36, 43, 46-47, 51; *see also* literature
politics 56, 81, 173; and American studies 9-11, 13-14, 24, 33, 36, 43-46, 48-49, 54-55, 57-59, 65, 72-73, 76, 78-79, 88, 94, 102-104, 109-110, 113-115, 121-123, 128, 131, 134-136, 138-158, 163-164; political philosophy 9-10, 28, 49; political science 36, 88-89, 93, 98, 100, 118; U.S. 30, 33, 43, 45, 52, 69-71, 74, 88, 90, 95, 98-99, 120-121, 124-126, 129, 144-145, 147-148, 160-163, 165-166, 168-169, 171
Pollock, Jackson 144, 168
Pop Art 77
poststructuralism 81, 172
Powdermaker, Hortense 86
Pratt, Mary-Louise 102
precariat 7, 172; *see also* class
A Promised Land (Obama) 5

Puritans 10, 30, 40, 64, 170, 172-174; belief system of 24-25, 43, 46-48, 74; writings of 21-23, 29, 39, 46-47

QAnon 161-163
Quakers 48, 74, 165
queer theory 157; *see also* LGBTQ

race 54, 76, 87-88, 95, 109, 123, 125, 147, 149-151, 163, 179; racial hierarchy 6, 8, 29-30, 47-48, 51, 57, 67, 69, 82, 90, 115, 139-141, 145, 162, 168-171, 177-179; *see also* African Americans; Asian Americans; Latinx; Native Americans; white
Radway, Janice 16, 111, 127-128, 150
recreation *see* sport
regionalism *see* subnational American studies
religion 22, 45, 47, 94, 179; and American studies 74-75, 101, 151; *see also* Puritans
Requiem for a Nun (Faulkner) 68
Ringmann, Matthias 18-19, 126
Rocky Mountains 31, 45, 50, 75
Rowe, John Carlos 16, 112, 114, 136, 167

Saldívar, José David 125-126, 136
Saldívar, Ramón 125
Salem witch trials 43, 175
Salter, Michael 90
Salzburg Seminar in American Civilization 55-57, 62, 85, 129, 145
scrimshaw 77, 173
sermons 36, 46
sexuality 88, 147-148, 165, 167; and American studies 14, 54, 59, 109, 122-123, 146, 150-151, 157-158; sexual assault 90
Shakespeare, William 51, 111
Sheeler, Charles 52
Shockley, Martin Staples 35
Shohat, Ella 165

Silko, Leslie Marmon 153
The Simpsons 46
slavery 5-6; history of 29, 69, 74, 123, 141, 155, 169, 175-177, 180; resistance to 69, 165, 170, 176-177; slave and neo-slave narratives 6, 44, 66-67; *see also* African Americans
Smith, Captain John 25-28, 37
Smith, Henry Nash 45-46, 48-54, 56, 59-60, 62-65, 68, 75, 107, 121, 129, 169
Smith, Sydney 34
Snyder, Gary 134
social sciences 12, 55, 62-63, 82, 84-90, 93, 99-101
sociology 45, 47, 72, 89; and American studies 12, 87, 93, 101, 103, 105, 114, 118, 138, 140; of sport 87-88
Sollors, Werner 67, 94
Somerville, Alice Te Punga 154-155
'Song of Myself' (Whitman) 29
'Song of the Open Road' (Whitman) 139
South, American 4, 33, 42, 68-69, 74, 78, 82, 160, 165, 169-171, 175-178; and American studies 86, 120, 123, 135-136, 138-143, 160
space *see* geography
Spiller, Robert 14
sport 38, 41; and American studies 11, 81, 87-88, 104, 138-143
Stam, Robert 165
Steinbeck, John 74, 128, 131
Stella, Joseph 53, 75
Stowe, Harriet Beecher 44
Stryker, Roy 10
subnational American studies 13, 85, 108, 118-123, 131, 135-136, 158, 165; *see also* Midwest; South; West
Supreme Court 55, 90, 176-177, 179-181
Sweet Home Alabama (Tennant) 120
The Swimming Hole (Eakins) 66

Tafuri, Manfredo 78-79
television 46, 95, 98-99, 180, 182; and American studies 63, 75-77, 82-83, 93, 118
The Tempest (Shakespeare) 51
Terry, Megan 99
theatre 90, 99, 104
The Theory of the Leisure Class (Veblen) 140
Thoreau, Henry David 34, 52, 66, 173
The Three Burials of Melquiades Estrada (Jones) 124
Tillyard, E. M. W. 47
'To his Mistress Going to Bed' (Donne) 21
totalisation: in American studies 12, 51, 93, 96, 106-110, 115, 120
Trachtenberg, Alan 53, 64, 75, 107
Transcendentalism 34, 73-74, 86, 117, 153, 173
transnational 173; *see also* global American studies; globalisation
transpacific *see* Pacific Ocean
Travels with Charley (Steinbeck) 128, 131
Tretheway, Natasha 78
Trinh T. Minh-ha 103, 135
Trump, Donald 23-25, 70-71, 90, 159, 161, 163, 166, 182
Twain, Mark 48-49, 52, 82, 139
Twin Peaks (Lynch and Frost) 82

The Unanswered Question (Ives) 144
Uncle Tom's Cabin (Stowe) 44
urbanisation 7, 73, 79-80, 162
U.S. Capitol *see* Washington, D.C.
Usonia 127
Ustopia 23
utopia 22-24, 43, 85, 157, 170

Veblen, Thorstein 140
Vespucci, Amerigo 18-20, 174
Vietnam Memorial Wall 99-100
Viet Nam War 108, 129, 147-148, 179-180; in American studies 96-101, 103, 113-114

Vietnam War, The (Burns and Novick) 98-99
Viet Rock (Terry) 99
violence 4-6, 69, 90, 97, 148, 155-156, 163; 'slow violence' (Nixon) 154
The Virginian (Wister) 121
Virgin Land (Smith) 45, 49-52, 54, 68, 75, 107, 121, 169
visual culture 2, 6; and American studies 12, 50, 52-53, 63, 75-83, 92-95, 98-99, 118, 122, 160-163; visual arts 55, 77, 99, 144; *see also* architecture; film; painting; photography; television

Wacquant, Loïc 87-88
Walden (Thoreau) 86, 153-154
Waldseemüller, Martin 18-19, 126
Walker, Kara 6
Wall Street 86-87, 181
Wall Street Crash 71, 178
Warhol, Andy 77
Washington, D.C. 1, 4, 7, 9, 24, 69-70, 99, 172, 176, 179-181; storming of U.S. Capitol (2021) 159-164, 182; White House 5, 79, 144-145
Washington, D.C. government charwoman (Parks) *see American Gothic* (Parks)
Watkins, Mary 125
Watson, Ella 1-7, 9-10, 29
Wayne, John 98
Weber, Joe 97
West, American 7, 33, 61, 154, 158, 171, 176; and American studies 45, 48-51, 65, 75, 80-82, 107, 120-124, 136
West, Cornel 5, 72-73
westerns 49-50, 75, 80-82, 121, 124, 169; *see also* 'dime novels'; 'West'
'What's in a Name?' (Radway) 16, 111, 127-128, 150
white: Americans 4, 25, 30, 33, 50, 61, 69, 72, 81, 86, 108, 120, 138, 147, 170-171, 176-177, 180, 182;

bias in American studies 14, 44, 54, 59, 66-67, 97, 103, 109, 146, 148-149, 157; supremacism 5-6, 9, 34, 69, 71, 123, 141, 160, 162-163, 166
White House *see* Washington, D.C.
The White Place in Sun (O'Keeffe) 94
Whitman, Walt 29, 49, 65-66, 139, 171, 173
Wiegman, Robyn 112, 116, 158
Wigglesworth, Michael 23, 25, 46
Wild West clubs 7
Willard, Emma Hart 31, 33
Williams, Raymond 156
Winthrop, John 23, 37
Wise, Gene 84-85, 148
Wister, Owen 121

women's studies *see* feminism
Wood, Grant 2-4
World War I 5, 40, 178
World War II 8, 34, 38-39, 44, 144, 169, 178-179; and emergence of American studies 11, 14, 36, 38, 59, 146, 148, 158, 171
World War Z (Brooks) 131-132, 134, 151-152
Wright, Frank Lloyd 127
Wright, Richard 6
Wyoming, University of 151

Yale University 30, 71, 79, 89
Yokota, Kariann Akemi 30, 37

Zombie, Rob 81

For Product Safety Concerns and Information please contact our EU representative GPSR@taylorandfrancis.com
Taylor & Francis Verlag GmbH, Kaufingerstraße 24, 80331 München, Germany

www.ingramcontent.com/pod-product-compliance
Lightning Source LLC
Chambersburg PA
CBHW050525170426
43201CB00013B/2089